THE TURBULENT DREAM

THE TURBULENT DREAM

Passion and Politics in the Poetry of W.B. Yeats

GEOFFREY THURLEY

University of Queensland Press
St Lucia • London • New York

© University of Queensland Press, St Lucia, Queensland 1983

This book is copyright. Apart from any fair dealing for the
purposes of private study, research, criticism, or review, as
permitted under the Copyright Act, no part may be reproduced
by any process without written permission. Enquiries should be
made to the publishers.

Typeset by The University of Queensland Press
Printed and bound by The Dominion Press—Hedges & Bell, Melbourne

Distributed in the United Kingdom, Europe, the Middle East,
Africa, and the Caribbean by Prentice-Hall International,
International Book Distributors Ltd, 66 Wood Lane End, Hemel
Hempstead, Herts., England.

For permission to reprint extracts from W.B. Yeats's works
acknowledgments are due to Anne and Michael B. Yeats, and
Macmillan Publishers, London Ltd. and to Macmillan Publishing
Company, New York, for extracts from *Collected Poems* by
W.B. Yeats copyright 1912, 1916, 1918, 1919, 1924, 1928, 1933, 1934;
renewed 1940, 1944, 1947, 1952, 1956, 1961, 1962 by Bertha Georgie Yeats.
Copyright 1940 by Georgie Yeats, renewed 1968 by Bertha Georgie Yeats,
Michael Butler Yeats and Anne Yeats.

National Library of Australia
Cataloguing-in-Publication data

Thurley, Geoffrey.
    The turbulent dream.

    Includes index.
    ISBN 0 7022 1962 2.

    1. Yeats, W.B. (William Butler), 1865–1939 –
Criticism and interpretation. I. Title.

821'.912

Library of Congress Cataloging in Publication Data

Thurley, Goeffrey.
    The turbulent dream.

    Includes bibliographical references and index.
    1. Yeats, W.B. (William Butler), 1865–1939—
Criticism and interpretation. 2. Dreams in literature.
I. Title.
PR5908.D73T48   1983   821'.8   83-5728
ISBN 0-7022-1962-6

To Wendy

Because I am quick as a flame
on a stick, the woman I love
is broad-thighed, tender, soft: a god
could only want such gentle strength.
　　　You are asleep. I reach
for quiet balance, you being absent.

You did not know, nor did I see
myself, how my poor heart in rage
went trembling through each man of middle age,
and every young man stronger than
　　　myself who spoke to you.
Leathern heart that doesn't know itself!

So, sky being purged of the error
of light, and all that bulk that made
the evening great, I leave for a while
the modern beat that has outgrown
　　　the heart to bring to mind
such times as have not been
stirred by desire or troubled by a dream.

Contents

PART ONE

Thesis: Fantasy

(i) The fin-de-siècle: "Ephemera"

The "decadent" art of the late nineteenth century can fairly enough be regarded as symptomatic of a general social malaise. As such it might seem easy to dismiss Maeterlinck, Wilde, Huysmans and the rest of the officially decadent as sickly by-products of a socio-historical process — signs that society and culture were in need of revitalization or rejuvenation through revolution. Yet this would be to over-simplify and to distort the facts of the case. For every artist, in a sense, is in rebellion against the things which offended the decadents. The act of poetry, that is to say, is as much an expression of repugnance and revolt as of interest; it is an act of retrieving as well as of reflection. What we mean by "L'art pour l'art", therefore, is an intensified pursuit of the indignant part of the poetic process. The revulsion against materialism, crassness, greed and insensitivity, originally salutary to artistic expression, grows beyond measure and devours its other half, which is delighted with what it sees in the world.

As to the crop this excessive indignation reaps, aestheticism breeds ultimately a disproportionate interest in the manner of saying or doing. The artist's instruments are what sustains his fervour in times of hunger and famine. If the artist has less of, say, Beethoven's intense feeling for life, he finds little that demands expression. If his indignation and revulsion enclose him within himself, his spirit has no variable sustenance: the source of supply (the raw fund of living) is voluntarily cut off, and the artist is driven to expend himself on what is nearest to him and most pleases him — which is to say, his technique. This accounts for the shuttered unhealth which vitiates decadent literature. We do not feel shut in with Pope or with Wordsworth. In the latter, the poet's self is referred consistently to a natural as well as to a philosophical background; in the former, the perfection of an inherently simple form is demanded by a constant, racy interest in the contemporary scene. The caste-mark of the decadent, on the other hand, is an interest in form, resulting from a radical lack of interest in the rest of creation, which revolts the poet. The English Victorians mastered a great number of verse-forms, displaying an excessive and gratuitous preoccupation with different ways of saying much the same thing. Formalism can thus be defined as a mode of artistic compensation, a means of marking time with the appearance of moving forward: Swinburne and the later Tennyson invent new or new-looking instruments so as to be able to sustain themselves at the position which had been reached by the great Romantics.

In striking contrast to this kind of virtuosic formalism, when admiration for ostentatiously proffered techniques constantly obscures matter, stand the technical preoccupations of Gerard Manley Hopkins. Hopkins's preoccupation with technique is quite contrary to Tennysonian virtuosity. Hopkins saw clearly that new tools would have to be forged for poetry to continue, and his concern with this problem is always subordinate to his need to satisfy the demands of a strenuous spirituality.

It is perhaps the strenuousness that needs to be emphasized. The intensity of the spiritual wrestling which make Hopkins's mature poetry the direct counterpart of the philosophy of Kierkegaard, is matched by the freshness and surprise with which he encounters, again and again, the wonder of creation. When we turn from Hopkins's poetry to that of the Symbolists and their English contemporaries, it is just this contact with reality that we miss. We miss it, as it were, by design. For it is the natural consequence of decadent turning-aside, the cultivation of indignation and revulsion at the expense of joy and delight, which would perhaps seem to denote an acceptance and an approval of that society which pays for the books in which the poems will be read. It is a complicated relationship, yet a clear and logically determinate one. The poet produces books, yet despises the society which consumes them. He is trapped in self-contradiction from which he can escape only at the expense of his "life". Despair is the inevitable end-product: the poet refuses to celebrate because he knows his celebration will be caught up in the cycle of production and consumption which causes him despair. Despair therefore is simply less contradictory than joy.

This is, of course, only one aspect of the case — the sociological. More deeply, despair is the authenticating response of the poet of all ages — the choice of significance rather than emptiness: it is the mode by which man comes up against his being and his death. It is this aspect of the matter which Kierkegaard and Hopkins variously examine. Unfortunately we cannot make a neat distinction between this "real" despair of the poet and that apparently discredited mask of despair donned by the decadent: the latter can fade back into the former at any moment. What we can do is to describe the various aspects of *fin-de-siècle* despair, in the hope that this will enable us to sift what is of value from much that can seem, to a hasty view, merely mannered and artificial, the despair of the salon. Sociological enquiry can help us to do this, since it establishes the common features of different poets and suggests the social and historical facts that helped produce them.

The essence of *fin-de-siècle* poetry, and of Symbolism (which is often taken to be the same thing), is indicated in a metaphor of Stephane Mallarmé which provided W.B. Yeats with the title of one of his *Autobiographies*, "The Trembling of the Veil". The poetic imagination, Mallarmé had assumed, transmitted hints of what lay — even to the poet himself — beyond a veil of appearances. Thus the Symbolist was concerned with interpreting inert matter to yield hints of Truth. Symbolism assumed that there was a world lying beyond the veil of things, and that this world was the real world, the world of Truth with which the poet must be concerned. This is an ancient metaphysical belief, of course, stemming from Plato in the western tradition and from the Vedic scriptures in the eastern. The *fin-de-siècle* was characterized by a resurgence of philosophical Idealism — Bergson, Meinong, Bradley, McTaggart and others — as well as by a new interest in "the mystic east". I am far from believing that sociological analysis, interpre-

ting this resurgence as a mere *trahison des clercs,* a wish to
escape the revolutionary message history was proffering,
can explain these phenomena satisfactorily. There is no
doubt, however, that they must in part reflect the withdrawal of the western intellectual in the face of the
onward march of positivist philosophy, capitalist
materialism and an apparent diminution of the meaningfulness of existence, and it is this aspect of the case that I
think best illuminates the earliest published poetry of
Yeats himself.

This poetry is, as every critic stresses, covered in a
narcotic mist: it is enveloped in that "twaelaight" which
Bernard Shaw ridiculed in the Irish literary revivalists.
It expresses repeatedly the desire to dream instead of act,
to sleep instead of wake. The major direct influence
behind Yeats's poetry here is not Shelley, or William
Morris, but Tennyson. It was Tennyson who legitimized
the Victorian poet's evasion of contemporary actuality,
and he articulated his withdrawal in a number of brilliant
allegories — in particular "The Lady of Shallott", "The
Lotos-eaters", "Mariana", "The Palace of Art", and
"Tithonus". These suave and beautiful allegories depict
self-destruction, immolation by decline, or merely escape
by turning-on. "The Lotus-eaters" shows the doughty
seafarers overcome by the passive hedonism of the
islanders, whose narcotic reverie they elect to join. In "The
Lady of Shallott", the artist-subject dare not look directly
at the external world, but only at its reflection in a mirror,
weaving her impressions of it into a tapestry which tears
open when she finally does stare directly in the face of
reality. If "Ulysses" had given vigorous early expression to
the Victorian intellectual's sense of exasperated energy
and constricting horizons, "Tithonus", with its lovely
eloquence, expresses the elegiac mood of late nineteenth-
century man:

> The woods decay, the woods decay and fall,
> The vapours weep their burthen to the ground,
> Man comes and tills the field and lies beneath,
> And after many a summer dies the swan.

Me only cruel immortality
Consumes; I wither slowly in thine arms,
Here at the quiet limit of the world,
A white-hair'd shadow roaming like a dream
The ever-silent spaces of the East,
Far-folded mists, and gleaming halls of morn.
                    Tennyson, "Tithonus"

Tennyson's white-haired persona haunts the western mind in various forms: in Conrad's hero lost in the Belgian Congo; and, in life itself, in the figure of Frederick Delius, a dying monument to the modern artist's self-destructive pursuit of an ultimate aesthetic pleasure.

The poets who influenced W.B. Yeats the most as a young man — Morris, Swinburne, Rossetti, Dowson, Lionel Johnson — were imbued with the Tennysonian philosophy of melancholy withdrawal, of sad despair in the face of an ugly actuality. Yeats was already, at twenty or twenty-one, expert in the desponding cadence that shuts off the future, and indeed any development in society whatever. Thus we see him creating that dream-world of misty pleasures and far-off streams, often enclosed in the woodland that is the real terrain of Symbolism. Yeats's early verse negates all change except decay: it foresees no future because it detests the present. It examplifies, that is to say, the doctrines of Symbolism — that the concern of art is with a dream-world, a world of noumena lying "somewhere" — beyond the veil or the forest.

It is hardly surprising that he gave consummate expression to the mood in a poem about ageing — "Ephemera".[1] Like Tennyson's "white-hair'd shadow", the speaker and his companion in Yeats's poem exist on the fringes of dying, in a wooded world itself decaying: their love is "waning" (the word occurs twice, in lines 3 and 4), and they pace "along the faded leaves". Passion has "worn" their hearts; the stars seem "far away" and so does their "first kiss", "and ah, how old my heart!" The poem is a conversation-piece, modelled perhaps on Verlaine's "Colloque sentimental", though closer in meaning to Richard Dehmel's "Verklärte Nacht", which the young Schönberg was busy translating into rather better music than the original deserved. Yet it is really an exercise in Tennyson's "Tithonus" manner:

> The woods were round them, and the yellow leaves
> Fell like faint meteors in the gloom, and once
> A rabbit old and lame limped down the path;
> Autumn was over him: and now they stood
> On the lone border of the lake once more:
> Turning, he saw that she had thrust dead leaves
> Gathered in silence, dewy as her eyes,
> In bosom and hair.

The Tennysonian philosophy, with its eloquent resignation, its sophisticated despondency, its despair of futurity, is assumed naturally, as it were, unthinkingly. It is therefore best seen as stylistic: Yeats has inhabited, with the skilful mimicry native to a young poet, the persona of an older poet. To this extent, we can say reasonably enough, that this is not the "real" Yeats. Yet we would be very foolish if we failed to discern in "Ephemera" not only a consummate work of art (it is as perfect a poem as Yeats ever wrote), but also one in which a good deal of individuality is displayed.

Most notable, is the *correspondance* of the leaves "like faint meteors". Yeats used this analogy twice again (in "The Wanderings of Oisin" and in "The Indian to his love") and it is a subtle and effective piece of symbolization, depending on a natural effect being sensitively captured. As such it is a kind of symbolic device more generally associated with the late Romantic poets: it owes its effect to the visual parallel between the few leaves remaining on the boughs and the falling of a meteor in the sky. It is a symbol, therefore, different in kind from at least two other sorts in the passage cited above. The leaves like meteors elide with the already fallen leaves the woman has thrust "in bosom and hair": we need no nudge from the poet to identify these with age or the premonition of age. Thus, leaves symbolize age in a different sense from the way in which they analogize meteors. Different again, finally, is the superb image of the "rabbit old and lame" that "limped down the path". This too shares traditional symbolic capacities, for "autumn was over him". But the rabbit becomes "symbolic" only through the narrative mechanism, and has significance only within the framework in which it is set. It is, in Roland Barthes' term connotative, gathering resonance only within the system of the poem itself. This connotative richness, to be sure, has both archetypal and cultural significance outside the poem. Rabbits do not have any emblematic meaning, like doves or eagles, but there is a certain "appropriateness" in the animal's occurrence here, an appropriateness not lost on earlier writers who might have influenced Yeats – George Eliot and Thomas Hardy, in particular. At the moment of her seduction by Arthur Donnithorne, Hetty Sorrel "hates the leveret that runs across her path"; later "the hare looked black as it darted across (Donnithorne's) path". A similar effect is obtained by Hardy at the moment of Tess's seduction in *Tess of the D'Urbervilles.* "Above them rose the primeval yews and oaks of The Chase, in which were poised gentle roosting birds in their last nap; and about them stole the hopping rabbits and hares."

We can hardly praise too highly the young Yeats's subtle distillation of this literary archetype into a self-declaring yet enigmatic symbol in "Ephemera". It shares the distinction of the whole piece, which ends with a muted cadence:

> . . .   our souls
> Are love, and a continual farewell,

It is a flawless piece, suave in its blank-verse naturalness, subtle in its manipulation of different sorts of symbolic device. Yet it has a tone which we know not to be authentically Yeatsian. The very perfection of an already perfected idiom prevents the emergence of that essentially querying, intellectual manner which was more native to Yeats. This does not matter. But we cannot help being more interested in a more flawed poem in which this individuality already struggles to declare itself.

(ii) "The Song of the Happy Shepherd"

At first sight, the poem which opens Yeats's *Collected Poems* is an innocuous and derivative piece of escapism which confirms the modernist's opinion of the young Yeats as a fay dreamer. Here are the Keatsian "woods of Arcady" ready to transport the reader to "faery lands forlorn". They belong to a conveniently dead past, a Golden Age of mists and regrets. The poem proposes, too, the predictably Tennysonian manifesto:

> Of old the world on dreaming fed;
> Grey Truth is now her painted toy;

On page one of his *Collected Poems,* Yeats proclaims the realm of dream dream is a nutrient, as it is in "The Lotos Eaters", in which Tennyson most richly and powerfully expressed, with that marvellous strength of languor he commanded in his prime, the central "decadent" idea, that reality is a thing to be avoided at all cost. The scientific advances of positivism are merely a "painted toy". For "there is no truth/Saving in thine own heart." This sounds like Kierkegaard's "truth is subjectivity", and the Romantic derivation of that insight is confirmed in Yeats's rejection of scientific claims to objective knowledge:

> . . .   Seek, then,
> No learning from the starry men,
> Who follow with the optic glass
> The whirling ways of stars that pass —

The knowledge of scientists and philosophers is rejected because "dead is all their human truth". Again, this lends itself to a Kierkegaardian interpretation: their human truth is dead because it is partial, objective fact masquerading as Truth, as Knowledge. But of course this would be giving Yeats the impossible benefit of the doubt. The Truth that is proffered as superior to this scientific objectivism is nothing more than the meandering reveries of the young Keats:

> Go gather by the humming sea
> Some twisted, echo-harbouring shell,

And to its lips thy story tell,
And they thy comforters will be,

This is a formula for mindlessness, not a superior vision.

It is not for this stale art-science dichotomy that the poem is interesting or remarkable. Yet the essential structure of the dichotomy is, I think, essential for the central meaning that does come through the poem: there is something recalcitrant in Yeats' handling of these modish Tennysonian motifs, something that resists the air of vague Arcadian glamour the poet seeks to cast over the poem. It is visible first in the powerful syncopation of line 9: "To the cracked tune that Chronos sings". The skid of unstressed syllables that throws us onto "tune" stands out the more strongly for the orthodoxy of the text-book iambus that precedes it, "In dreary dancing past us whirled". Neither is line 9 remarkable only for its rhythm: its dissonant sounds ("cracked tune . . . Chronos") shake us out of the iambic patter of the surrounding verse. We shall see later that such rhythmic and sonic disturbances are central to Yeats's deepest poetic meanings. Something in this line makes us attend a little more carefully than we might even to the modish-sounding line that ends the sentence, "Words alone are certain good." At first glance this runs smoothly with the anti-positivistic stance of the whole poem. Language is robbed of its disturbing powers of reference and commitment: the poet must merely weave his web, like the Lady of Shallott, and not seek to stare "Grey Truth" in the face. But the meditation on dead kings that follows leads to more interesting matter. What lives is merely the *reputation* of the kings, so that the deeds for which they are remembered have disappeared into the words that preserve them. So, "Words alone are certain good." The poem succeeds now in placing itself within the modern world, a world of "the stammering schoolboy" who becomes the focus of things, as indeed he had been in Baudelaire's "Le Voyage". The poem acknowledges itself as being the product of the age of "education", rather than of glory or myth. Thus a slightly more real significance attaches even to the regret for the "antique joy" that was said to be "over".

Since, moreover, our reality is linguistic, and the reputations we remember are at bottom mythic, perhaps the poet is right in wondering whether

> The wandering earth herself may be
> Only a sudden flaming word,
> In clanging space a moment heard,
> Troubling the endless reverie.

Yeats has shifted the focus of his poem along a scale, leading from the Keatsian Arcady of the opening, through the world of the schoolboy studying history and classical myth, forward to a cosmos in which all the foregoing loses itself. There is a tangible meaning, a thrust of real sense, therefore, in the description of the earth as "a sudden flaming word": it is not a conceit, but a suggested ontology. The whole of creation is a great Logos. What is peculiarly Yeatsian about the treatment here is the association of this ontology with violence: it is a "flaming" Word. Our retrospective sense that we are on the brink of some of Yeats's most important thematic content, is surely confirmed beyond all possible doubt by the line that ends the first section of the poem, "Troubling the endless reverie."

All poets have their "personal" words — words which inscribe their private code, like their particular gene-structure or their finger-print or signature. Such lexical frequencies occur in every writer, and, though always of interest, they may not always be important. Poets have their mental tics, their less directed signature-words, which may contribute to our understanding of what Anton Ehrenzweig called "the hidden order of art", may establish authorship and identity. But these may not necessarily tell us anything important about the valuable significance of a poet's structures. A computer read-out is likely to be unable to distinguish between the really significant verbal frequencies in a writer's work, and the "personal" but uninteresting ones. I shall wish to speak throughout this study of a stock of root-words in Yeats — words which function with a particular poetic force. In doing so I am not concerned with frequency *per se,* nor with the poet's "creative personality" (whatever that might be). I am concerned with words which function with particular poetic force, and which provide perhaps a matrix of his entire poetic output. It may well be that only certain types of poet rely upon a stock of such root-words. If this is true, Yeats is certainly among them.

The difference between "Ephemera" and "The Song of the Happy Shepherd", I have suggested above, is the difference between greater and less individuality. "Ephemera" is undoubtedly the better poem, but its superiority is based upon its too complete assumption of a current poetic language. Aesthetically, this is perfectly justifiable: originality in itself is not valuable in art, and all art to some extent derives from a common stock of inherited idioms and practices. Besides, "The Song of the Happy Shepherd" is no less derivative a poem. It comes from a variety of ill-digested sources, the lighter Keats in particular, and then, the earlier Milton: the last section of the poem imitates with touching impotence the clear, neo-classic gravity of "Lycidas" ("And still I dream he treads the lawn"). Stylistically, then, "Ephemera" is purer and better. Yet the very clumsiness of the "Song" — its inability to forge a style out of its influences — leaves the way open to the "real" W. B. Yeats to make a first appearance "Troubling the endless reverie." The music here is not Keats or Milton or Tennyson, it is Yeats, and the verb "to trouble", and the noun "reverie" are the first words we can confidently designate as Yeatsian root-words. Wherever these words occur later in Yeats (and they will do so, again and again) we shall find Yeats close to the heart of his own matter.

At this stage, to be sure, there is a looseness, an un-directedness: the adjective "endless" is unfunctional. It does nothing, and testifies only to the young poet's desire to stay inside the dream of reality. Rhythmically, too, the adjective contributes nothing: it is tied to the poem's iambic grid — "the endless" — while "troubling" and "reverie" break the iambic surface, creating the "troubling" effect that is the essence of the whole passage. Our difficulty here is that the verb "trouble" does *trouble*: that is, Yeats's meaning and his diction coincide completely, and it is tricky to make critical comment that has not already been made by the poet himself. We shall come to this aspect of the root-words in due course. For the moment, let us pause to look at *reverie*. Nothing testifies to Yeats's curious genius more emphatically than his persistent, and persistently successful use of this worn-out piece of operatta-ese: *mon reve,* "reverie" — the words were already, by the eighteen-nineties, irredeemably implicated in the world of the lighter French opera or the drawing-room ballad. Yet Yeats dwells upon its root — to dream, and exploits its rippling movement to create an effect of disturbance within flow.

In the present instance, its use reinforces the image the poem as a whole presents of the universe as itself the product of some vast Dreamer's fantasy. Moreover, this not un-typical nineteenth-century vision (testifying to the poet's desire to sleep, and be able to hide from the horrible facts of urbanized reality), is given more than usual force later on in the poem by another characteristic Yeatsian connection:

> Then nowise worship dusty deeds,
> Nor seek, for this is also sooth,
> To hunger fiercely after truth,
> Lest all thy toiling only breeds
> New dreams, new dreams; there is no truth
> Saving in thine own heart.

Diction again tells us that Yeats is into a stride that is already peculiarly his own: "toiling" and "breeds" in particular are verbs he is always going to rely on in important contexts. They too belong with Yeats's root-words. But it is the movement of thought which is important here. When Yeats urges us not to "hunger . . . after truth" he is sounding one of the central ideas of his later poetry: out of hunger or lack, man dreams; his dreams make him toil to realize them; the toil breeds new courses of action, which in turn cause new dreams, more toiling . . . and so it goes on, an endless cycle, of dreaming and doing.

This syndrome is perhaps the most fundamental in all of Yeats's poetry, and we meet it here in the first poem in his *Collected Poems*. The poet is unable to impose his movement on language for sustained periods at this stage: by the end of the poem we are back in Lotos land with "poppies on the brow", being urged to dream. Yet there is already the core of a deeper meaning to the notion of dream than would have appeared likely. Even at this early stage, dreaming is a more complicated and significant activity than allows us to dismiss the whole ethos of *Crossways,* and wait patiently for the mature poet to "wake up", stung out of his somnolence by the tart ironies of modernism. To hold such a view of Yeats is, indeed, to have sacrificed any possibility of a proper understanding of his work.

(iii) Labours of dream: Fergus, Cuchulain

It is probably only with hindsight that we can understand the importance of this motif in Yeats, yet we must use all the resources available to us. "The Song of the Happy Shepherd" divulges a valuable early glimpse of the original poet within the accomplished versifier of "The Wanderings of Oisin". Yeats shows his peculiar earnestness, as well as his originality, in the way in which he begins to sift a more concrete concept of dream from the general late Romantic otherworldliness — that hatred of the material and the progressive so suavely expressed in "Ephemera" and other early lyrics such as "The Indian to His Love". Gradually, in the poems that follow, Yeats begins his critique of dream, selecting from the mist of enchantment that covers his landscape, certain more problematic elements. The idea of enchantment appears early and is pervasive throughout the first two columes of verse Yeats published, *The Wanderings of Oisin* and *The Countess Cathleeen*. What we might call Yeatsian man begins to emerge from "the murmuring greenness" in certain of the poems included in the section of the *Collected Poems* entitled *The Rose*: "Cuchulain's Fight with the Sea", "Fergus and the Druid" and "The Man Who Dreamed of Faeryland".

When Cuchulain fights with the "bitter tide", we meet the first of many obsessional characters who appear throughout Yeats's poetry. The tide and its indefatigability were put there by God, but the idea of fighting it came from within Cuchulain. It was implanted in Cuchulain by the Druids, who were afraid that when Cuchulain woke up to the fact that he had killed his own son, he would run amok and kill them. The narrative mechanism is fortuitous, but the content expressed through it — the obsessiveness — is not. Yeats's choice of myth is significant. He was, it is true, only interested in a particular aspect of the myth: another writer might have emphasized the Knutish vanity, for instance, or the Sisyphean exasperation of the labour to effect the impossible. These aspects of the story did not interest Yeats: it was the obsessedness that fascinated him.

So it is with "Fergus and the Druid". Fergus, the successful man of action, sees himself suddenly as a "foolish labourer/Who wastes his blood to be another's dream". His life has brought him no satisfaction; the reason given for this is that he has wasted himself for other people's dreams. But this is really a distraction from what is, for Yeats, the centre of the myth — the fact of wasting life (of blood) in the pursuit of dream. Out of this dissatisfaction, Fergus demands the Druid's bag of dreams. To deter him, the Druid points to his own "thin grey hair and hollow cheeks". Such details were later to be used by Yeats with devastating effect, to establish the image of the dream-wasted, spiritually hungry man. For the Druid is himself an image of dream-ridden man, and knows that Fergus will derive no profit from the bag of dreams he is going to get. The whole poem is a rehearsal of major Yeats themes. Once again as in the Cuchulain poem, the myth itself points in various directions: it suggests a satire on kingly or earthly power, which is really irrelevant to Yeats. A poet's true maturing consists in eliminating the unwanted implications of basic myths and themes. In the good poem there will be no fortuitous elements, and it will not be possible to say of "Leda and the Swan", for instance, that the myth-subject is a mere peg upon which to hang something else. Indeed, we may take leave to wonder whether this is ever really the case with a good poem. Ultimately the poem will not tolerate the irrelevant directions of a myth or theme and the poet's success will be decided in part at a prior stage, with the very choice of subject, myth or theme, and the ability of this theme to cohere with personal and other factors. The poet must learn to recognize his real subject-matter or terrain, and have something of Milton's patience and humility in choosing it.

"Cuchulain's fight with the Sea" and "Fergus and the Druid" bring Yeats's deeper concerns with other aspects of dream closer to the surface. A further stage of awareness is represented in "The Man Who Dreamed of Faeryland", which is altogether a new achievement. The technical mastery and a greater flexibility enable Yeats to comment on his evocations of "the Land far away". In other words, the Land far away is set in a considered, criticized context. It is no longer mere wish-fulfilment, a Romantic desire to escape. As such the poem is in a different category from "The Lake Isle of Innisfree", "A Faery Song" and "The Stolen Child". It is a sardonic, at times Blakean review of various sorts of siren voices which keep the man from ease in life, and finally from peace in the grave. It is interesting that irony here releases Yeats, it does not inhibit him, as it inhibits the poets of the nineteen-thirties and forties. A Blakean mischievousness animates the malicious natural voices:

> A lug-worm with its grey and muddy mouth
> Sang that somewhere to north or west or south
> There dwelt a gay, exulting, gentle race
> Under the golden or the silver skies;

And again:

> . . . one small knot-grass growing by the pool
> Sang where – unnecessary cruel voice –
> Old silence bids its chosen race rejoice,

For all its eloquent beauty, the knot-grass's legend disturbs the dreamer so that "The tale drove his fine angry mood away." This ability to release the "heroic" *Oisin* manner within a context of irony clearly marks an important stage in Yeats's evolution. His subject-matter is clarifying itself: it is the disturbance of consciousness entailed in dreaming which interests Yeats, not the content of the dreams themselves.

(iv) The labour of love: Helen and the Rose

Yeats's *oeuvre* can really only be viewed with confidence from the vantage-point of his death. Judgements about the significance of individual works and what they can tell us about the poet's development are likely to betray us as they reveal themselves to be made on the strength of alterations and revisions made late in life. This is especially relevant to any attempt to show the growth of Yeats's thought. The *Collected Poems* of 1949 shows divisions of the poems into certain "books". But these books often exist only as divisions made in collected editions, and do not represent stages in actual publication. In the present instance, it is certain decisions Yeats made in putting together the *Poems* of 1895 that concern us. It was in this book that Yeats invented the "collections" now familiar to us as *Crossways* of 1889, and *The Rose* of 1893. The poems in these collections appeared in either *The Wanderings of Oisin* (1889), or *The Countess Cathleeen* (1892). The re-titlement of the poems as *Crossways* and *The Rose* respectively assumes a particular interest: it shows Yeats in the process of deliberating upon the meaning and direction of his *oeuvre.* In particular, to call the shorter lyrics in *The Countess Cathleeen The Rose* betrays an intelligent awareness of development: in focusing the "symbol" of the rose, Yeats had made an important step forward.

The opening invocation of the collection, "To the Rose upon the Rood of Time", assigns no clear symbolic role to the flower: it is merely "Red Rose, proud Rose, sad Rose of all my days", and the ensuing poem informs us of the poet's intention of singing "old Eire and the ancient ways". The symbol of the rose is of course far too richly and complicatedly emblematic for it to function as a symbol in the genuine modern sense — as an item of external reality made resonant through the poet's own emotional experience of it. Yet the Symbolists as a whole were intoxicated by the ancient rich emblems of Christian culture. The Rose, in Yeats as in Aleksandr Blok, can stand for many things: it is above all the rich unattainable focus of earthly dream, and in itself the embodiment of what is loveliest. Yeats's roses do not have the sensuous richness of Keats's "globed peonies"; they have the air of being oppressed by their own richness. As such, the symbol gathers the poet's mind together, concentrates, makes a nucleus.

A more pointed address to the "ancient ways" is made in the first of the rose poems in the 1893 collection, which is called "The Rose of the World". Significantly enough, Yeats begins with a line that Lionel Johnson would have been proud to write: "Who dreamed that beauty passes like a dream?" A beautiful if somewhat extravagant late Romantic gesture, one would think, a rhetorical question paying its homage to Keatsian Beauty by making itself unanswerable. Yet it is not merely the recurrence of the notion of dream that alerts the attentive Yeatsian to the presence of more serious matter in the poem. The volume itself, besides its dedicatee, proclaims its ostensive purpose with a nice bit of St. Augustine, roughly translatable as "I loved you late, Beauty so ancient, yet so new/I loved you late". Yet the disturbing power of the beautiful woman evoked in "The Rose of the World" goes beyond the merely psychological torments reserved for the despairing lover in Romantic mythology. In fact, Yeats contradicts the apparent unanswerability of his opening question by pointing to the all too tangible consequences of the beauty:

> For those red lips, with all their mournful pride,
> Mournful that no new wonder may betide,
> Troy passed away in one high funeral gleam,
> And Usna's children died.
> "The Rose of the World"

In a Note in *Collected Poems,* Yeats says that the Indian and faun-satyr poems of *Crossways* were products of his late youth, because, from the time he wrote "The Wanderings of Oisin" at twenty, his "subject-matter became Irish".[2] Yet the theme which, from its first appearance in "The Rose of the World" dominated and finally united all the strands of Yeats's creative genius, was not Irish but classical: the Trojan War, both as a narrative archetype and a human syndrome, became for Yeats the paradigm of all human passion, both personal and political. There are few more remarkable instances in literature of a poet's recognizing his central theme so early and exploring it so tenaciously. From this first appearance, the Trojan War will never be long absent from Yeats's poetry. It will appear finally, with its accustomed properties — "topless towers . . . burnt" and "that face" — in "Long-legged Fly", where it represents one of the three great human drives, War, Love and Art. If the Rose is Yeats's first really effective symbol, The Trojan War is his permanent thematic nucleus.

Significantly, Yeats's way into this theme is the identification of the Rose with Helen's lips. In the Note from *Collected Poems* from which I have already quoted, Yeats goes on to say that "the quality symbolized as The Rose differs from the Intellectual Beauty of Shelley and of Spenser in that I have imagined it as suffering with man and not as something pursued and seen from afar."[3] Yet in "The Rose of the World", the world suffers *because* the rose does. Helen is at once victim and cause — cause indeed because victim. She is victim because she is so exceptional:

for such beauty, nothing on earth is adequate. Her red lips are "Mournful that no new wonder may betide". Because of Helen's bored disillusionment, "Troy passed away in one high funeral gleam". The association of Helen's beauty with imagery of height is a significant one, incidentally, that we shall have cause to return to. No less important is the fact that the image of height is immediately juxtaposed with one of effort. Because of Helen's high beauty,

We and the labouring world are passing by.

The syndrome is characteristically Yeatsian. Because of the woman's high beauty, men labour — in ships, rowing from Greece to Troy, where they will battle for the prize. We remember the association of "The Song of the Happy Shepherd" — the hunger after truth, the dream, the toiling, the new dreams.

The general association of love and violence — what we might regard as the heart of the Trojan story — is rather more rhapsodically celebrated in "The Rose of Battle", which is significantly called, "Rose of all Roses, Rose of all the World". For this Rose, too, the ships are waiting with "thought-woven sails" — another Trojan reference. The same elements and associations — beauty, height, fire and toil — appear in "The Sorrow of Love", a tighter, more strategically organized re-doing of "The Rose of the World":

> A girl arose that had red mournful lips
> And seemed the greatness of the world in tears,
> Doomed like Odysseus and the labouring ships
> And proud as Priam murdered with his peers;
> > "The Sorrow of Love"

The whole syndrome is subtly associated with the brawling of sparrows in the eaves and is said in a later re-working[4] to "compose man's image and his cry". (The "pity of love", by the way, in the companion poem, is a whimpering sort of emotion, manifestly not to Yeats's liking: Better the world in flames than the moping emotion.) As in "The Rose of the World", the legendary ephemerality of

beauty ("Who dreamed that beauty passes like a dream?")
is contradicted by the endlessly ramifying consequences. It
is almost as if the woman wants the world to burn so that
her beauty may be remembered. Whether this is so or not,
it is with consequences that Yeats is now fundamentally
concerned. From this time onwards, Yeats was to regard
all human behaviour as inherently and necessarily
historical and dialectical, taking place in a process which
brings it into being, and is then affected by it. The trouble
is, of course, that we cannot usually dictate what the
consequences of our acts will be. Neither can we know,
really, why we do what we do, so that we cannot really be
said to know *what* we do. If the springs of our acts remain
hidden from us, so does the essential nature of the acts
themselves.

We could sum this up by saying that for Yeats all
behaviour was more or less dream-like, carried out with the
curiously blind purposefulness of the somnambulist. This,
in essence, is the meaning of the Trojan War for Yeats. We
have seen it paralleled in Fergus's desire for the bag of
dreams (which expresses, as it were, man's need to be
governed by something other than his own will), in
Cuchulain's absurd fight with the sea, and in the various
delusions of the man who dreamed of fairyland. Above all,
it is foreshadowed in those lines from the "Song of the
Happy Shepherd" which associated the "fierce" hunger of
man with his consequent doings. Another intimation of
Yeats's basic vision of human behaviour comes in "The
Rose of Battle":

> *The sad, the lonely, the insatiable,*
> *To these Old Night shall all her mystery tell . . .*

The Rose of Battle, then, is the rose of all the world
because it too has heard "God's bell" — that "sweet far
thing".

We have, then, first dream, and then disturbance; from
disturbance, action — this is the dialectic of dream. In the
Trojan War the source of the disturbance was Helen — she
whose red lips were "mournful that no new wonder may

betide". If the Trojan War was Yeats's central mythic structure, Helen was the central element of that myth. And Helen was, as we know, a particular woman, Maud Gonne. Once Yeats had seen and fallen in love with Maud Gonne, we can say, his poetic fate was sealed; she never left him in peace until he died. To a certain extent, Yeats's entire evolution as a poet may be charted in the poems he wrote to Maud Gonne. Yet what is perhaps most remarkable in what might be regarded as an extraordinary case of obsession is that although the poet never ceased at some profound level of himself to love the woman, he never really wrote a wholly satisfactory love poem to her. To explain this rather curious fact, we have first to consider, in order to refute, a false explanation.

This is that Yeats's love for Maud Gonne was of the pre-Raphaelite variety, afraid of fulfilment and wholly dependent on distance to maintain its own credibility. In fact, no attentive reading of the poems allows of such a view of the matter. In dealing with Yeats's love for Maud Gonne we are not confronted with that disembodied Romantic love which fears actual contact lest its own frailty be exposed. Neither can we conclude that Yeats was frightened lest fulfilment be less satisfying than desire. That is not the emotion that comes through the poems. Yeats quite rightly kept Maud separate from sex: there was no tendency for her to elide with Crazy Jane, whose very name suggests the low role Yeats was to allot sexual need when it finally arose in him. Maud Gonne herself was probably simply puzzled by Yeats's shyness. She would undoubtedly have jettisoned him as lover, just as she jettisoned Captain MacBride, the more conventionally macho lover-spouse she took after turning the poet down. Yet there is nothing effete or unhealthily idealized about the emotion that wells through the Maud Gonne poems. On the contrary, it is powerfully physical. So what is the explanation of the fact that, as Harold Bloom points out,[5] Yeats never wrote a love lyric as good as Dowson's "Cynara"? Is it that he simply didn't love anyone that much? Or is it that the love he sustained for so long for

Maud Gonne meant something different to Yeats from
what it meant to Dowson? It is not a question of concern
with the "strength" of the feeling: it is a religion of love
rather than love for a particular woman that informs the
passionate declamation of "Cynara". And it is this content
which is absent from Yeats, not any strength of feeling.
The reason, therefore, why Yeats never wrote a love poem
as good as "Cynara" is not that he loved Maud Gonne less
than Dowson the nameless harlot within "Cynara", but
that he was interested in saying different things: Maud
Gonne was Helen of Troy, but Helen of Troy for Yeats
is something other than the instigator of a Romance love
tragedy. Yeats's assumption, of course, was that she was
something other for Homer as well, and that the *Iliad*
concerns matters of more moment than the nature of
Love.

Maud-Helen was, at the same time, the supreme high
being, the principle of that Eternal Feminine that is so
dominant in late nineteenth-century culture generally,
and the source of profound disturbance. As goddess of
Love she is the source of dream, and the Trojan saga begins
as Paris' pursuit of the dream at the risk of no matter what
consequences. The consequences themselves, however,
transcend the merely personal: they become political, and
the whole saga is in essence political. It was several years
before Maud Gonne became associated for Yeats with
politics, but the immediate identification with Helen as
source of disturbance is of the greatest significance. In
the *Rose* lyrics, Maud Gonne was the embodiment of
proud beauty, an incomparable human being for whom
tawdry reality was simply not good enough – or shall we
say, just good enough to burn for her. She is implicitly,
therefore, the cause of discord, hatred and bitterness; and
those so prettily pouting lips, "mournful that no new
wonder may betide", will soon express the extreme of
exasperation. We have an excellent instance of the
transformation of cultural themes through adaptation to
changing historical circumstances here. Initially, Yeats
would seem to have adopted the structure of the fated

Romantic love so typical of the *poétes maudits* who influenced him. Almost at once, he begins to exploit the myth to say something different: Maud-Helen becomes not merely the goddess of love but the nexus between passion and politics.

This, of course, brings us to the question of Yeats's political affiliations. At the time of which I am now writing — the first five years of this century — Yeats was a member of two different organizations: one political (the Irish Republican Brotherhood) and the other mystical (the Order of the Golden Dawn).[6]

The two movements overlap and commingle in Yeats's verse, so that it is almost impossible to know when the interests of one (the political resolution of "the Irish problem") end, and those of the other (vaguer, but equally concerned with an ultimate revelation to do with Ireland) begin. Perhaps any discussion of Yeats's politics should begin precisely with this fact, for it was to be his greatest distinction as a poet to unravel both the mysticism of politics and the politics of mysticism.

Again, Maud Gonne appears as the key-figure: as Helen united love and politics in Homer, suggesting that the drive behind the one became the motivation of the other, so Maud Gonne lay at the heart both of Yeats's visionary mystique of Ireland and of the Golden Dawn. She was the Rose, and the Rose was both Ireland and the unattainable but revered Truth. Yet genuine and profound as Yeats's love for the woman was, he shows his curious perceptiveness in nothing so clearly as in the clarity with which he discerned their different aims in life. Much earlier than one might imagine, a note of regret infiltrates his tributes to her. As early as "The Folly of Being Comforted" and "Adam's Curse" (both from *In the Seven Woods* of 1904), Yeats informs his "love poems" with subtle dissonances.

It would be easy to explain the episode in terms of the dreamy unpolitical poet, unable to descend from that mythical ivory tower and involve himself in the turmoil of politics (that is, "real life"). But, again, a close reading of Yeats makes such a view impossible. At no point does

Yeats give us the impression of being unable to grasp the quick of the political matter, or unwilling to commit himself once he had. What we are concerned with is not the traditional (and largely mythical) aloofness of the poet, but on the contrary, the poet's concern with things ridden roughshod over by the political animal. And to unravel this tangled skein, we must attend again to Yeats's handling of the dream-motif. For his Helen was the living embodiment of one dream — the Romantic — yet it was another, that of a free Ireland, which drove her forward. What were Yeats's views of the political question? And how did his Helen react to it?

(v) "To Ireland in the Coming Times"

The earliest indication of Yeats's attitude towards the political question comes in the last poem in *The Rose*. At first sight Yeats appears to take advantage of the poet's time-honoured role as being "above such things". He seems to postulate a singer-role for the poet, incompatible with the more mundane political requirements:

> I cast my heart into my rhymes,
> That you, in the dim coming times,
> May know how my heart went with them
> AFter the red-rose-bordered hem.
>> "To Ireland in the Coming Times"

We know all about that particular evasion of a full participation in the affairs of men: it has never been the way of the great poet. Yet Yeats's lines have more than wistful evasiveness. There is a certain richness to the mimesis of the first line quoted, in the progression through "cast", "heart" and "rhymes". The "rhymes" receive the "heart" with a real fullness. Whatever the basis of Yeats's attitude might on analysis turn out to be, the feel of the verse tells us that it is not evasion. The "red-rose-bordered hem" is of course the old Ireland, sung in many a charming rhaeme of the twaelaeght. The lines in fact suggest a clear affinity between Yeats's two interests of the time, those of the Order of the Golden Dawn, with its prophecies of a mystic culmination of the Irish destiny, and those of the politically harder-minded Irish Republican Brotherhood. When we go back over the poem itself, we shall find that this is indeed the clue to Yeats's attitude. "To Ireland in the Coming Times" is nothing less than an apology in advance, an explanation — with small chance of being accepted — of what was *not* going to be his position in these matters. Yeats's Ireland in this poem is "a Druid land". The poet commits himself to the mystic visionary dream island that existed "before God made the angelic clan" (the English? — a bitter pun for an Irish poet to make). He wishes for Ireland not freedom or home rule, but precisely those values he was later to wish for his daughter in a more famous poem:

And may the thoughts of Ireland brood
Upon a measured quietude.

Accordingly, he dissevers himself from the ambitions of those who will inevitably destroy such things — the patriots who are seen as ranters and ragers. With all humility, he makes his pronouncement, his characteristic opposition to "the elemental creatures"

That hurry from unmeasured mind
To rant and rage in flood and wind;

To this ranting and raging, he offers those values later to be argued in "A Prayer for my Daughter":

Yet he who treads in measured ways
May surely barter gaze for gaze.

We have here an excellent example of Yeats's steady evolution as a symbolist. Not only isolated verbal "symbols", substantives such as *star* and *wind* and *night*, but verbs, *barter, rant, rage,* adjectives, *unmeasured, measured,* and entire dramatic figures (the little drama of the ranters and ragers, and of the pacing meditative man), are now made to play roles in Yeats's symbolic poems. The act of bartering "gaze for gaze", can be used to signify a certain value — that of the open honesty sacrificed in the ranting and raging. Yet the poem succeeds in conveying a certain inevitability about the coming of the ranting and raging: it is the first of Yeats's poems, perhaps, in which we can detect the presence of foreboding, a certainty of the violence to come. Yeats is aware of the fact that the things he loves, and which he wishes for Ireland, may themselves be passing on to a place

> . . .   where may be,
> In truth's consuming ecstasy,
> No place for love and dream at all;

This white light of ecstasy "consumes" (the occurrence of this key-verb is significant here) not only the things he loves, but those "benighted things" that go to and fro around the poet's desk as he writes. Even so early, the poet is haunted. Surely the poem's title, "To Ireland in the Coming Times", justifies our seeing in these closing lines a reference to the violence Yeats felt must come. The poem contains both a warning and a preference for the old Ireland.

> Ah, faeries, dancing under the moon,
> A Druid land, a Druid tune!

It seems significant that Yeats fell short of syntax here: the lines are a mere sigh, that at once conceals and discloses the poet's sense of the unreality of the desire expressed. Nevertheless, the juxtaposition of this, the dominant "faery" motif of the early volumes, with the premonition of violence — together with the poet's own more straightforward declaration of position in the earlier lines — makes the poem important.

Associated as he was with the political movement, and, more enthusiastically and thoroughly, with the cultural revival promoted by Lady Gregory, the truth is that Yeats's work was to constitute a bitter rebuttal of the nationalist cause. By means of the nationalist position, Yeats was to define first himself, and then the nature of

his role as poet. "To Ireland in the Coming Times", therefore, is not evasive, but a genuine assurance of spiritual
support in spite of persisting irreconciliabilities and
contradictions between his poetry and the political cause.
We may be sure that Yeats was well aware that such a
"position" and such sympathy are repulsive to the
nationalistic zealot. It was genuine for all that.

Less advanced in its thinking, yet in its own way significant, is "The Dedication to a Book of Stories Selected
from the Irish Novelists". Even here, where Yeats gets as
close as he ever does to the Hollywood-Irish utterance (it
has *Eire* — a form not favoured by Irishmen — exiles,
greenery in abundance, and a dripping charm), there is a
significant hardness about the condition evoked. "Eire"
has "barren boughs". It is, moreover, a "country where a
man can be so crossed" (no Hollywood lyricist ever wrote
more awkwardly than that!), where a man can be "so
battered, badgered and destroyed/That he's a loveless
man". Yet all this — casually versified as it is — is then to
be dissolved in "laughter", the "saddest chimes are best
enjoyed". Here, in other words, where Yeats appears most
closely identified with suffering Ireland, he seems also
most determined to sublimate the condition in a literature
of laughter and sad charm. Finally, Yeats writes the Irish
off the map:

> We and our bitterness have left no traces
> On Munster grass and Connemara skies.

We shall see later that this general association of Ireland's
political sufferings with the past, and with a kind of soul-
fully sublimated literature, is deeply significant in Yeats.

(vi) The Wind among the Reeds: The Secret Rose and the hidden goal

As yet this characteristic hesitancy in Yeats's politicality
remains undeclared. It emerges largely in the form of a
certain guardedness as to matters about which his friends

tended to be wildly emphatic. In proof of this, his next volume — *The Wind among the Reeds* of 1899 — is full of a repressed violence. The key-note of all Yeats's early verse is, as has been said often enough already, the desire to remain within the confines of "dream". We have seen the idea of dream criticized, sharply at times, in a number of poems, and have observed Yeats beginning to outline the salient features of a theory of human behaviour in which dream plays a dominant role. Still, these poems are themselves set within a mist of enchantment, of Irishry — much as the English reader of the time expected. At the centre of this poetry is the belief that

> . . . everything that's lovely is
> But a brief, dreamy, kind delight.
> > "Never give all the heart"

In *The Wind among the Reeds,* the verse is rich with the heavy weight of passion put to sleep — "the Shadowy Horses . . . their hoofs heavy with tumult," "The Horses of Disaster . . . hiding their tossing manes and their tumultuous feet." This sense of drugged violence is related to a sense of glory and greatness having passed irrevocably — the loveliness "that has long faded from the world."

> The jewelled crown that kings have hurled
> In shadowy pools, when armies fled;
> > "He Remembers Forgotten Beauty"

The whole volume is heavy with the same obscure sense of an apocalypse crying for expression:

> *Until the axle break*
> *That keeps the stars in their round,*
> *And hands hurl in the deep*
> *The banners of East and West,*
> *And the girdle of light is unbound,*
> *Your breast will not lie by the breast*
> *Of your beloved in sleep.*
> > "He hears the Cry of the Sedge"

"Maid Quiet" has taken herself off, with the result that

Now words that called up the lightning
Are hurtling through my heart.
                                    "Maid Quiet"

"The Travail of Passion", moreover, that has been associated with the Trojan episode hitherto, is related to the Christian passion: "Our hearts endure the scourge, the plaited thorns, the way/Crowded with bitter faces, the wounds in palm and side". This particular poem ends with a parody of Swinburne's most extravagant decadence: "Lilies of death-pale hope, roses of passionate dream." But we know by now that the appurtenances of passion and dream are not handled lightly by Yeats. With this in mind, we may be prepared to regard the "elemental powers" the poet invokes elsewhere a little more seriously. "The Powers" have "pulled the Immortal Rose". What exactly does Yeats mean here? Is it too fanciful to see here too that awakening sense of violence so often met with in the book:

And though the Seven Lights bowed in their dance and wept,
The Polar Dragon slept,
His heavy rings uncoiled from glimmering deep to deep:
When will he wake from sleep?
        "The Poet pleads with the Elemental Powers"

It is an arcane poem; the symbolism, though clear in itself, is obscure of function. Yet its coherence with other poems in the book seems in itself to constitute an interpretation. For the poet has wished his beloved dead in one poem; at peace in another; and in a third mourned "for the change that has come upon him and his beloved, and long(ed) for the end of the world":

I would that the Boar without bristles had come from the West
And had rooted the sun and moon and stars out of the sky
And lay in the darkness, grunting, and turning to his rest.
        "He mourns for the Change that has come upon him
        and his Beloved, and longs for the End of the World"

These are magnificent poems, and they are love poems. I do not wish to translate them into symbols of another meaning. But the passionate allegory they form takes place in a still larger body of work, the poet's *oeuvre* as we have it now, and this *oeuvre* itself bears consistent and important relations with historical facts. Thus it seems fair to emphasize the motifs of awakening violence, of the poet's efforts to "charm" that violence to rest, and to attempt to relate these motifs to the poet's larger schemes. And the conclusion that one is forced to draw is that Yeats found the prospects of "the" awakening — whatever it might turn out to be — deeply disturbing. The whole of *The Wind among the Reeds* is no less than a kind of charm to keep the forces of violence asleep. The forces are both passionate and political; as he has wished his beloved were dead in one poem, in another he wills for her a pacifying power she does not possess in reality:

> But let a gentle silence wrought with music flow
> Whither her footsteps go.
> > "The Poet pleads with the Elemental Powers"

Elsewhere, the forces of violence seem indisputably political. There is the militaristic symbolism of "He bids his Beloved be at Peace" for one thing, and the ger-eagles of "The Unappeasable Host" for another. Besides, such an association is woven into the very fabric of the Trojan story, and the two strands cannot be disentangled. The whole volume had opened with the Sidhe "hosting" — an energetic image of Bacchanalian women bringing violence and discord. The loved woman, moreover, is clearly not to be protected: on the contrary, she is at the heart of the violence. Consistently, she is represented as one who dreams "about the great and their pride"; she is the "white woman that passion has worn/As the tide wears the dove-grey sands"; She is the

> White woman with numberless dreams,
> > "A Poet to his Beloved"

The woman is Maud Gonne, and the dreams are those of the Irish patriot. The general sense of apocalypse that pervades the entire volume is explicitly related to Irish political dreams in two poems. "The Valley of the Black Pig", Yeats's note tells us, refers to prophecies "of the coming rout of the enemies of Ireland, in a certain Valley of The Black Pig, these prophecies are, no doubt, now, as they were in the Fenian days, a political force." And, "Periods of trouble", Yeats goes on to remark, "bring prophecies of its near coming."[7]

Yeats is less helpful in his lengthy Note to "The Secret Rose",[8] giving us a great deal of irrelevant information about Irish legends and their source, and telling us nothing about the real meaning of this beautiful, powerful and important poem. The Rose returns, now surely in its most explicitly inexplicit form, as the focus of men's dreams and aspirations, as the Absolute that beckons both through the lips of a beautiful woman and through the wounds of Christ. Yeats's opening line finally places the Rose in its mystery: it is now "far-off, most secret, and inviolate". For it, moreover, men go to any lengths: they have sought her "in the Holy sepulchre", yet also "in the wine-vat". Those that have sought the Rose and failed are said to "dwell beyond the stir/And tumult of defeated dreams". By now, we can read this in all its richness of reference. The Rose is the focus of those dreams men live by and die for. Men have named it "Beauty". It drives them to "vain frenzy". One man — Cuchulain again — lost "the world and Emer for a kiss". Another "drove the Gods out of their liss" — and, as a result, men died — "till a hundred morns had flowered red/Feasted, and wept the barrows of the dead." Fergus returns as "the proud dreaming king who flung the crown/And sorrow away." Another "sought through lands and islands numberless years,/Until he found . . . A woman of so shining loveliness/That men threshed corn at midnight by a tress,/A little stolen tress."

It needs no great percipience to detect the common thread in all the members of this highly characteristic Yeatsian catalogue: all are men seeking, driven on, under the domination of some dream or other and achieving either their extinction or their ultimate happiness. At the beginning of the poem, Yeats had begged the Rose to enfold him in his "hour of hours". This seems to indicate some crisis in the poet's personal experience. At the end of the poem, this sense of crisis assumes a more public, apocalyptic cast:

> . . . I, too, await
> The hour of thy great wind of love and hate.
> When shall the stars be blown about the sky,
> Like the sparks blown out of a smithy, and die?
> Surely thine hours has come, thy great wind blows,
> Far-off, most secret, and inviolate Rose?
>   "The Secret Rose"

It does not seem possible, with or without hindsight, to interpret these lines in other than political or historical terms. A more personal reading, in terms of the individual man's emotional life, is surely mere bathos. The Rose's great wind, we note, is full both of love and of hate. The dreams men dream are not all lovely. It is surely beyond doubt that the dreams Yeats is referring to here are those of his fellow Irishmen.

This is the most overtly political apocalypse evoked in *The Wind among the Reeds,* and it marks an important moment in Yeats's work: he is, consciously and unequivocally, dissevering himself from the violence. He defines himself against its objectives. At the same time, if this should seem over-generous to a poet who was obviously experiencing a good deal of turmoil and doubt within himself, we must admit that there is a tendency in these poems to evade the present and the future, to evade the real political issue, by means of recourse to mythology. At the end of his life, we shall see that Yeats castigated his own class for simply refusing to take Irish politics seriously. Here, he hymns the past in order to disdain the present, and thus the future:

> . . . I have forgot awhile
> Tara uprooted, and new commonness
> Upon the throne . . .
>   "In the Seven Woods"

The Rose is deferred to the ultimate recesses of the unimaginable, which can by definition never be realized on earth. Thus the suggestion of political violence (if the Rose is taken for Ireland, the sparks that fly about the sky are struck from the anvil of "Ireland's wrong") is sublimated and raised to a pitch where it is practically ineffectual. So that Yeats's question — "When shall the stars be blown about the sky . . . ?" is rhetorical. By availing himself of a stylistic convention, in other words, Yeats subtly removes his poem from the sphere where it properly belongs, that of political and historical actuality.

If we wished to place the nature of Yeats's politicality at this stage, we could do no better than compare the alternately hesitant and sublimated tone of *The Wind Among the Reeds* with the passionate fervour of James Clarence Mangan's "My Dark Rosaleen". Mangan's poem was cryptic, in that it could be read intelligibly without being understood on the level — the political — upon which it ought to be read. If you do not know that the poem is by an Irishman about Ireland, you can still read it as a passionate love-lyric. Only some quality in the fervour alerts us to another dimension in the poem. No woman on earth — not even Yeats's Maud or Homer's Helen — ever justified such a profound intensity of devotion. This is not the psychosis of late Romantic love, but the driving passion of patriotism:

> My dark Rosaleen!
> My own Rosaleen!
> To hear your meet and sad complaints,
> My life, my love, my Saint of Saints
> My dark Rosaleen!

The casual nineteenth-century reader might have thought its fixated intersity reminiscent of the author of "Annabel Lee" and "Ulalume". In fact, it was the failure to find a correlative adequate to the expression, that made Poe a second-rate poet whose exasperation craved ever more luridly lit celebrations of its own *nevrosité*. Mangan's poem, which is far above the run of the poet's work, is no less passionately intense a declaration than Poe's "Annabel Lee"; but where Poe's love strikes one as being (in D. H.

Lawrence's words)[9] "terribly obscene", Mangan's poem is fresh and vigorous. The political goal exists in the realm of the Absolute, and the poem is profoundly poetic in so far as it is political, and political in so far as it is profoundly poetic.

(vii) Reaction: "At Galway Races"

Historical reasons in part explain why such an absolute commitment of the poet to the political was not possible in Yeats's time. The goal, in the first place, had come much closer to realization: Gladstone had brought Home Rule close to reality, and the English were now tiresome bullies rather than a satanic barrier to the Absolute, as they were for Mangan. The poet requires the ultimate, absolute dimension before he can give any theme poetic realization. For Yeats, as for Joyce, the question of Irish independence now seemed a mere matter of time, and therefore not fit subject for poetry. This is partly why Yeats never wrote a good "patriotic poem". The poets of the Romantic period proper — from Shelley to Mangan and Mickiewicz — felt themselves able to conceive the political in absolute terms, and, conversely, the absolute in political terms. For the poets of the later nineteenth century this was not possible. Politics had become too much a matter of economics.

For this reason alone, Yeats was gradually to feel himself something of a traitor to the Irish cause. Like Joyce, he was too conscious that an orthodox commitment to the cause of independence did not call out the poet in him. To some extent, this parallels his attitude to love poetry. Just as Yeats never wrote a patriotic poem on a par with "My dark Rosaleen", so he never, as we have seen, wrote a love poem as good as "Cynara". He was, in fact, from a relatively early stage in his life a poet of qualification and hesitation, a brooding wary man who was at the same time intensely alive and committed in his language. Necessarily, he failed his republican friends from the outset. The prosecution of the aims of political activism increasingly seemed to Yeats to involve precisely that kind of blinkered hag-ridden obsessiveness he had already written about in "Cuchulain Fights with the Sea" and "The Man Who Dreamed of Faeryland". Thus, the "political" poetry he wrote takes the theme of Irish emancipation, but subjects it to a process of mediation from which it emerges transformed into something else — that congress of themes associated with dream and obsession. It is the same thing with his love poetry. Indeed the one led to the other, the passion to the politics, the politics to the passion. His Helen — who united both things in herself — had become the victim of the dream-obsession she inspired in others. There is evidence here of an early defection in Yeats: he should have given in to her entirely, as to the politics. In fact he did neither, but stood waiting on the threshold, pondering and probing.

Now, there was an important social factor in this situation: Yeats was not Irish, but Anglo-Irish. We must be careful not to explain his subsequent behaviour entirely by this fact. Men often act against the interest of their own class, and their decisions must in the end by respected for what they say they are. This is especially true in Yeats's case, since he continued to give forthright and lucid expression to those values which he felt increasingly to be threatened by the sort of politics in which Maud Gonne indulged. Maud Gonne, indeed, gave him endless matter for rumination, and again and again provided Yeats with his subject. For she too was Anglo-Irish, more Anglo- than Irish, in fact. She was in all respects a typical product of the English ruling-class, with an army childhood and an imperial background. She would have made an excellent model for Britannia with her dreadnought chin. She was in fact that most intense of all political types, the offspring of a ruling class who takes it upon herself to embrace the cause of the people her own class is oppressing, and becomes revolutionary out of disgust with her own caste. In every other respect but the actual cause she chose, she was a true daughter of England, domineering, practical, capable of self-sacrifice: she was of the stuff that Empires are made. Necessarily, therefore, she was at some profound level in reaction against herself, and this makes for an extreme of aggressiveness and bitterness. As an upper-class Englishwoman, moreover, she could not *be* Irish, she could only take the part of Ireland (in a play, or whenever opportunity arose).

The intensity of exasperation which Maud Gonne irradiated in her daily dealings irritated and saddened Yeats by turns; but it was of the utmost importance to him as a poet. Here, before his very eyes, was the embodiment of dream-ridden, restless humanity, never at peace, ceaselessly disturbing itself, blinded by hate and love. For Yeats the ultimate aim of all consciousness was to *know*: not to feel, or to sympathize, but to know. The things most hateful to him were ignorance and self-deception. What he saw in the increasing ugliness of Maud Gonne was the action of a systematic and progressive maiming of the organ of knowledge: there was quite simply more to things than she allowed. We have seen that he tended to baulk the political question lurking within his poetry by deferring it to the realm of the mystical or the symbolic. He substituted a mythical Ireland — the land of Finn MacCool and Tara — for the present reality. Where he addressed things more directly — as in "To Ireland in the coming times" — he showed himself hesitant and self-doubting. In the poetry that followed this, there are signs of an increasing awareness of the reasons for being hesitant and for preferring self-doubt to the kind of blind asseveration he saw at work in those around him. He could not, as Maud Gonne could, resign himself to the destruction of a social order for which he felt love and profound attachment. Those things that were black-and-white abstractions to the political activist were for him living realities, the substance and value of life itself. Yeats shows his distinction of mind precisely in his ambivalence towards those matters which were for the patriot cut and dried. In art, this is the professional realism of the poet: dedicated to the absolute register of things, the poet is bound by birth to honour

those things which are real. The Absolute is only to be
attained through the completest faith to the actual. The
matters which the patriots and activists bandied about
carelessly in upper-case slogans, Yeats examined for what
they were. What was under examination now was the
civilization threatened by the attacks of the Land League
and the activists around Maud Gonne. Such is the power of
the political dreams of the activist that the real consequences of the dreams he pursues are swamped, lost to
view.

If Yeats felt that his task was to understand the truth
beneath the abstractions, he was certainly not immune to
the raw emotions involved. He had no doubt as to the
justice of the Independence cause: Ireland should be free
of English rule. But he was Anglo-Irish, free-thinking,
descending from Yorkshire Yeatses of the seventeenth
century, intermarried exclusively with other English
families; and this made him different from the Catholic
with an Irish name and no taint of West Briton in his
stock. When we read through *Autobiographies* and realise
that in all the range of his relatives and acquaintances there
is scarcely an Irish name (it is all Pollexfens, Butlers,
Ormondes, Russells, Millingtons), we cannot refrain
from wondering what this represents in terms of the man's
attitudes. Within the peaceful coexistence of Catholic and
Protestant in the Republic of Ireland — itself a great
tribute to Irish tolerance — the two streams flow in
harmoniously clear separation. The Protestant Ascendancy
is the economic name for the culture that produced W. B.
Yeats, and when we come to consider his poetry we
cannot leave this out of account. He was simply too sane
and too interested in the truth not to be aware of the
importance of these things to him. He shows his distinctiveness as a poet in the fastidious wariness with which he
entertained the implications of emotions and causes (love
and politics) which his lesser contemporaries found all-
absorbing.

Unlike his Russian contemporary, Aleksandr Blok,
whose persisting seriousness led him to embrace the cause

of the Revolution which would destroy his own class, Yeats learned to understand himself by dissociating himself from the political activism which would logically end the Protestant hegemony. Blok's contemporaries flirted with radical politics, then gravitated back to the class-interests of the intelligentsia: Blok persisted in being a revolutionary poet. Yeats took the opposite course. He had, to say it again, no doubts on the fundamental question. There is no hankering in his work for a perpetual West Britony. Yet there is a profound ambivalence in much of the poetry. Consciously and intellectually, Yeats's mind was made up: Ireland should be free. He nevertheless began to feel that he could not fulfil himself as a poet by blinkering his mind to the realities involved in bringing independence about by violence and agitation. To the real political activist, such feelings are irrelevant, mere squeamishness, the end justifying the means, such scruples are the hall-mark of the bourgeois mandarin. But this is of course exactly what Yeats was; the bourgeois mandarin has his point, especially when he is also a considerable poet. For Yeats the "end", so clear and unambiguous for the Fenian, was unknowable: he felt that time or English fair-mindedness would, eventually, in the not-too-distant future, bring independence about. "To Ireland in the Coming Times" had raised the troubling question, what will *we* be when we get there, if we get there by warping ourselves with hate and fixation?

It was in this poem that Yeats first expressed the fear that something permanently valuable in Ireland was under threat, obscurely but definitely, from those very forces which were working towards its liberation. The poem postulated a vague soulfulness ("A Druid land"), yet this very vagueness was a value. The dreaminess of the old Ireland seemed menaced by the blindness, bitterness and narrowness that are the other side of idealism: idealism is the dream of political activism. The political question resolved itself more and more clearly into that propensity to dream which he had from the earliest diagnosed at the root of human behaviour. The white woman of numberless dreams became increasingly worn, and this spelt trouble for the culture Yeats loved. His new poems betray his increasing sense of alienation from the political and social ambitions embraced with such fervour by Maud Gonne and the nationalists. "At Galway Races" strikes a note often heard in the later Yeats, that distaste for the world of "the merchant and the clerk" which blossomed (if that is the word) into the somewhat strident heroics of the thirties. In this latter vein, Yeats was not an attractive figure. The Nietzschean contempt for the ordinary and the non-heroic which animates such poems as "Lapis Lazuli" and "Vacillation" comes too close for comfort to the naive hero-worship which made writers like Gabriele d'Annunzio, Pound, Stefan George and Bernard Shaw go in for Hitler and Stalin. Nietzsche was in some ways an important positive influence on Yeats; but he was in part responsible for the rather callow heroics of some of Yeats' later verse, verse which does no justice to the poet's real distinctiveness of mind. One can sense in the later poems a semi-conscious refusal to see the truth about the modern experience which militates against the full use of the poet's mind. This is different from what we see in "At Galway Races". Here a wonderful freshness redeems the scorn for the commercialism of the twentieth century. In some of the late poems there is a terrible emptiness at the centre, producing not the nostalgic joy but the factitious Nietzchean *Fröhlichkeit*, than which there is nothing on earth more ghastly. In "At Galway Races" there is a positive presence: the poem celebrates the fact of men held together by one joyous impulse.

Now this is the closest Yeats ever gets to celebrating a Shelleyan abandon. It is also perhaps the first instance of Yeatsian man seen in his positive aspect. For the effect of joy in the poem derives from the fact that the people in it are all dominated by one emotion: they are "all of the one mind". Thus, "abandon" in fact is just what we don't have: abandonment in Yeats is merely positive domination, transcendance of the ordinary plane of reality through subordination to some powerful overmastering "impulse". If Shelley's poetry all the time tends towards the splitting-open of its own techniques, Yeats's characteristically fulfils itself in containment. This is especially true of "At Galway Races". The technique, with its often risky "bad" rhymes ("course is/horses"), loosely and effectively ropes everyone in together. It is itself an image of just that happy subjugation the poem as a whole celebrates. Equally easy is the simplicity of the "observations": it is enough for Yeats to point to "the riders upon the galloping horses", and then "The crowd that closes in behind". Somehow the absence of any striving-after-effect here is of the essence of the easy good breeding that is at the heart of the poem's values. The poet can move easily into his nostalgic regret — "We, too, had good attendance once," — with none of that rankling bitterness that appears sometimes later on in the poet's life. What is Yeats talking about here? Is "good attendance" the servants the Anglo-Irish élite can no longer count on, or simply the fact of good company? Whichever social fact is meant, the effect is not of selfish disgruntlement, but of generous regret. Again, it is the language that bears this out: "we", who had "good attendance once", were also "hearers and hearteners of the work". There is a kind of maximized ambiguity here. Language could hardly contain less specific reference, yet be more effective at transmitting a sense of social well-being. The words are made to combine by that overriding yet not bullying force which effortlessly draws the whole poem along, constituting itself an image of that generous social hegemony extolled throughout the poem. A conservative social philosophy can rarely have been presented so sympathetically or convincingly. A number of later poems — "The Cat and the Moon", "An Irish Airman Forsees his Death" — seem similarly to emanate from a hidden rhythmic spring expanding throughout the poem to produce an effect of ease and vitality without one's being obliged to acknowledge the poet's skill at any particular point. The language — as Irish estate agents say of the land they wish to sell you — is in good heart.

The regret is given only five lines, the glass of memory eventually being clouded over by the clerk's and merchant's "timid breath". Then the poem modulates into the future by means of an imperative:

Sing on: somewhere at some new moon,
We'll learn that sleeping is not death,
Hearing the whole earth change its tune,
Its flesh being wild, and it again
Crying loud as the racecourse is,
And we find hearteners among men
That ride upon horses.
"At Galway Races"

There are several important characteristic devices of rhythm and syntax here. Most remarkable perhaps is the triple suspension within the lines "Hearing the whole earth change its tune/Its flesh being wild and it again/Crying aloud ... " The sense is, as it were, jacked-up at "death", and Yeats inserts a series of suspensive clauses introduced by the present participle, none of them repeating the other in syntax; the subject of "hearing" is "we", of "being" (earth's) "flesh". The subject of "crying aloud" is also "earth", but in such cases, the verb *to be* bears a different kind of relation to the subject from any other verb, so that Yeats' effect is at first unclear. The resultant effect of a kind of abundant gallop is increased by the rhythms. "Hearing" inverts the stress-pattern that has been fairly consistent throughout the poem hitherto, at the same time as it suspends the onward movement of the sentence grammatically. Such effects are available to Yeats precisely because of the weight he habitually places upon the downbeat of his rhythmic units. We shall see later that these two effects working in conjunction – the suspension of sense by the use of the present participle and the inversion or disruption of the stress-pattern of the stanza – play a profoundly important part in Yeats's poetry.

The "bad" rhyme returns slightly modified "the racecourse is/upon horses", – looping the whole poem together with something of the not too tight, not too professional galloping of the country horsemen themselves.

The "banality" also achieves a kind of apogeum: Yeats need say no more by way of description than "men that ride upon horses" for the poem to reach its resolution. With men galloping the poem began; with men galloping it ends; only now they are not the men introduced descriptively at the beginning. They now stand for "hearteners among men", the community and order that have gone from the earth, and therefore epitomize the reasons for rejoicing and regretting at the same time.

Within the loose comfortable envelope of the verse, however, there is a more sombre motif. The joy of the crowd at the races is related to the earth's changing tune, and to the wildness of its flesh. The poem has celebrated the positive aspect of domination: the men at the races are joyously subjugated, and it is "delight" that has made them "of one mind". There were to be relatively few later occasions when Yeats was able to celebrate such domination-by-delight. Domination has already begun to emerge as the salient feature of Yeatsian man, and it is significant that he should find domination by delight here in the form of an ancient and essentially noble ceremony: it is the ancient sanity of the community in which horse-riding is natural and enjoyed that subtends the mastering delight. (Ceremony in Yeats, incidentally, rarely means the kind of ossified dead ritualization of "life" that sometimes seems to be understood by the word, but rather a certain ease, born of years of custom, unthreatened by violence and change, and therefore able to breathe at freedom). In the case of "At Galway Races", this ease and delight seem to be "in tune with nature" in a way which is not often encountered in Yeats. Yeats was generally with Blake and against Wordsworth in his opposition to the idea of man's finding happiness by somehow "getting-with" Nature, and in his general scepticism to the idea of the "natural man". Here, nature is visited first at the new moon — a significant fact, surely with its connotation of the demonic and the magic. And the earth's flesh is "wild", "crying aloud as the racecourse is". There is no doubt that the event looked forward to, or at least willed and invoked, is positive. Yet it is surely interesting that the earth or nature here is as it were possessed: it sleeps, it dreams, its flesh is wild and it cries aloud. This is rather that demonic Nature of Coleridge than the deep harmonic principle of Wordsworth. At any rate, there is no denying that Yeats is celebrating in this poem a condition remarkably close to that state of possession he was to deplore or lament in so many later poems: man subjugated or driven, and nature wild.

The continuity of the poem with "To Ireland in the Coming Times" and many other earlier poems is evident. The old and the established order is presented in its most positive aspect, and is implicitly or explicitly under theat. This positive order is also, we shall see, presented to us as a dream, the dream of civilization, as opposed to the nightmare of barbarism. Yet the matter is more complicated than such a formulation suggests. Yeats is to be more precise in his inspection of the dreaming man characteristically indulges in than this clear dichotomy indicates. Man does not have a specific organ of dream: dream is of his intellectual and spiritual nature, and it is complex in its workings. The dream of order and joyous delight celebrated in "At Galway Races" is threatened in the poem merely by the encroachment of the insidiously small-minded commercialism eroding the base of the old civilization. But the culture Yeats was always to identify himself with, and never to betray, was under threat from a more high-minded and at the same time more destructive consciousness — the political consciousness of the kind represented in Maud Gonne. This consciousness works not by insidious encroachment but by "agitation".

"Agitation" is another key-word in Yeats. It receives its first important statement in another poem from *The Green Helmet,* "Upon a House Shaken by the Land Agitation". This poem is the proto-type of those great elegies Yeats was to write late in life, "Coole Park, 1929" and "Coole Park and Ballylee, 1931". Like some other Yeats poems, this one takes the form of a series of rhetorical questions. The fact is not without significance, surely. The questions implicitly expect the answer in the negative ("how" cannot be answered by yes or no, but the equivalent answers expected here are negative — "it wouldn't", or "in no way", or "not at all"), but questions they are, not statements. Such questions admittedly come naturally to an Irishman, who characteristically answers a question by putting another suggesting its idiocy. There is, at any rate, no doubting the power and directness of Yeats's implied statement within his rhetorical questions. Each question carefully modulates so as to answer these queries raised by the earlier, and the poem ends with a straight-forward statement of the values implicit in the questions — "high laughter, loveliness and ease". Yeats was perhaps the last major European poet who could name openly the "values" he was inwardly prepared to stand by. There is in fact a considerable — if not an absolute — difference between those values somehow "implied" in and through a literary text, and the value named and identified by the poet. There is always the possibility of course that history may subvert the poet, trusting to something else in his text or tale rather than to the "named" values. It is difficult to see how this could happen in the case of Yeats's poem in this instance, since the naming of the values proceeds out of the preceding text naturally and inevitably. Neither Rilke nor T. S. Eliot felt able to give a name to those values they believed in. In Yeats they are not only given a name — made honest as it were — but are given the verbal support that guarantees their integrity from the outset:

> How should the world be luckier if this house,
> Where passion and precision have been one
> Time out of mind, became too ruinous
> To breed the lidless eye that loves the sun?
>   "Open a House Shaken by the Land Agitation"

Alliteration ("passion . . . precision"), punning ("one/ won"), and the resourceful exploitation or foregrounding of the cliché ("time out of mind") — these essentially rhetorical yet natural devices of language co-operate to give the values enshrined in the poem, as in the house, clean plastic definition.

It was of course the existence and persistence of the house itself and the way of life represented in it that made this linguistic support possible. Yeats speaks for a real society here. Neither Rilke nor Eliot knew any such support. They were lost children of alienation: they created symbolic landscapes and disappeared into them. Rilke's Austro-Hungarian castles were charade houses, with little or no visible support in political or societal actuality. Yeats's ancestral houses stood in actual ground, and they were — still — animated by a vigorous life. Yeats was, that is to say, in the literal sense, an "old-fashioned" poet: the old world fashioned him, and he was able to assume its reality if not unthinkingly, at least authentically. This emerges artistically in certain plastic values, which are testable on the page. His endorsement of values out of alignment with the "progress" of society as a whole necessarily partook of a certain defensiveness, but there is in it none of that hollow ring of the man deceiving himself or blinded to historical realities. On the contrary, his defensiveness is a token of his open-eyed intelligence about the matter. His social philosophy — briefly that social hierarchy is justified or not in the excellence of its end-product — manifests itself also as eloquence. Eloquence is perhaps the literary virtue neither Rilke nor Eliot could afford themselves. Eloquence appears as a kind of art-speech equivalent to the social reality it expresses. So we find Yeats here proposing

> . . .   a written speech
> Wrought of high laughter, loveliness and ease?

It is such poetry that intimates Yeats's approach to those matters which were ultimately to draw from him the finest poetry of which he was capable.

(viii) "A Woman Homer Sung": agitations

What we can call the two major threads of Yeats's early poetry — the love poetry inspired by Maud Gonne-Helen of Troy, and the political poetry expressing a vague sense of unease about the future of a valued culture – come together at about this time. For that vague Romantic sense of disturbance associated with Homer's heroine in *The Rose* now appears in overtly contemporary form. In "A Woman Homer sung", the poet confesses himself seized by a love strangely unlike love, and more like possession. If another man approaches her, the poet shakes with fear, yet resents it as "bitter wrong" should any man fail to pay her homage. Like the owner of a precious old master, he is afraid of losing her, never at peace in his "possession", yet trembles and curses should the visitor not admire enough. He cannot "enjoy" her: the second stanza states his function as to provide a "glass" in words for her. The last stanza of the poem returns to the time of the first (the second line of each stanza is "When I was young") by providing the "glass" of which the second has spoken:

> For she had fiery blood
> When I was young,
> And trod so sweetly proud
> As 'twere upon a cloud,
> A woman Homer sung,
> That life and letters seem
> But an heroic dream.
>   "A Woman Homer Sung"

It is a magnificent tribute, the verse as light and breathing as that of the previous stanza, with its Blakean verbs ("I wrote and wrought") had been forged and industrious. The "heroic dream" of the Trojan War is here expanded to include the poet's own life ("letters"), and as such emerges as the more general type of human endeavour that it becomes in Yeats. The alarms expressed in the first stanza, with its dread of being dispossessed, were clearly real ones. The tone of the whole tribute in fact is subtly different from those early celebrations ("He Wishes for the Cloths of Heaven", "He remembers Forgotten Beauty"). The woman stands for disturbance in a more literal sense.

"No Second Troy" shows the poet free enough to register for the first time an awareness of qualities in the dream-woman which are inconsistent with the rapt adoration of the Romantic worshipper. It is here also that that obscure prophetic quality of some of the earlier poems ("To Ireland in the Coming Times" and "The Secret Rose") is related to the beautiful woman and to actual social and political details. Once again the poem takes the form of rhetorical questions. What is especially interesting is what the poet is prepared to concede in his questions. The beautiful woman, it now appears, has "filled (his) days/With misery". We had not suspected this before, except in the pleasurable sense in which the Romantic lover was conventionally supposed to tremble and shake with passion. His earlier lamentations had been provoked by age (or a premature sense of age), or by the "eternal" truths of love. What we have here is something different — specific and real grievances caused by faults in the beloved which previously had not been allowed to exist. The Beautiful Woman, who is at once distinguished from and related to Helen of Troy by the poem's title, has been doing things the poet finds troubling. The identification, that is to say, of Maud and Helen, is in process of becoming both more than and less than a trope. She has, in the first place, "taught to ignorant men most violent ways"; she has taught them to hurl the little streets upon the great/Had they but courage equal to desire". This is Yeats's first direct reference to Maud Gonne's political activism, and it is a most significant moment in his poetry. From being a vague source of unease, she has been named as an instigator — an agitator. The nature of her activities is repugnant to the poet: he does not like the "violent ways", as we should have been able to predict from "Upon a House Shaken by the Land Agitation" and "To Ireland in the Coming Times". He is disturbed for more than one reason that the inhabitants of the "little streets" are being urged to turn against those of the great. (Yeats scorns the poor for not having the courage of their convictions here, though rather inconsistently he doesn't praise them for having it later.)

This is specific and actualized political poetry. Yet what

is most remarkable is that, at this stage, Yeats was still sufficiently indifferent to the issues involved to be able to offer them as fuel for the poem's bonfire: they become elements in the hyperbolic tribute the poem's rhetorical questions imply. The reason why he "cannot" blame her, the reason why she has encouraged the poor to attack the rich, is that there is no object worthy of her desire:

> What could have made her peaceful with a mind
> That nobleness made simple as a fire,
>   "No Second Troy"

Once again we have the image of fire, always associated at this stage with Troy and Helen, to symbolize both the Absolute of beauty and mind untrammeled by sordid reality, and the evil consequences of agitation and disturbance. It is followed here by a superb simile: her beauty is "like a tightened bow". The figure evokes at once an unforgettable picture of the woman's beauty (one that is borne out by the photographs of Maud Gonne herself — Brittania-like as that jaw is), and captures its dangerous quality. In the image of the bow, in fact, Yeats has collapsed cause and effect of the Helen syndrome: her beauty is like a tightened bow, and because of it the bows of war are bent.

Nothing about this remarkable poem is more remarkable than the fact that history chose both to complete it for Yeats and spoil it at the same time, by transforming his final rhetorical question into a real question, to be answered in the affirmative:

> Was there another Troy for her to burn?

The line is offered as a final hyperbolic tribute, supremely flattering because its formal question requires no answer. Yet the vengeful agitations fanned by the woman who unites the themes of love and violence, passion and politics, were finally to produce the bloodshed and bitterness of actual war, and the second Troy was Ireland. The beauty is again a weapon of destruction: history and the poet's own acumen turn the hyperbolic tribute into accurate prognosis. Yeats's association of Maud Gonne with Helen of Troy was more justifiable than he had known. His poem worked against itself, and in undoing itself fulfilled itself.

It is in the poems of this period, then, that passion and politics emerge as inextricably interrelated in Yeats. Of course, the original choice of Helen of Troy as focus had rested upon such an association. But there is a great difference between the intuitive and Romantic view of Helen (launching her thousand ships and initiating the burning of the towers) and the conscious perception, in these later poems, that the passions that animate the lover and those that drive the idealist or the agitator are deeply allied. Yeats never wrote a love poem as "good" — as passionately headlong — as Ernest Dowson's "Cynara". Yet there can be no doubt that Maud Gonne meant far more to him than the harlot in Dowson's poem meant to him: indeed it is the essence of Dowson's poem, which is a true Romance love poem, that the particular woman does not matter: what matters is Love. And it is to this that Dowson is so headlong in his commitment. Yeats could never give himself to Love in this way. There was always a range of further emotions. These emotions concerned man himself in his dealings with his fellow-men and with his own deepest needs. In particular, they concern his capacity for dream and for being driven by dream. Love itself remained a central theme for Yeats precisely because it was the most spectacular instance in human culture of man's capacity for being possessed by a dream. The whole litany of love is made up of terms which apply equally well to those dreams Yeats was beginning to see at work in the activities of the people around him. The lover is "possessed", *ob*sessed, driven; he is no longer "himself", he behaves abstractedly, foregoes his usual pleasures, works against his own immediate interests, even to the extent of not eating; his comfort is irrelevant to him — more, it is disgusting, associated with that ordinary world which knows nothing of love. All these stock properties of the Romantic lover Yeats saw curiously distorted in the behaviour of men and women in love not romantically, but politically.

(ix) The ideology of dream

The book in which these important political and societal poems appear, *The Green Helmet* (1910), sounds also a sourer, less Romantic note, a note which has endeared it to modern critics. It was the experience of working in the Abbey Theatre from 1904 to 1910 that gave Yeats the perspective he needed to develop. He is now to be found complaining about "work" (a thing unknown from the earlier books):

> . . .   My curse on plays
> That have to be set up in fifty ways,
> On the day's war with every knave and dolt,
> Theatre business, management of men.
>   "The Fascination of What's Difficult"

The truth is that this third decade of Yeats's life had been a trying one. His youth was gone, and he was big enough and intelligent enough to register the awareness of the fact in his poetry, even though his whole aesthetic had apparently been geared to keeping poetry free of such realities. Now what we are witnessing here is, of course, the phenomenon of growth: we would have less respect for Yeats if he did not tell us these things. But there is a big difference between growth and *growing-up*; between changing, that is, and merely waking up out of a delusory state of mind. By and large it seems fair to say that modern criticism has been eager to celebrate Yeats as a man who eventually matured to the extent of being able to see that his earliest verse had been foolish and empty. Yet such an account destroys Yeats's *oeuvre* by concentrating attention exclusively on his later poetry as a poetry of confession. The truth is that the later poetry only makes sense in terms of its relationship to the earlier: the dream-quality of the first Yeats is absolutely central to the meaning of all his later work.

In the process of evolving, Yeats deliberately distanced himself from the early work in a way which perhaps suggests to commentators of a certain disposition that we, too, can spurn these books. A careful inspection of Yeats's metaphors makes this impossible. "The Coming of Wisdom with Time" is the best instance of this kind of poem:

Though leaves are many, the root is one;
Through all the lying days of my youth
I swayed my leaves and flowers in the sun;
Now I may wither into the truth.

This may seem to offer, at first sight anyway, good ammunition for those critics who want to discount Yeats's early work *en bloc*. In fact it does nothing of the sort. The leaves and flowers are just as important as the roots and branches — more important, even, since they are arguably its *raison d'être*, its evolutionary justification. This poem does not offer a rejection of the early work, though it does constitute a distancing from it, a determination to honour the change that has come about in the man. The tree will produce later crops, more leaves and flowers: what the poem suggests is that when the foliage is dead, it is indecent to go on proffering it as if it were alive. In cultural terms this means that the style must change with the changes in the man (the tree as a whole). This poem, therefore, offers a metaphor for the creative work which Yeats was always to honour. "The root is one", we note. It is not to be mistaken for the subject and purpose of the poet's work. Poetry is concerned with super-structure, not base. Certainly, Yeats accuses himself of having lied; but lying is difficult to define. All poetry (as fiction) can be viewed as lying, from a certain point of view, and Yeats certainly had at no time any sympathy for the view that poetry's main purpose is to "tell the truth", — not, at least, in the sense likely to be intended by the cultural empiricist impatient with all this aery-faery fantasy. Yeats was to proceed not by the rejection of fantasy in favour of "the Truth", but by the closer and more thorough inspection of the faculty of making fantasies — of dreaming.

In doing so, he was honouring an ancient conception of the poet's function. This is the Apollonian conception of the poet as interpreter of dreams. We can do no better at this point than go straight to Nietzsche. Early on in *The Birth of Tragedy,* Nietzsche quotes Hans Sachs's instructions to the young Walther in *The Master-singers:*

> My friend it is the poet's work
> Dreams to interpret and to mark.
> Believe me that man's true conceit
> In a dream becomes complete:
> All poetry we ever read
> Is but true dreams interpreted.[10]

Just what a "true" dream might be, is something of a mystery. But the general conception is clearly expressed and comes close to a satisfactory definition of Yeats's general methodology. By this stage some indication of the ways in which, even as a young poet, Yeats was beginning to interpret dreams, has already been given. We are concerned with more than the characteristic *fin-de-siècle* weakness for substituting a wish-fulfilment world for the real one. The dislike of a harsh reality certainly formed part of the young poet's *Weltanschauung.* But his "awakening" — signs of which we have already witnessed in "The Coming of Wisdom with Time" — does not take the form simply of a mature recognition that the world lies "out there", cold, harsh and forbidding, like the waking world after a dream. Such an awakening would cancel the Apollonian function altogether, and this, as we shall see, would be to destroy the substance of Yeats's mature poetry. What the poet comes to recognize is not merely that he had been foolishly dreaming, in flight from "reality", but that those abstract, hard-headed, pragmatic and positivistic men around him — against whom his own poeticality had been unconsciously defined — were themselves in the grip of certain dreams, ideals, drives, ambitions; that his own dreams, moreover, constituted policies, which could be formulated as well as theirs. The faculty of dreaming, therefore, is of the utmost importance in Yeats, and his lifelong preoccupation with it is a serious — if not the most serious — part of his poetic achievement. We might even come to regard the concern with dream as the identifying feature of Yeats, and to trace to this fact not the inherent disabilities of the poet brought up under the wing of William Morris, but the source of a sustained and profound enquiry into the nature of twentieth-century life. To justify this view, we require of course a more serious conception of dream (fantasy) than is often assumed.

For such a view of the dreaming faculty we have plenty of authority. Nietzsche was himself the acolyte of Schopenhauer, whose distinction it was to have given perhaps the first articulate expression to what later became known as the Freudian theory of dream as wish-fulfilment.[11] And of course it is Nietzsche's investigation of the dream-art of Apollo to which Yeats is, in the first instance, indebted. But we must note that the dream remains — in *The Birth of Tragedy* at least — the province of the night. It is dream as the man in the street understands it — nocturnal dream, taking place in sleep — that Nietzsche characterizes beautifully in the opening pages of *The Birth of Tragedy*. Brilliantly as Nietzsche analyzes the "plastic art" of the Apollonian dream-interpreter, he does not make the transition to that broader, second meaning of dream to which the nocturnal wish-fulfilment fantasies are so deeply analogous. The dreams of success, happiness, empire, ambition which motivate so many of our conscious actions were certainly understood by Freud as "day-dreams". And indeed Freud made the connection between the innocent day-dreaming of the errand-boy and what goes on in novels and plays. Freud's treatment of art is somewhat reductively philistine, but there is no doubt that he understood that the drive that makes us dream at night does not go to sleep during the day.[12] The activity of the day-time dream, however, is not confined to those abstracted fantasies we allow ourselves to indulge in when nothing else is pressing for our attention. What is much more fundamentally directive than the impulse to day-dream and wish our lot better than it is, is the vaster, unconscious dreaming that shapes societies, and the lives of the individuals within them. It would not be difficult to show that our entire lives in their general shape and direction were dominated by different and often conflicting dreams. Not merely our "fantasies" (and it is significant how this favourite word of Yeats's has acquired a technically precise meaning that underlines the common origin of the two types of dreaming), but our ordinary rituals and purposes follow the lines of dream. All the things we do contribute towards the fulfilment of some dream: we "save or pray", as Yeats later suggested, even when we are without some greater purpose. Such dreams shape not only private lives, but the directions taken by whole societies, and even civilizations. We acknowledge the influence, for example, of the "American Dream" in shaping life and foreign policy and big business in the United States. The Hollywood movie — in its primitive, innocent phase, at least — almost exclusively dramatized the American dream, until failing box-office returns informed it that this dream has lost its currency and should be jettisoned for the critical anti-dream. At the other end of the cultural scale, Scott Fitzgerald's art is devoted, equally exclusively, to the articulation and criticism of the American Dream. It was Dickens who expressed most broadly and sensitively the broader dream of capitalist man — his Great Expectations. Even today we cannot say to what extent life in "the West" (the West that threatens to become the whole world) is governed by the dream of success, of improvement, and, more alarmingly by the atrophy of that dream with affluence.[13] Certainly life in "highly motivated" societies such as West Germany and Japan is driven, from moment to moment, by the motor of material improvement; and material improvement expands to embrace almost the whole of existence. The failure of Soviet art to outlive its revolutionary phase arguably derives from the failure of Soviet man to replace the Revolutionary dream with any alternative. Mere material subsistence — especially under the increasing awareness of the better-off neighbours on the other side of the Curtain — has not proved enough. Neither has the consciousness of living in a more equitable society (to give that society its maximum due). Marxists in non-Marxist societies still dream of a society in which the rewards of labour are distributed "from each according to his ability, to each according to his need".

It is dream in this sense that dominates Yeats's poetry, and it is as an interpreter of such dreams, in the true spirit of Apollo, that he commands our respect. Fantasy, we might say, provides the thesis of Yeats's dialectic. Initially it has several shades of meaning within it. It represents first the typical late nineteenth-century intellectual's refusal of engagement in the processes of a society he despised, a society increasingly bent on nothing but material aggrandizement. Such a society erodes the basis of the culture the intellectual must believe in. Secondly, the fantasy is that of the Irish or Anglo-Irish writer or intellectual who refuses to acknowledge the reality of British overlordship and appeals to a "greater" reality, or to a mythical past of Irish heroes. Fantasy in this sense was induced in the Irish by the fact of never having had the means of their own political management in their own hands. From this point of view, fantasy or dream appears as a subtle form of ideology, which has as its psychological counterpart that mockery which is what most distinguishes Irish from English humour, and which makes it most difficult for Englishmen to know when Irishmen are being serious.

Lastly, dream appears in a more specifically Yeatsian mode as the defining property of Yeatsian man. In this respect, we must look at Yeats's diction, rhythm and theme to discover in them the discursive properties of a "human condition". Yeatsian man is characteristically dominated, driven, impelled, or, in a word, enchanted. This is the connection between Yeats's passion and his politics. For both political man and man-as-lover are under the dominion of an idea or a person. In Romantic love, the woman stands as the mere embodiment of Love itself, or, according to the more severe view, Love itself stands as the surrogate for Death. Both, similarly, are under the sway of dream, like Cuchulain fighting the tide, or Fergus after he has got the dream-bag from the Druid. The dream has already — in *The Green Helmet* — begun to manifest both positive and negative aspects. Positively, dream appears as the configuration of societal and cultural forces summed up in the word civilization. Yeatsian man is at his best when dominated by customs and rituals that have not only the virtue of longevity and persistence behind them, but a certain sanity within them — order, horse-riding, good manners, respect. Negatively, dream appears in the envious agitation of political activism — the little streets striving to overturn the great.

PART TWO

Antithesis: Terror

Introduction

It is clear that no conceivable process of awakening could cancel the "reality" of those dreams or fantasies which obsess man so much. What we are confronted with, in fact, is not a capacity for being deluded, which we could contrast with an admirable common sense, but with the very nature of being human. It is in our humanity to dream, and perhaps the most dangerous fallacy confronting us is that of supposing that leading a full, mature life is in every respect like being literally awake as opposed to being literally asleep. Being awake, or fully conscious, also means being preoccupied with certain goals, drives and dreams: that is what makes us different from the animals.

That this is W. B. Yeats's opinion, is suggested in that otherwise puzzling little quotation from an "old play" which is used as an epigraph for his next volume, *Responsibilities*: "In dreams begins responsibility". What this means is simply that our lives are governed by the dreams and projects we conceive or inherit; and therefore that we must be prepared to stand by those dreams which we at some level choose to live by. We are responsible for nothing more than for our dreams. Yet as Yeats had already seen, there is apparently nothing we are less able to control. The poetry of his next period will concern itself with this dilemma.

(i) Allegories of dream

The poems in *Responsibilities* fall into three main groups: poems repudiating with some contempt the Ireland of the present; a Maud Gonne group; and a miscellaneous group of mythological or parabolic poems concerning hermits, beggars and dead kings. The volume begins with a sardonic admission that, although "close on forty nine", the poet has no child — "nothing but a book" — and it closes with a disgusted repudiation of the "Celtic twilight" manner and of his own fame. Yeats steps out of his earlier manner as if out of a suit of armour he has spent years forging. To this extent the book completes the process begun in *The Green Helmet,* and must be seen rather as a bridge to *The Wild Swans at Coole,* in which Yeats's middle or antithetical period receives its most powerful expression, than as innovatory in its own right. If it does not mark time, it makes little ground. In some respects even, the book reiterates the motifs and attitudes of Yeats's first period, and certain of the poems are actually contradicted by later poems.

The mixture of modes displayed in the volume is more than an expression of Yeats's uncertainty about his position in a new intellectual climate, though this cannot be ignored. When *Responsibilities* was published in 1914, Yeats was conscious of being an old-fashioned poet in the new modernist environment. Not only to Ezra Pound and the young T. S. Eliot, but to the Georgians, Yeats already appeared something of a dinosaur, a relic of the decadence. The uncertainty the poet seems to have felt is reflected in the sometimes uncomfortable switches of tone from allegorical enchantment on the one hand, to a new "realism" on the other. The poet who speaks of beggars and dead kings can seem inconsistent with the poet who speaks of his own work as "but a post the passing dogs defile". Pound, predictably, took this latter image as marking Yeats's emergence from post-Romantic archaism to fully-fledged modernism.[1] That is nonsense, of course, and of a sort which, if accepted, would completely distort the significance of what Yeats later achieved. Yeats never acknowledged the validity of that naive realism which Pound seems to have held to (though a sufficiently archaic figure himself in other respects, with his "thou's" and "lovest's"). In fact the enchantment that appears in poems like "The Hour before Dawn" and "The Three Hermits" is not a reversion to an older, washed-out manner; it represents a significant thematic continuity.

One of the things which has stood in the way, perhaps, of a proper recognition of Yeats's genius has been the dominance in critical circles of a perceptual realism best

summed up in the phrase "telling like it is". Although a
clear visualizer of scene, Yeats lacks all but entirely that
genius for "exquisite particularity" (in Leavis's phrase)
which has been so important in modern criticism. He is
always, apparently, preoccupied with something other
than the given scene. He displays little or no interest in
that characteristic Romantic quest for the objective
correlative; nature is never watched for its clues. It is
indeed regarded, if at all, with suspicion. For Yeats was
above all an arcane poet, whose gifts and limitations — his
subtle rhythmicality, his indifference to the "seen" and his
fascination with the hidden — all worked collaboratively
together. Too much can be made of Yeats's tiff with
George Moore at this stage of his life.[2] Moore was an
exceptionally spiteful man to tangle with, but the
"objective" art he represented himself was less challenging
to Yeats than the new poetry of Pound and Eliot, with its
urban rhythms and its perceptual "touch". It is against this
that we must set Yeats's proud art, not against the slightly
sensationalist and sentimental naturalism of the author of
Esther Waters.

Of the allegorical poems in *Responsibilities,* "The Three
Beggars" is by far the most important. The riddle proposed
by King Guaire is essentially Yeatsian: "Do men who
least desire get most,/Or get the most who most desire?"
By this time, we understand that the relationship between
desiring and conduct — or, to put it another way, between
dreaming and the consequences of dreaming — lies close to
the heart of Yeats's interests. The three beggars predictably
swallow the bait — the bait life proposes all of us in some
way. Having described their illusions first, they set about
the oddly hellish task set them by the King, of falling
asleep first. The poem becomes horribly intense: the pre-
requisite of being the first to sleep is not being the last
awake, so the beggars keep themselves awake in making
sure that their fellows don't sleep:

> They mauled and bit the whole night through;
> They mauled and bit till the day shone;
> They mauled and bit through all that day

> And till another night had gone,
> Or if they made a moment's stay
> They sat upon their heels to rail,
> And when old Guaire came and stood
> Before the three to end this tale,
> They were commingling lice and blood.

There is an anticipation here of the troopers belabouring each other in "Meditations in Time of Civil War", of course, and it is no fortuitous coincidence; Yeats has given a foreshortened but none the less perceptive allegory of a world in which men were just about to begin biting and tearing each other for some delusory dream of advantage. Not merely our modern acquisitive society, but the militaristic adventurism encouraged by that society, is fairly mirrored here. Yeats rounds his allegory off with an effective irony: when the King comes back and announces that the time is up, so that none of them can win the prize, all three beggars

> Fell down upon the dust and snored.

The whole tale is beautifully offset by the italicized commentary on the "old crane of Gort", seen and heard at the beginning and end of the poem delving for food in the river by which the beggars sit and fight. Yeats sees to it that we are fully aware of the contrast between the sane, silent vigil of the bird looking for trout and the crazed wrangling of the men driven on by the dream-bait.

"The Three Hermits" is a tranquil antithesis to this sardonic parable. The hermits are, again, pitiful images of man: they talk of prayer and God but crack fleas and fall asleep while they pray. The central argument of the poem is a throw-back to the Oriental "wisdom" of Yeats's earliest Golden Dawn days: when the first hermit laments that the nearness of death still does not stop him falling asleep in the middle of prayer, the second points out that our deaths mirror our lives and that, as in Hindu scripture, the imperfect or unfulfilled man is simply recycled after death until he completes the job and achieves nirvana. The third hermit merely sings "unnoticed like a bird". It is difficult not to think of the more famous Chinamen of "Lapis Lazuli" at this point. There too gaiety and longevity go hand in hand with an insouciant music. What is perhaps more interesting is the second hermit's observation that the nirvana — escape from the hellish "crowds" that plague us at birth — must be achieved through "passion". We have had many hints as to Yeats's distaste for a certain range of angry and agitated states of mind, and passion has usually been associated with the idea of being driven beyond control. What, then, does he mean by "passion" here? Clearly it is something positive — "most holy" because "most living" — that transcends the failure of the weak-willed. Equally clearly it does not mean — by juxtaposition *cannot* mean — the insensate striving brutally parodied in "The Three Beggars".

The question is too important to be answered easily or lightly. I am not myself sure that Yeats himself provided an "answer" to it in all the length of his poetic career, nor that it is a question that can be answered, being too closely related to the quick of poetry and poetic experience itself to be formulated. Some approach to the question is made in "The cold heaven". Before moving on to this beautiful and powerful poem, however, it will be as well to say something about the last of the three beggar allegories, "The Hour before Dawn". Like the other two poems, this one suggests that it is to Yeats that Samuel Beckett looked when he set about creating his own allegoric world of beggars and tramps. Even the humour reminds us of Beckett. When the "cursing rogue with a merry face,/ A bundle of rags upon a crutch" (Molloy is here in embryo, surely) stumbles into the hole in the ground where the "great lad with the beery face" is lying asleep, he congratulates himself on having a wooden leg: "Were it not/I have a lucky wooden shin/I had been hurt". Once again, as in "The Three Beggars", an allegory shapes itself. The sleeper lies beside a tub of beer, and when the tramp makes as if to help himself to some of it, the sleeper awakens to inform him that the beer has magic properties: the drinker has only to mention a period of time he wishes to sleep, and he will sleep that long afterwards. The tramp replies that he wants to sleep only until the winter has gone,

> Or till the sun is in his strength.
> This blast has chilled me to the bone.

The sleeper says that this had been *his* plan at first, but that he gradually came to want less and less consciousness (ordinary waking life), and so slept longer and longer — "nine centuries/But for those mornings when I find/The lapwing at their foolish cries/And the sheep bleating at the wind/As when I also played the fool." Nothing in life, then, with the possible exception of these moments of spring, is worth waking for. The beggar is enraged and says that if it were only spring, with a South Wind, he would be happy not to sleep. The sleeper's reply really anticipates Yeats's later lyric, "The Wheel". What you really want, he says, is to die:

> For all life longs for the Last Day.

The enraged beggar falls on him, like the beggars in the earlier poem, and pummels the other, but

> . . . might have pummelled at a stone
> For all the sleeper knew or cared . . .

Once again a sardonic irony closes the allegory, leaving us with a bitter freshness: the poem is enclosed with the promise of the South Wind. Certainly we could have no better example of the direction in which Yeats is moving than in his new way with the properties of fairyland: this is no land of heart's desire, but a hard, bleak mirror of our own existence.

A similar hard bleakness pervades "The Cold Heaven", but here with a thrilling zest. Once more we have man "driven wild", but, as in "At Galway Races", the domination is positive. The source of the possession in this case is nothing but experience of the natural world. The poem begins in a spasm, a *frisson* of ecstasy, of the kind that every poet recognizes as lying close to the heart of poetry itself:

> Suddenly I saw the cold and rook-delighting heaven
> That seemed as though ice burned and was but the more ice,

We knew from *Crossways* that Yeats always identified a certain pristine severity — the stars, the night, the moon, winter — with spiritual truth and life. Here is that truth, that life. Because of it,

> ... imagination and heart were driven
> So wild that every casual thought of that and this
> Vanished, and left but memories, ...

The cold heaven does not only delight the rooks (though it delights us in delighting them): the poet too is "Riddled with light", driven into an imaginative trip, an insight into "the after-life". Is this what it's like? he seems to ask. Am I now like the dead, stripped of that which clogs and that which is banal? Such a reading is consistent with "The Three Hermits", with its suggestion that only the man of "passion" escapes the dreary cycle of life and rebirth, and also with the beery sleeper's observation that what men really want is to die. To die is to be lost to the staleness and the flatness of most human experience. The passion celebrated in "The Cold Heaven" is the passion of the intense spiritual experience which vaults beyond the merely phenomenal and tedious by experiencing it with ecstasy. The ecstasy itself is a kind of death, since it destroys every vestige of the normal man. The poem ends, to be sure, soberly, with a chastened "Ah!" The poet as it were stops on the brink of his discovery: the heaven that delighted the rooks is now unjust.

The supple alexandrines of "The Cold Heaven" set it apart from the rest of *Responsibilities.* Its intense yet natural white light (it is an important part of the poem's effect that it is felt to be *outer,* referring to real country roads and real skies, not inner ones) is a kind of visual equivalent of the coldness that runs, however, through the entire volume. Yeats's recognition of a kind of soul-landscape in Sligo has begun to determine the temperature of his poetry. Gone are the warm colours of the early Tennysonian poems: everything now is cold, black, rock, water. This is a fact about Yeats that critic and reader simply have to accept.

It is no use lamenting the absence of warmth and good old human ordinariness. Yeats would have no claim on our attention if he were incapable of deep, subtle and powerful human feeling. But the spiritual values which determine the direction he took (the passion of an intense purity of feeling and thought as against a more ordinary "human" tenderness) must be granted their own validity before the poetry can be appreciated for what it is.

In other respects, too, *Responsibilities* shows how far Yeats had moved into his own territory. The contempt for the commercial classes expressed *en passant* in "At Galway Races" and "No Second Troy" emerges now in a defiance which is almost, at times, truculent. Poems like "Paudeen" and "To a Wealthy Man" do not immediately commend themselves for their social humanity. Yet neither do they, as George Moore said they did, assume that "strange belief that none but titled and carriage-folk could appreciate pictures".[3] Not only conservatives like Yeats, but socialists like Bernard Shaw, were aware that if it were up to "the people", there would be no British Museum, let alone a national theatre. There is in fact a curious harmony between an essentially "aristocratic" critique of modern society such as Yeats's, and those of radicals like Lukacs and Marcuse. The Left has always adopted a tone of hauteur towards the cultural aspirations of the middle class. George Moore was honest in his jibe at Yeats's aristocratic disdain, but it is interesting that Yeats's scorn for the new middle class should put him shoulder to shoulder with the intellectual Left.

By far the most problematic expression of Yeats's sometimes unpalatable social philosophy, however, is "September 1913". Here too there are the by now almost ritualized references to "greasy till", the "half-pence and pence". The scrimping and saving, moreover, are related not to the Protestant Ascendancy, who might be thought to represent not only the spirit but the tangible success of the work-ethic, but, by implication, to the Catholic majority who add not only half-pence to pence, but "prayer to shivering prayer". The result of this abjectly obsessive concern for praying and saving, is that they have "dried the marrow from the bone". At a stroke Yeats redeems and transforms the faintly snobbish scorn with the insight of the poet: the notion of drying the marrow in the bone is one of a cluster of important Yeatsian motifs reflecting the physical manifestation of spiritual or mental processes. Such a relationship – of mind to body – is central to his thinking. Perhaps we should say less that Yeats saw the mind in terms of the body, than that he saw that physical "effects" are in fact themselves essential to the mental or spiritual processes. The effects of wasting, of drying up, of becoming old and wrinkled in tune with the obsessional mental preoccupations – these become part of a complex system of psycho-spiritual analysis in Yeats. "September 1913" argues that "Romantic Ireland's dead and gone,/It's with O'Leary in the grave." This is not a new motif in Yeats: we have seen him lauding the past before, in an effort perhaps to ward off unacceptable change. What is new is the tone – dry, rough, dismissive. New also is the sense of futility that attends his nostalgic celebration of the dead nationalist heroes: "And what, God help us, could they save?" There is a marked difference between the backward glances of "In the Seven Woods" – still heroic in their fresh bitterness – and the frank dislike of the contemporary reality of "September 1913". Any poet must have a view of eternity, and his bitterness is frequently the mode by which this expresses itself. At any rate, Yeats now sees the heroic sacrifices and deaths of the great Irish patriots – Fitzgerald, Emmet and Tone, and the "grey geese" (glorified mercenaries in fact, rather than patriots) – in terms as distantly and definitely mythological as the doings of the Danaan children and Cuchulain. The strivings of the patriots, moreover, is described in thoroughly Yeatsian terms as "All that delirium of the brave". They too were driven, though by more honourable forces than the scrimpers and savers scorned earlier in the poem. By a natural transition, Yeats then associates the patriots with a version of the Helen-motif: were we able to see them now, he says, we would think them mad — as if "some woman's yellow hair/Has maddened every mother's son". With beautiful poise the poem rocks to balance: "They weighed so lightly what they gave." Here is that by now familiar idea of the disparity between the cause and the effect: the patriots behaved as if their lives were of no more consequence than the miserable aims of the penny-pinchers for whom they died.

Mention should be made of a remarkable technical feature of the poem, the consistent para-rhyming of the fifth and seventh lines of each stanza: the sequence of rhymes reads *bone/gone, spun/gone, Tone/gone,* and *son/gone.* The rhymes thus fall into two pairs — *bone-Tone, spun-son.* It is a remarkable display of the rhyming art. This rhyming subtlety plays an especially important part in the sombre rest achieved at last: "But let them be, they're dead and gone". This is the only time the refrain "Romantic Ireland's dead and gone" is varied at all and the effect derives from the muted close afforded by the half-rhyme, *son-gone.*

A contrast of a different kind structures "Paudeen". If in "September 1913" the contrast was between two different dreams — that of the sordid acquisitiveness of a bourgeoisified Ireland, and that "delirium of the brave" — "Paudeen" reaches again for that "passion" so thrillingly caught in "The Cold Heaven". The poem enacts the poet's escape from the "obscure spite" of the commercial reality out onto a height where "a curlew cried and in the luminous wind/A curlew answered". Once again the characteristic symbolism — night, the stars, nature in its most chaste and severe mode — is made to frame a moral vision:

> . . . on the lonely height where all are in God's eye,
> There cannot be, confusion of our sound forgot,
> A single soul that lacks a sweet crystalline cry.

That is what Paudeen misses in life; you don't have to be a

conservative social philosopher to sympathize with the moral reasoning here.

This passionate escape is sharply distinct from the agitation now more than ever discerned at the heart of Maud Gonne's activism.

The brief but pungent sequence of Maud Gonne poems in *Responsibilities* — "That the Night Come", "Friends", "Fallen Majesty", "To a Child Dancing in the Wind" and a "Memory of Youth" — bear the same relation to the tributes of *The Green Helmet* as "September 1913" does to "In the Seven Woods". In the first place, there is a sense that the essential emotional link — created solely by Yeats's devotion, since the lady had become increasingly cool towards him — has now been finally severed. It was to be replaced later with another sort of link, that of an increasingly pitying regret, but the warm, passionate devotion has vanished altogether. Secondly, the lady has now, apparently, moved into the past. Where "No Second Troy" looked to a rhetorical future, "To a Child Dancing in the Wind", and, still more, "That the Night Come", record facts.

"To a Child Dancing in the Wind", moreover, is the first of those poems which reveal Yeats's later tendency to see the past in the present: his reverie-istic contemplation on the figure of Maud Gonne's daughter recreates the child as the mother:

> Has no one said those daring
> Kind eyes should be more learn'd?
> Or warned you how despairing
> The moths are when they are burned?

She too will destroy her Yeatses. The next stanza explicitly forecasts not only this, but also the dereliction of the daughter after the pattern of the mother:

> O you will take whatever's offered
> And dream that all the world's a friend,
> Suffer as your mother suffered,
> Be as broken in the end.

"A Memory of Youth" and "Fallen majesty" both place

the hyperbolic manner of the earlier tributes in an equally emphatic context of disillusionment: we remember that magnificent tribute in "A Woman Homer Sung" who "trod so sweetly proud/As 'twere upon a cloud". Here, too, the woman's incomparable beauty is expressed in the way she walked. But now the poet acknowledges how much he had contributed to her own image of herself — how, in a sense, he himself had created her. Bernard Shaw called Maud Gonne "outrageously beautiful",[4] but could she possibly have conceived herself in as exalted a way as the poet conceived her?

> Believing every word I said,
> I praised her body and her mind
> Till pride had made her eyes grow bright,
> And pleasure made her cheeks grow red,
> And vanity her footfall light,
> Yet we, for all that praise, could find
> Nothing but darkness overhead.
>   "A Memory of Youth"

"Fallen Majesty" expresses the poet's sense of himself as "recorder" of "what's gone", somewhat after the spirit of the Shakespeare sonnets. Once again the intensity of the emotion reasserts itself, as one had not suspected it capable:

> . . .   A crowd
> Will gather, and not know it walks the very street
> Whereon a thing once walked that seemed a burning cloud.

Again and again this will happen as we move through Yeats's poetry. When we think he has made his final crushing judgement on the woman, the old passion forces its way to the surface in some magnificent phrase. And we begin to see why Yeats never wrote a "Cynara": the passion is in the re-creation of itself — in some intense pitying stewardship of the Absolute. In this case, the use of the word "thing" is especially felicitous. Jessie Chambers records that D. H. Lawrence was fascinated by the way Rochester calls Jane Eyre a "thing"; "You couldn't say that in French", Lawrence said.[5] With his marvellous intuitive sense of the possibilities of language, Lawrence had put his finger on a profound truth: the resources of the language and the possibilities of expression are deeply related. Yeats foregrounds his passionate hyperbole by inserting the humble, impossible word "thing": how indeed would a French translator handle that?

The change in direction that is visible in the Maud Gonne poems of *Responsibilities,* however, is irreversible, and towards an increasing severity. This is best illustrated by "That the Night Come". Here Yeats cleverly mixes two modes, one Romantic and hyperbolic, the other mordant and allegoric. The poem takes the form of an imagined epitaph, and draws upon a heroic metaphor to express its subject. The woman celebrated in it is seen as having brought destruction upon herself, as the Romantic lover brings about her own end by being in love with death. This is a significant change from "No Second Troy", where the bored beauty brings about chaos in a *Götterdammerung* of ennui: the violence assumed at the end is, as it were, better than the world deserves. In "That the Night Come", she woos destruction because of the disorder in her soul: she "could not endure/The common good of life", and so, like the king in a legend filling the gray wastes of his marriage day with noise and entertainment, she invites the destruction, as he, by cancelling time, brings night and love (and death) more rapidly. The tone of the poem is considerate, but its conclusion is trenchant.

Trenchant enough to serve as an adequate prelude to the most considerable poem in *Responsibilities,* and arguably the greatest poem Yeats had yet written, "The Magi". It is in this poem, I think, that we are entitled to greet the emergence of the great poet of the next fifteen or twenty years.

(ii) "The Magi": Dionysiac disturbances

The reasons for such a judgement are various. In rhythm, versification, and philosophy, "The Magi" marks perhaps the greatest single advance Yeats was ever to make; most of the major themes of his first four books of verse receive here their most powerful and deeply organized expression. The theme of the poem is possession, possession as numerous earlier poems had defined it. The Magi, of course, traditionally belong with our warmest emotions: they wait for Christ, and therefore witness and inaugurate the new age. Yeats was always agnostic – a "free-thinker", in the old phrase. He had, moreover, witnessed the destructive power of Christianity in the Church's hounding of Parnell. He had also become aware of the distance, intellectually and spiritually, between himself and the Catholics who naturally led and dominated the drive towards Irish independence. "To a shade" – included in *Responsibilities* – is a passionately disdainful tribute to Parnell, and refers to those who brought him low as "an old foul mouth", that "set/The pack upon him". "The Magi" suggests how far Yeats's distaste for Christianity as a disquieting and inherently anti-civilizational force had progressed by the outbreak of the First World War. The Catholic bigot elides with the political agitator in the figure of the magus who stands not as a herald of the miraculous and life-enhancing revelation, but as the fixated prophet of disorder. The Magi, in Yeats, are "the pale unsatisfied ones"; their clothes are stiff and painted; their "ancient faces" are like "rain-beaten stones"; and, most significantly of all, their eyes "are fixed". Such are the details which render the image of what we can call either the idealist or the fanatic. The word *fanatic* – stressed upon the first syllable – is later to play an important part in Yeats's poetry. The word itself does not occur in the earlier poetry, but the lineaments of fanaticism are inscribed unforgettably in "The Magi".

The poem itself is a masterpiece of Yeatsian prosody. It takes the form of a single sentence. The main verb occurs in the first line and the direct object in the second, yet the fulcrum is delayed until three lines from the end: for the poem turns upon the single past participle *fixed*. Fixity is the poem's subject, and the syntax and prosody make sure that we experience it. The word is immediately followed by two masterly suspensions of the kind we have noticed above more than once. Again, as in "At Galway Races", Yeats places one suspension within the other, varying the syntactical relations. The subject of "hoping" and "being" is the same, 'the pale unsatisfied ones'. Yet the effect created in each case is different; "hoping" is transitive; they hope *to find* something, but what they hope to find is suspended by "Being . . ." and the verb's having no transitive function creates an effect of balance, before the grammatical object, "The uncontrollable mystery on the bestial floor" arrives to finish thought, syntax and poem with tremendous power. The effect of unleashed violence could hardly be more powerfully created.

The effect is not created solely by the characteristically wristy syntax, however. There is a still more significant lexical contribution. Among the words I have put into the class of lexically significant elements in Yeats are "trouble", "reverie" and "impulse". These words all unite rhythm and meaning: they function powerfully in Yeats's poetry because their rhythmic effect mirrors and furthers their meaning. The meanings, naturally, are especially important in Yeats. "The Magi" provides the best evidence we have so far had reason to notice of Yeats's deliberate exploitation of his limited stock of root-words to explore a wide range of related emotions and meanings. The effect of the syntactic suspensions in the last three lines of the poem is heightened by the sound, meaning and rhythm of the words "turbulence", "Calvary", "uncontrollable" and "mystery". Clearly there is also a phonemic dimension to the effect created: the repeated "l" sounds, the "-bl" sound, and the echo of *Calvary-mystery* all collaborate to create an effect of liquid disturbance. "Unsatisfied" — occurring for the second time in the poem's eight lines — has by contrast a flat stone-like sound. The fixity of the eyes and the stoniness of the Magi's attention are causally related to the liquid turbulence. Thus the inner drama of the poem is mimicked on the level of sound.

But the centre of this phonemic maelstrom is the word *turbulence,* and this word belongs to the stock of Yeats's root-words. The occurrence of words containing the *turb-*root (from Latin *turbare* — to turn) invariably signals a certain force of disruption in Yeats. There is no more important verbal element to be found in all his poetry: *disturb, perturb, turbulence* and their grammatical derivates, play a key-role in the poetry of this, Yeats's tragic, or antithetical period, and it is "The Magi" which inaugurates it. All the other poems in *Responsibilities* have their formal parallels in the earlier books: they generally go beyond them, but they still repeat the methods and meanings of the first-period work. The beggar-hermit allegories for instance, belong with "The Madness of King Goll" and "The Man Who Dreamed of Faeryland". "The Cold Heaven" is a superior version of poems like "The Lover tells of the Rose in his Heart". The Maud Gonne group have their formal models in *The Green Helmet* — "No Second Troy" and "A Woman Homer Sung", in particular. There is, of course, no possibility of establishing exactly where an artist begins and ends a particular phase of his career; and in the long run there are no phases, only the whole body of work, at the same time complete and fragmentary. Yet the difference between "The Magi" and everything else in *Responsibilities* is, I think, great enough to be called absolute, and to suggest that here a new state of synthesis is reached: here Yeats has changed gear. It has no parallel in the earlier work, and it does not merely look forward to the poetry of Yeats's greatest years, it *is* that poetry.

It does this not only on the level of technique, but of meaning. Yeats is engaged here on what is perhaps the central theme of his middle years, and the sense of a new rhythmic control and responsiveness is part of the process. We may describe Yeats's second, tragic or antithetical period in terms either of the new, critical attitude towards his own verse ("The Closing Rhyme", for instance, or "The Coming of Wisdom with Time" from *The Green Helmet*) or of the emergence through rhythmic disturbance of dark and violent forces which shatter, or try to shatter, the calm mirror of his verse. The new rhythmic responsiveness of "The Magi", therefore, bespeaks Yeats's complex attitudes towards those matters which were beginning to occupy the centre of his attention. These matters had an emphatically political cast: Irish political activity lay within Yeats's constant preoccupation with violence and an approaching catastrophe. Yet it would be superficial and short-sighted to reduce Yeats's poetry and thought here to the political: it is rather more like the development of Shakespeare from the political preoccupations of the great Histories to the Tragedies themselves, which also, it should be noted, have plots about deposed kings, the abuse of power and the social contract. Politics lies in the foreground of Yeats's awareness, but it became eventually a "paradigm of things".

To speak of dark forces in this context is immediately to invoke, again, the figure of Nietzsche. Yeats had been a student of Nietzsche since John Quinn introduced him to the German philosopher.[6] At no point did Nietzsche usurp the influence of William Blake and Shelley on Yeats. On the contrary, Yeats was shrewd enough early on to realize that Nietzsche's thought "runs but even in a more violent current in the bed Blake's thought has worn".[7] There is no question, therefore, of explaining anything in Yeats by the influence of Nietzschean thought. On the contrary: we can go to the poet to correct the philosopher, not to the philosopher to explain the poet. I have described Yeats above as an Apollonian poet, one, that is, whose concern was to create dream-form in order to shape the inchoate or obscure. At one stage, however, the influence of "the strong enchanter" is heard in a cry to certain forces to awaken:

Sing loudly, for beyond the wall of the world
That race may hear our music and wake.
                    "The King's Threshold"

I have suggested above that this strain is basically alien to Yeats: we hear it — or something very like it — in the overtly political poems of Yeats's Russian contemporary, Aleksandr Blok, where it is backed up by the poet's full intellectual awareness. There is little or no conviction behind the student's cry for the new race in "The King's Threshold", an insignificant play which throws little light on Yeats's major poetry. In fact, it is interesting that Yeats had, around the time of the composition of "The King's Threshold", *circa* 1901, confessed to a weariness with what he regarded as the Dionysiac strain in his own earlier verse. He found in Nietzsche's *Birth of Tragedy* confirmation of his own feeling that "the soul has two movements primarily: one to transcend forms, and the other to create forms".[8] Nietzsche, he went on, in the same letter to John Quinn, "calls these the Dionysiac and the Apollonian respectively. I think I have to some extent got weary of the wild god Dionysos."

In fact, Yeats's Dionysiac strain was always rather tame: it may be felt in "The Song of the Happy Shepherd". But the poet's real attitude towards those forces the wild god was supposed to help us unleash is much more maturely expressed in "To Ireland in the Coming Times", where they appear as repulsive and destructive. The truth is that Yeats was a natural Apollonian, concerned to keep the ugly and meaningless at bay by the creation of beautiful form. But the Apollonian must *know* the dark forces, otherwise his forms are uninteresting. The really impressive thing about Yeats is the complexity of his relationship to those dark forces — the Dionysiac forces of intoxication and recklessness, those which Nietzsche describes as co-operating with the Apollonian formal urge in Greek tragedy, and which he sees as essential to the creation of any complete poetry. If the defining limitation of the Dionysiac is chaos, that of the Apollonian is sterile perfectionism — the easy plasticity of the aesthetic. (The two poles might in fact also be described as the impressionist and the expressionist.) Nietzsche writes: "Lest the Apollonian tendency freeze all form into Egyptian rigidity, and in attempting to prescribe its orbit to each particular wave inhibit the movement of the lake, the Dionysiac flood-tide periodically destroys all the little circles in which the Apollonian will would confine Hellenism."[9] This is related to a theory of Greek tragedy itself which is problematic and not always clear. But Nietzsche's main drift is apparent: the Apollonian must be mastering and concerting *something,* something moreover that requires mastering, otherwise his "art" is mere decoration. The dangers of adopting Nietzsche's formulation uncritically, however, without a due recognition of its relationship with actual life, are manifold. Nietzsche can be reduced too easily to a formula, in which the forces of the vital/ unconscious/animal/intoxicant "co-operate with" those of control, order and responsibility to produce "complete" poems and plays.[10] Art cannot be arrived at so easily. Neither are the so-called "Dionysiac" forces to be tapped and unleashed by an act of the will: false-Dionysism is rampant in German culture throughout the *fin-de-siècle* and the early decades of the twentieth century. It is rife in the young Rilke, and even in certain effusions of the older Rilke, such as "shatter me music with rhythmical fury". This is Nietzsche for the salon, a frisson for the ladies, of the sort pilloried by Thomas Mann in the bard of the Kridwis circle, Daniel zur Hohe, whose poetic dreams "dealt with a world subjected by sanguinary campaigns to the pure spirit, by it held in terror and high discipline . . . ."[11]

To beg to be shattered by forces bespeaks no fear of them and no respect for their reality: it is the cry of an effete society, surfeited with the good things of civilization. Nothing is more impressive in Yeats than the way in which he begins to transmit through his verse the violence of certain forces — forces which must be what Nietzsche calls the Dionysiac — without surrendering to the temptations of pseudo-Dionysism. Far from yielding to them or welcoming them, Yeats to the contrary remains on guard against them, and articulates the antithesis of his own dialectic in analyzing the forces which begin to disturb the mirror of his poetry. For if he does not submit to the Dionysiac forces, he is too much the poet to repress them.

In acknowledging their presence in himself, he came to recognize their workings in others and in the political life of society itself. Initially reluctant to acknowledge the violence within himself, he sustained his meditation upon the nature of dream, love and Ireland until he came to full knowledge of it. We have noted above that Yeats was Apollonian not only in the need to impose a certain formal purity upon the inchoate, but in his gradual assumption of the role of dream-interpreter: as early as *The Rose,* he had been interpreting man's dreams. The epigraph of *Responsibilities* — "In dreams begins responsibility" — makes it clear how conscious Yeats had become, in the intervening years, of the nature of his role. Apollo's function was to interpret the utterances of the Pythian oracle, we remember; and the utterances of the oracle were invariably preceded by an ecstatic trance. The interpretations Yeats now begins to deliver himself of, in this, the antithetical phase of his evolution, are accompanied by rhythmic disturbances of an increasingly frenzied kind. Trance and frenzy are later to appear in his work as often as disturbance, turbulence and reverie: Yeats's utterances, too, are preceded by trance-like states.

All this of course is consistent with his preoccupation with magic and his membership of the Order of the Golden Dawn — something otherwise inexplicable. It is as well to remember, perhaps, that Yeats's interest in the occult went along with a healthy Anglo-Saxon scepticism: he was at many times expelled from seances for scepticism.[12] In general his *fin-de-siècle* interest in the supernatural — what Mallarmé called "the inquietude of the veil of the temple" — reflected nothing more than the confusion of the western intellectual. But there was always something peculiar about the tenacity of Yeats's interest. The reality of certain psychic states — trance, reverie, possession, frenzy — was known to him too powerfully, and was too deeply connected with his poetic self, to be merely the result of an intellectual fad. Probably, there is a vein of truth running through even the most transparently obvious charlatanism: the doctrines and formulations of occultism are in general absurd, but the states and phenomena which these formulations are intended to honour seem to stem from deep layers of the mind. It is impossible to separate the mystagoguerie of Madame Blavatsky and Macgegor Mathers from the serious concerns of William Blake, Jakob Boehme and the entire hermetic and cabbalistic traditions. Too much of what is humanly important is invested in, and woven into, these various traditions for them to be dismissed out of hand.

In Yeats's case, the proof of such a contention is, I think, attested by the role of rhythm in his verse: we are not concerned with ideas or doctrines merely versified, but with rhythmic currents and disturbances which constitute, as it were, their own verification. Any idea can be set in verse, but no poet can fake his rhythms. Yeats was — one might almost say — primarily a master of rhythm. That is why analysis of his stature and meaning as a poet can never afford to spend too long on his "ideas" — that is, on those intellectual sprigs he borrowed from random sources, some occultistic and scarcely respectable, others from the highest strata of European culture. Yeats himself, it is true, fairly early expressed himself dissatisfied with the less structured obscurantism of the occult-mongers, and in need of "the kind of exact analysis that drives me back to poetry with my vigour renewed."[13] He meant the more academic philosophy of Kant and Hegel. But even this served — as his words testify — as fuel or stimulus rather than as content. The "content" is the rhythm, and the movement of his verse. In Yeats's case, this involves also the meaning of the words.

Of course, this is always true of a poet's rhythm. Any good poetry comprises image, verbal harmony and rhythm, all collaboratively creating the total verse-entity. But this fact should not blind us to the differences that exist between one poet's rhythms and another's. T. S. Eliot was also a great master of rhythm. Indeed, he is one of the few poets who have left us a lucid account of the genesis of poetry in the rhythmic strata of the mind.[14] Yet the great ground-swell of Eliot's rhythms, with their ambulatory propulsion, does not, as Yeats's does, depend for its effect on the co-operation of the meanings of particular key-words with the surrounding rhythmic and metrical structure. Naturally, Eliot's words contribute their meaning to the effect of the whole: there is no isolated "rhythm" in poetry, rhythm proceeds from meaning. But they do not create it, in the way that Yeats's create his. Eliot's words ride the ground-swell of the rhythm — they are indeed launched by it, at its behest. Paradoxically, it is the Puritanic Englishman, with his prufrockian dignity and cult of good sense, who is the more Dionysiac. There is, indeed, scarcely a paragraph in Yeats where the rhythm is allowed to release the imagery as Eliot's is released in these lines:

> Along the reaches of the street
> Held in a lunar synthesis,
> Whispering lunar incantations
> Dissolve the floors of memory
> And all its clear relations,
> Its divisions and precisions,
> Every street lamp that I pass
> Beats like a fatalistic drum,
> And through the spaces of the dark
> Midnight shakes the memory
> As a madman shakes a dead geranium.
> 　　　　　　.T.S. Eliot, "Rhapsody on a Windy Night"

There is almost a palpable intention, a determination here that an obsessive rhythm destroy the structure of consciousness. How different is the deliberate subtlety of Yeats's rhythm, with its characteristic reliance upon the meanings and metric inscapes of certain recurrent words. For Yeats's rhythm in a sense depends upon the fact that his words are repeated again and again, in slightly different circumstances. It cannot be accidental that Yeats's "style" has proved so eminently copyable, where Eliot's is not copyable at all, though it can be parodied.[15] To imitate Eliot is simply to travesty this or that passage, and every-one, more or less, has had a crack at it, from Henry Reed to Vladimir Nabokov. Even Eliot's prose — as John Updike has shown — is susceptible of parody, though it would be difficult to say in what it consists. The truth is that Eliot was a true modernist, and had no style at all: style was what was left out, not what went in. Yeats, on the other hand, is all style: he is among the most mannered and repetitious of poets. T. S. Eliot is a disguised Dionysiac poet, a real double-agent, one whose cover, that of the infinitely respectable man of letters, member of the Anglican church and the Conservative party, allowed him to preach discipline and order from the pulpit for more than forty years while habitually destroying that social order in his verse. Yeats by contrast is a conscious and apparent Apollonian. His rhythm, with its characteristic rocking effect, is the external manifestation of that collision of subterranean currents with surface forms which, it becomes increasingly apparent, as we move through *Collected Poems,* constitutes his true subject-matter. It is from this point of view that "The Magi" is of such significance. Here, for the first time, we find Yeats grappling with forces he had hitherto acknowledged, but hardly *rendered* through his verse. The theme of the poem, moreover, itself expresses this awareness: the poem is organized at all levels, lexical, semantic, rhythmic and thematic. The fixity of the Magi creates that "uncontrollable mystery on the bestial floor". Note, too, how the poet signals his attitude towards the fanatics from the first words of the poem. The opening words hold them at length, get them in focus, so that their power and danger can be seen for what they are: "Now as at all times I can see in the mind's eye . . . "

I have said that Yeats was the last major poet of Europe who felt able to name the values he stood by and wrote in the name of. Now we can see that Yeats's attitude towards the Dionysiac forces is revealed in the fact that he invariably uses an overt, explicit vocabulary to refer to them. Swinburne, for instance, who was, of all Yeats's older near-contemporaries, the most consistent in his Dionysism, who indeed represents a most interesting confusion of the true and the false Dionysiac streams, allows his rhythms to dictate the wayward course of his imagery. Swinburne's imagery takes second place to the rhythm not because he did not think about what he was doing, but because he worshipped the Dionysiac urge, and would not stand in its way. Eliot, in his subtler, more guilt-laden way, also let the Dionysiac urge take hold of his symbols, though he probably gave them more time to form themselves in the pre-conscious mind than Swinburne, and thus appears more "in control". Yeats, by contrast with both poets, invariably uses a loaded, explicit diction when his poetry is rocked by the violence of subterranean forces. Thus, in "The Magi", we find him judging ("placing", in Leavis's favourite usage) the "turbulence" inaugurated by the Passion of Christ precisely in designating it "turbulence". The rhythmic disturbance set up by the lexical elements of the Dionysiac — "Calvary's" and "turbulence" together — is thus ridden by the controlling diction. The poet tells us that the forces are to be guarded against and mastered precisely in giving them their names. The judgemental element in the meanings of the words defines the Dionysiac forces: to describe a motion or a force as "turbulent" implies that the speaker is both outside it and morally opposed to it.

In general, this will be found (with a single exception) to apply to all Yeats's Dionysiac disturbances: the words by which he transmits its forces are themselves words if not of overt censure, at least of objective definition, which carry a distancing or critical overtone. All the root-words of Yeats's vocabulary share this critical quality, and perform the dual function of expressing the Dionysiac and defining it at the same time: in giving shape to the forces, Yeats controls them. They therefore express, embody and enact the Dionysiac: they are genuinely dithyrambic words, in that their rhythms disturb the flow of the verse, yet they are not part of a Dionysiac cry. This could be expressed by saying that lexically these root-words of Yeats's — the *-turb* words, *reverie, trouble* — are Apollonian; rhythmically they are Dionysiac.

It would be inaccurate to call Yeats ambivalent about

it: the Apollonian control represented in the semantic anchorage of the words prevails over the dithyrambic. Yet the curious complexity of Yeats's responses to so many of the important things in life derives, as we shall see, from his acquaintance and familiarity with matters which are not normally regarded as acceptable and constructive in the body of society. The best illustration of this, again, is his lifelong interest in magic. He would not have been the great poet he was if he had not had knowledge beyond the scope of the socially constructive consciousness.

Because of this intricate inter-relationship of meaning and rhythm, the problem of analyzing Yeats's Apollonian dithyrambos is difficult. But some attempt must be made, if only to indicate the direction such an enterprise ought to take. Earlier, I gave, as an immature essay in the rhythmic mode I am concerned with now, a line in "The Song of the Happy Shepherd":

> The wandering earth herself may be
> Only a sudden flaming word,
> In clanging space a moment heard,
> Troubling the endless reverie.

It is notable that apart from the inversion at the beginning of the second line quoted ("Only a"), the first three lines here are regularly iambic. The fourth line includes two of Yeats's most important root-words, "troubling" and "reverie". The particular collocation here is of the greatest interest, since it is precisely the relationship between "reverie", (or day-dreaming as we say), and "trouble" that Yeats is exploring in "The Magi". Equally important is the metric disturbance set up by the words. Where "Only a" was a mere inversion of the expected metre, "Troubling the" introduces disturbance of idea as well of movement; it is of the essence of poetry that the mere occurrence of stresses and slacks is not in itself enough to constitute rhythm. As Dr. Johnson showed, any metre can be copied, stress for stress, without producing the effect of rhythm that is so powerful when a great poet with aforethought disturbs the flow of his verse. It is the defining fault of metrists to believe that poetic rhythm is obtained by particular alternations of stressed and unstressed syllables, or at best with the interruption of such patterning by judicious confutations of the expected. But it is not merely the disturbance of the expected pattern that constitutes poetic rhythm; it is rather the introduction of idea and sound *in combination with* disturbances of stress pattern. Quite innocuous verse can be found to interrupt the expected stress grid — very little verse conforms to the iron regularity of doggerel — and the source of the power of good poetic rhythm must be sought elsewhere.

In the lines from "The Song of the Happy Shepherd", it is the occurrence of the word "troubling" with its idea, sound and rhythmic inscape that produces the effect of profound disturbance in the line. The adjective "endless", I have observed above, helps to re-establish the iambic grid sooner perhaps than the mature Yeats would have allowed: if we isolate the unit "thé end-less ré-" we find that we have the only iambic elements in the line. We are not allowed to do so, of course: we cannot, no matter how badly we read, isolate the prefix "re-" from the rest of the word, and so read that word itself iambically —' "ve-rié". The final syllable will not be stressed in this way. The word asserts its gently disruptive influence over the paragraph as a whole: "réverie" must be read as a dactyl, and so, in a sense, connects up with the dactylic "tróubling the" at the beginning of the line. But the effect of the line as a whole is not of an iambic grid disturbed by the super-imposition of dactyls fore and aft. It is that rather of a regular surface broken by a subterranean current: the disturbance set up by "tróubling" — in lexical meaning as well as in rhythm — appears manifest in the undulation of "réverie".

As such, the passage must be read as an early instance of Yeatsian Dionysism. How much more important this is in the case of "The Magi", where the rhythmic pattern of the whole poem is so much tougher and more resilient. It is not possible to reduce this poetry to mere regularities disrupted by irregularities. We are dealing with a major poet working near the top of his powers, and so are concerned with an entire rhythmic pattern that is subtle and varied throughout. But it is just this air of control, of wary vigilance — signalled in that opening deictic "Now, as at all times, I can see in my mind's eye . . . " — that makes the final disturbances so powerful. Note, too, the powerfully controlling effect of the four phrases (a high frequency in a poem of eight lines) containing the word "all". We find first, in line 1, "at all times"; then, in line 4, "with all"; in line 5, "and all"; and again, in line 6, "And all". The effect in each case is to place the maximum weight upon the "correct" iambic syllable: the word "all" receives full emphasis both because of its meaning (in everyday conversation we tend to use "all" with emphasis) and because of the support it receives from the weak syllable preceding it: "at", "with" and "And". In the fourth and fifth lines in particular, the phrases using "all" impose the strongest possible iambic pattern:

And all their helms of silver hovering side by side,
And all their eyes still fixed, hoping to find once more,

Now, it is interesting that in this poem, as in "The Cold Heaven", Yeats employs the alexandrine: the extra length of the line gives him the room to create the effect of disturbance the whole poem is in the end to offer. We notice that in the lines quoted immediately above, the strict iambic regularity imposed by the "all" phrases breaks up in the second half of the line, when the influence of the Magi's strange fixity asserts itself: "hovering" in particular rejects any place in an iambic scheme, even though the final phrases re-establish it; "-ing síde by síde" is copybook iambic. Equally disruptive is the juxtaposition of the two strong stresses "fixed, hóping" in the fifth line. Again the iambus asserts itself in "tó fínd once móre", but the disturbance has been felt within the long lines.

In the last two lines of the poem, however, the disturbance is not to be mastered: it is, as it were, placed within the vigilant attention established by the poem's opening words. Rhythmically, the Dionysiac disruption is complete:

Being by Calvary's turbulence unsatisfied,
The uncontrollable mystery on the bestial floor.

It is in fact only the insertion of the prefix "un-" that prevents the seventh line being wholly dactylic. The alexandrine allows of a dactylic grid, subdividing naturally into four threes. But try reading the line *without* the intrusive "un-". It cannot be done. The meaning and the rhythmic inscape of the words resist regular scansion. The suspensive present participle has already been noted more than once as a key-element of Yeats's prosody, prosody more than usually dependent on grammatical and syntactic structuring. Here it varies the suspension introduced by "hoping", weakly letting the turbulence have its head. This throws a great deal of weight on "unsatisfied". Twice in the poem the syllables of this word rap out: "unsatisfied". It is a tribute to Yeats's power that he can make so innocuous a state as dissatisfaction assume so foreboding and forbidding an air. The disturbance caused by the fixity of dissatisfaction reaches its apogeum in the poem's last line. This line cannot be scanned at all, and exceeds the number of "permitted" syllables not by the statutory extra syllable (we have had that in lines 2 and 3 and in line 7, if we give "Calvary's" three rather than two syllables), but by three. The line, if taken apart, in fact, retains its air of rhythmic poeticality, but has no recognizable metric shape: it belongs to no imaginable context but the one Yeats has so carefully engineered for it. We note that the meaning and rhythm together collaborate in the word "uncontrollable". The word itself is not to be controlled: it simply cannot be used in this poetic context; yet it is the only word to use. The word "mystery" represents, again, that hammered dactyl which is the motto of disturbance in Yeats. (So, from a certain point of view, does the main part of the preceding word: "-tróllable" is also dactylic, but I take it that the prefix "un-" and the word's first syllable "con-" make it impossible to read the word as a whole dactylically).

To the last syllable the line resists pattern: "on the bestial floor", shows a last heave of disturbance through rhythm, so that "floor", though in meaning, sound and stress an appropriate choice to end the poem, cannot be read as the last foot of an iambus: "bestial" needs to be read slowly, with three syllables. It is also the most overtly judgemental word in the poem. Earlier in the line, "mystery" reveals, perhaps, Yeats's ambivalence towards these forces, his well-known reverence for the mysterious as opposed to the factual and the explicable. Yet the use of "bestial" surely shows how conscious Yeats was of the nature of much of what he had dabbled in. He was always to be fascinated by magic, the occult, by mysteries. But he was, as we shall have occasion more than once to remark, fully conscious of the ambiguities of magic, even, perhaps of the evil they represented, and of his own function as a mediator or – yes, as himself, perhaps, a kind of double agent.

(iii) "Easter 1916": the paradox of enchantment

It is now clear how important it is to preserve a sense of continuity with the earliest phases of Yeats's poetic career. The preoccupation with enchantment in the first books has now reappeared critically, by antithetical opposition, as that strange fixity – trance-like, immovable – of the Magi. We cannot read the poem without referring to the numerous poems surrounding and preceding it which have dealt so subtly and humanely with various orders of dream-obsession. Taking "September 1913", on the one hand, and the various Maud Gonne poems on the other, it is reasonable to see in the fixity of the Magi a paradigm of that political fanaticism Yeats had long since come to find detestable in his Helen. He had been trying to dissuade her from politics for more than ten years. Many strands of his thinking and feeling in fact had been drawing together. Fanaticism, – political enchantment, if you like – is beginning to emerge as a central, if not *the* central theme, in Yeats's middle poetry. The rigid fixity of the fanatic is causally related to the "uncontrollable mystery on the bestial floor". Thus the "high" elements of human thought — man's capacity for idealism — directly stimulate the negation of his humanity: man becomes "bestial" out of his idealism. The Magi are intellectually fixed, yet the consequence is insensate violence, negating the intellect, and reducing man to the level of the beast. It is with this central paradox, what we might call the paradox of enchantment, that Yeats is primarily concerned in the poetry he now writes.

The paradox of enchantment led Yeats to his deepest and most genuinely tragic poetry. It will be most convenient and natural now to proceed directly to the analysis of "Easter 1916", towards which the arguments I have been advancing *à propos* of "The Magi" seem most obviously to lead us. I do not, however, wish to give the impression of driving a highway through Yeats's poetry, selecting only those things that seem relevant fuel for a theory. In an *oeuvre* as complicated as Yeats's, many lines converge and diverge, many poems are but the intersection of diverse strands, like the passing notes in polyphony. Yeats has also been well-studied — over-studied, one might think — and it is no part of my purpose to offer a "reading" of all or most of Yeats's poems. I mean only to extract for attention a certain theme; if it is an important theme, and my description of it is judicious, then it will cohere with others and perhaps throw some light on Yeats as a whole. Of the poems in Yeats's next volume *The Wild Swans at Coole* (1919), half a dozen at least require serious attention in any study of Yeats, no matter how fleeting its intentions. Among these are "Ego Dominus Tuus", the Maud Gonne group, "The Phases of the Moon", and "The Cat and the Moon". If, therefore, I turn to "Easter 1916", which appeared in the book that followed *The Wild Swans at Coole — Michael Robartes and the dancer* (1921) — it is not to dismiss everything else as of no consequence, but because of the naturalness of doing so in this context.

In *Responsibilities* Yeats refers to two different sorts of passion, one positive, the other negative. The positive emerges in moments of ecstatic apprehension — as in "The Cold Heaven" — and secures man his release from the wheel of mortality (as in "The Hour before Dawn"). The negative encloses man in his own blindness, in dreams which have become obsessional. William Blake is probably behind Yeats here: "To be in a passion you good may do," Blake wrote, "But no good if a passion is in you."[16] This is the difference between the man beside himself (as we interestingly put it), and the man transformed and refined by the fire of an exalted idea. In *The Marriage of Heaven and Hell,* of course, Blake had observed that "the tigers of wrath are wiser than the horses of instruction". Now this is a dangerous doctrine, especially for an Irishman. Yeats was fully aware of the dangers, especially in regard to Irish nationalism. He had tangled with Sinn Fein and the Catholics for many years, and can hardly have been unaware of the irony that *The Playboy of the Western World,* for instance, was a success — intellectually and financially — from its first performance in London, where it was reviled and execrated not only in Ireland but by Irish-American audiences in the United States. Moreover, it was with regard to the nationalist movement that so much of his important thinking was prosecuted: he was involved in these matters more deeply than he could express, and it was inevitable that he should be unable either to extricate himself from his nationalism or to identify himself wholly with it. From the time of *In the Seven Woods,* Yeats had been in the habit of calling Ireland and Irishmen blind and bitter. That nationalism, especially in Ireland, is a narrow and narrowing business, Yeats of all people needed no reminding. What, then, is the nature of the white heat of revolution? Is it black and blind, or white and transfiguring? It is between these poles that "Easter 1916" oscillates.

The title of the poem — presumably with deliberation — suggests a parallel with "September 1913". In that poem Yeats had said that "Romantic Ireland" was dead and gone, "with O'Leary in the grave". John O'Leary —

certainly one of the finest men ever associated with the
Irish nationalist cause and perhaps the first Catholic Irishman that Yeats ever really knew — had died in 1907. But
the death of the "Romantic Ireland" dated back to the
eighties of the previous century, when Parnell had held the
banner. From the downfall of Parnell, Yeats's disillusionment with nationalism really began, though he continued
to be associated with it for more than a decade. Harold
Bloom has observed that "the revolutionary martyrs of
Easter 1916 were to so profoundly shock the conservative
Yeats by proving that Romantic Ireland was not dead and
gone".[17] This is only in part true, and more than mere
conservatism is involved. The greatness of "Easter 1916"
is that it can register so delicately Yeats's profound
ambivalence. The question is, to what extent *is* this the
"Romantic Ireland" of Emmet and Tone?

From the first, Yeats had treated the Rising as a
"Comedy". The participants, from whom the poet is set
apart, wear "motley", the habit of the clown. We must
remember that, by this time, Yeats was a back-number,
as far as the nationalist movement was concerned. He had
been on the British Civil List since 1911, receiving a
pension of £150 per annum, for which he was nicknamed
Pensioner Yeats by the nationalist press.[18] He had also
been a member of the Royal Society of Literature's
Academic Committee since about the same date. This
estrangement is reflected in the jests and jibes and "polite
meaningless words" which the doings of the patriots with
their "vivid faces" inspire from the poet. Yet each of the
poem's four sections enacts the transfiguration of the
comedy into something beautiful and terrible which stills
the jokes in his mouth. Yeats first presents himself as
having been overtaken and surprised by the turn of events —

> Being certain that they and I
> But lived where motley is worn:
> All changed, changed utterly:
> A terrible beauty is born.

More than a personal failure is recorded here. Late in life, in his poem "Parnell's Funeral", Yeats admits that his entire class — the Anglo-Irish intelligentsia — failed Ireland by consistently refusing to take seriously the political (or, really, any other) matter. With characteristically dialectical reasoning, he was to assert there that "An age is the reversal of an age", and that when the heroes of that "Romantic Ireland", whose passing he had lamented in "September 1913", were killed, he and his class "lived like men that watch a painted stage", and that the "scene" "had not touched our lives". In Yeats's case, this characteristic tendency of the Irish intellectual is directly related to the graver failure expressed in the Rising itself. "Easter 1916" does not merely watch admiringly while the serious patriots get on with the job declined by the poet and his ilk. It expresses in its peculiarly subtle balance the poet's complicity in events with which he felt he should have been more actively concerned. For if the poem's first section registers the involuntarily admiring surprise, the second catalogues more grimly the elements of revolt. The catalogue begins, predictably enough, with Maud Gonne, who has spent her days "In ignorant good will,/Her nights in argument/Until her voice grew shrill". This is the first, though not the last, occasion on which Yeats saw fit to mention a particularly unattractive aspect of Maud Gonne's politicking — the shrillness of her argumentativeness. Yet here, ugly as he has found her zeal, she is transformed, along with those men — some promising, another "A drunken, vainglorious lout" who "had done most bitter wrong/To some who are near my heart" — whom the poet had not previously thought capable of any action worth recording. They had been — so the poet thought — engaged in a "casual comedy", but now resigned their parts in it for something not to be taken so lightly.

But what of this "terrible beauty" that is born? The phrase has passed into currency almost too easily. Is beauty ever really terrible? Still more pertinently, is the terrible ever really beautiful? The dangers of a facile Romanticization of the actual are manifold here, and Yeats comes perilously close to consigning the political from one zone of unreality (the comic) to another (the Romantically heroic) without really looking at it. But the poem does not affect us as facilely heroic, so that it is all the more important to do something like justice to its subtle poise. Precisely what it is *not* is the celebration of the arm-chair revolutionary, who jumps on the waggon once it has started moving, and hangs on for a few yards before dropping off when the excitement has gone and dull reality — or, still worse, retribution — supervenes. The point of the catalogue in the second section of the poem is that it facilitates Yeats's transition to his deeper meditation on the springs of the events at the same time as it honourably and honestly confesses to his own failure. We know by now that he cannot have been wrong about the woman's "ignorant good-will" or her nights of argumentation. The Dionysiac dactyls of "terrible beauty" send their rippling disturbance across the poem's texture: whatever response we are being asked for, it is not going to be unqualified.

Sure enough, the third movement of this most controlled of word-symphonies (the only one which lacks the "terrible beauty" refrain) turns away from the actual personalities and events in order to generalize. Yeats does so by means of that image which had lain at the bottom of "The Magi", that of the stone. We remember that the Magi had had faces like beaten stones, that their eyes and minds were fixed, and that therefrom came the disturbance — the "uncontrollable mystery". The third movement of "Easter 1916" makes no mention of Ireland at all. But its central symbol has a detailed Irish lineage:

> Hearts with one purpose alone
> Through summer and winter seem
> Enchanted to a stone
> To trouble the living stream.

The paradox of enchantment found no more overt or precise definition in Yeats, and he has done the job of relating his faeryland poetry to his political poetry himself. These four lines are also a particularly good example of

Yeats's rhythmic maturity. Both "enchanted" and "trouble" do their work of disturbing the current of the verse at the same time as they fix the relationship of terms: the enchantment and the trouble are related *via* the stone which the heart has become. Immediately, the involuntary admiration implicit in the astonishment reflected in the first two movements of the poem, with their heroic refrain, suffers severe qualification. The stone in the living stream of life is contrasted with the natural world — beautifully and simply evoked — which lacks mind and purpose and simply "lives". The disturbing quality of "Enchanted" is transferred to the strange fixity of the stone-heart. The "terrible beauty" the poet has appeared to envy in the "vivid faces" of the patriots transfigures them, we remember, "utterly". We cannot say quite that they are dehumanized. On the contrary, nothing is more quintessentially human than this possession. As much is suggested in the heart-stone metaphor: man is apart from the rest of nature as the stone from the stream, the birds and the horses — in the midst of all, but different from it. This is our human burden, to be more terrible in our essential nature than in our apathy. By constant repetition of a single motif, the mind is transfigured and made not inhuman, but, to borrow from Nietzsche again, "human, all too human". The unfulfilled intellectual, moreover, seeks to fulfil himself (or herself) in the violence he or she envies in others. This highly Dostoievskian theme runs through all those poems dealing with Maud Gonne in Yeats's new critical, antithetical vein. (They begin with "That the Night Come" and end perhaps only with "Long-legged Fly".) It is no accident that Yeats places the argumentative woman with her ignorant good will and her shrill voice at the head of the patriots in section two. He did not, of course, suggest any definite causal relationship between Maud Gonne and the Rising, nor did he ever think that the woman literally influenced the course of history. This is not really the point. The point is that the Helen-Maud association enabled Yeats to understand the deep affinity of love and hate, passion and politics, possession and inspiration. Above all, it was the means by which Yeats came to understand the occult connection between Ireland's dream-like quality (its "soul") and its strange fixations.

In "Easter 1916", the paradox of enchantment reveals its true identity: on the one hand there is the fixity of the stone-mind, of trance, on the other the possession of violence, of abandonment. The opposites in the poem — stillness and abandonment — are mediated in the text by the verb "troubles" — the word, of course, by which the Irish refer to the disturbances leading up to the establishment of the Free State and the Civil War. Once again, the word enacts its meaning rhythmically, and "places" it. But of course the context, with its motif of a "terrible beauty", qualifies the qualification itself: there is to be no head-shaking, regretful disapproval. Yeats had, in admitting himself surprised by the turn of events, also confessed himself impressed by some quality within the intensity. Again we approach this central problem in Yeats, of discriminating between the passion that destroys man by rendering him blind and fanatical, and the passion by which he transcends the merely mundane and material level of his existence. At the end of his life, in a rather bad poem, "Under Ben Bulben", Yeats was again to acknowledge a beauty or transcending quality in hatred:

> Know that when all words are said
> And a man is fighting mad,
> Something drops from eyes long blind,
> He completes his partial mind,
> For an instant stands at ease,
> Laughs aloud, his heart at peace.
> Even the wisest man grows tense
> With some sort of violence
> Before he can accomplish fate,
> Know his work or choose his mate.

I doubt if Yeats ever wrote worse than this (though he is as bad again later in the same poem, with his "indomitable Irishry"). But the lines nevertheless refer to a serious concern, a concern that is apparent in "The Cold Heaven" as well as in the transfiguration of the patriots in "Easter 1916". "Some sort of violence", of course, does make it clear that more than, less than, or other than actual physical violence is intended. At any rate, the problem exists, and it gave Yeats something he needed to balance his poem when he came to celebrate, or rather to record, the heroes of the Easter Rising. For the astonishment he experienced when the Rising occurred enfolds a critique of the violence which, balanced as it is, allows as little to the nationalist as to the loyalist. Love for Ireland motivates the patriots, but its "excess" bewilders them until it is indistinguishable from its opposite, hatred:

> We know their dream; enough
> To know they dreamed and are dead;
> And what if excess of love
> Bewildered them till they died?

The verb-sequence here is significant and characteristic. First comes the dream, then the bewilderment. "Bewilder" can be added to the stock of Yeats's root-words. Again, the word enacts its Dionysiac rhythm and controls it by its meaning: again, the vision is of man *out of control,* because under the domination of some dream, concept or ideal. The disturbance of rhythm ("bewildered" is not dactylic, but as certainly resists the iambic grid) is the means by which Yeats transmits yet controls the forces he now recognizes and fears both in society at large and, increasingly, as we shall see, within himself. If the opposition between Yeats's verse-movement and its disturbance by the dark forces, can be represented in Nietzsche's terms, as the conflict of the Dionysiac rhythm and the Apollonian diction, "Easter 1916" enables us to extend the Nietzschean parallel. Nietzsche sees the achievement of Greek tragedy as the opposition yet balance of the Apollonian chorus and the *dithyrambos,* in which, to quote Nietzsche, we see "a community of unconscious actors all of whom see one another as enchanted".[19] There is surely a close parallel between Nietzsche's "community of unconscious actors" who are "enchanted" with one purpose, and the actors in the comedy-turned-tragedy of the Easter Rising. Yet when Nietzsche goes on to generalize that "Enchantment is the precondition of all dramatic art", the parallel between the two writers turns into a mocking mirroring in which all values are inverted: it is not Dionysiac revellers Yeats sees around him, but the "vivid faces" of the patriots, their hearts transfigured into stones by "too long a sacrifice" and finally "bewildered" into hatred by excess of love.

The greatness of the poem lies in its ability to take and transfigure the Dionysiac terror without repressing it or destroying the contours of its form. At the end of the poem, there is an exact equipoise, expressing itself through the characteristic rocking rhythms of the short lines. The equipoise derives from the candour and honesty with which Yeats honours the occasion, without suppressing his deep misgivings about it. Maud Gonne, significantly, thought that Yeats's poem was wholly inadequate — itself adequate testimony, if one were thought needed, to Yeats's integrity and craftsmanship. There is only apparently an approach to the tone of rebel songs like "The Rising of the moon":

> I write it out in a verse —
> MacDonagh and MacBride
> And Connolly and Pearse
> Now and in time to be,
> Wherever green is worn,
> Are changed, changed utterly:
> A terrible beauty is born.

Once again, the judgemental element in the Apollonian diction — that "terrible beauty" — defines and contains the Dionysiac frenzy, so that the emotion involuntarily experienced and aroused by the intonation of the names, is converted into terms that place it. The poet's function, we notice, is to name, to number, to intone. Yet this primordial bardic function obliges the poet to be a witness in the fullest sense: the poetic-ness of the poem is its *integritas,* its wholeness. There is nothing for the gunman in Yeats's poem, any more than in O'Casey's plays, and that is why Maud Gonne did not like it. As far as the "Easter Rising" is concerned, Yeats was not alone in regarding it as the "heroic tragic lunacy of Sinn Fein"[20] rather than a concerted, spontaneous expression of popular sentiment. Regarded strictly in the light of *Realpolitik,* on the other hand, the Rising could be seen as a master-stroke, correctly predicting that England, in no mood to deal with an Irish rebellion with a World War on its hands, would mete out savage retribution, and therefore swing Irish opinion behind Sinn Fein. This is in fact, exactly what did happen: 73 out of 103 elected members at the election of 1918 were Sinn Fein or republican, and the Dail's first move was to vote for complete independence from England. None of this could have been anticipated from Irish opinion before the Rising. Seen in this way, the Easter Rising was neither heroic nor lunatic, and Yeats's poem does it more than justice.

(iv) Blok, Yeats, Nietzsche

The peculiarly subtle balance achieved at the end of "Easter 1916" demonstrates that Yeats's dissension from what we might call a Nietzschean view of things went much deeper than aesthetics. By Nietzschean, I mean genuinely Dionysiac: the Nietzschean reader will forgive me for what might seem a gross distortion of *Also sprach Zarathustra* if I take Nietzsche's philosophy as a whole to be Dionysiac, and Yeats's poetry and thought to represent a considered rejection of its essential spirit. The truth is, I think, that Nietzsche wrote in a situation which guaranteed that he would be read politically. I do not refer only to the vile distortions of his philosophy perpetrated under Hitler. I mean rather its broader relevance to the trend of Western society as a whole. Nietzsche's philosophical writings are imbued with a passionate contempt for contemporary society — that smug bourgeois society that had provided itself with an all-explaining mechanistic psychology and thought it had solved man's basic problems for good. In his attitude towards music, and his vision of an ultimately transfigured man, Nietzsche exerted a powerfully disruptive influence upon those who read him. It was inevitable that this Dionysiac spirit, which pervades also the words of Zarathustra himself, should be read societally, if not actually socialistically.

From this point of view, Nietzsche takes his place in the tradition of Romanticism. The Romantics were aware that there is an element of the barbaric in all real poetry, that poetry strengthens the roots of consciousness in re-affirming the pre-conscious ground of our being: our strength must come from somewhere, unless we believe it to have been invented by the Will. The Romantic assumption is that a major part of the function of poetry lies in its irreconcileability with what we have accommodated within rational frameworks. In times of stress, the rational frameworks break open, and then the deeper-seated drives in man are his ultimate redemption. In point of fact, Nietzsche postulated a union of Apollonian and Dionysiac drives: both tendencies ideally involve the use of the conscious and the unconscious parts of the mind. Yet Nietzsche's description of the soporific state of an excess Apollonianism confirms, I think, the suspicion that he regarded Western culture as a whole as being in dire need of Dionysiac revitalization. Man creates the perfect dream-image, Nietzsche says, because he cannot bear the pain of reality, but beware of dwelling too long or too exclusively on this plane; there are other parts of man that demand satisfaction. It was in the context of the excessive Apollonianism of Enlightenment reasonableness, of course, that Romanticism made its first affirmations of the Dionysiac spirit; and it is this trend, for all his scorn of the German Romantics themselves, that Nietzsche implicitly followed. And it is for this reason also that his Dionysiac spirit, and his essential rejection of an excessively rationalistic Apolloniansim should have led later writers to read him in societal terms: it was not a theory of art that was concerned but the rejuvenation of Western society.

Nietzsche had early sought the new Dionysiac spirit in the music of Wagner. Yet the outstanding Dionysiac work of the nineteenth century was Beethoven's Choral Symphony, with its vision of an ultimate brotherhood of man and of human consciousness dissolved in the One. Now Nietzsche gloried in the dithyrambic chorus of Dionysus: he saw it explicitly as expressing man's need to re-join the One, the Infinite, Nature, God — from which mind had alienated him.

If the Ode to Joy in the Choral Symphony is the greatest modern expression of this impulse, the theme itself is a staple part of Romanticism as a whole, from Schleiermacher to Carlyle. This drive took various forms, some of them vaporous and (literally) dissolute, others magnificent and open-eyed. Generally speaking, I think, we can say that this essentially Dionysiac aspect of Romantic art required a societal dimension to keep it from dissolving into the pseudo-Dionysism that has become for some critics synonymous with Romanticism itself. Such a societal dimension is implicit in Nietzsche himself, for his heroic individualism implicitly looks forward to a time when Mankind as a whole will be transfigured. In fact, we can say, I think, that the great Dionysiac writers were orientated towards a kind of visionary socialism: to achieve satisfaction, the Dionysiac drive requires a scale of fulfilment beyond the merely personal. The Dionysiac artist conceives the Ninth Symphony with its visionary millions kneeling in homage to the great spirit they have been able to release and honour in themselves. It sees the "endless beaches", of Rimbaud's "Saison en enfer" "covered with white nations in joy". To such artists as Rimbaud and Beethoven, actual political socialism usually appears a dismal and materialistic affair. But their vision is consistent with an apocalyptic socialism, though it may only be that socialism Marx foresaw as the final withering-away of the State itself. Controls and repressive limitations of personal liberty may be considered necessary within actualized socialism, because men are regarded as unable to be trusted with themselves: they are still subject to the vices of the untransfigured Adam.

When no such vision attends the Dionysiac tendency in the artist, we get the internalized ecstasies of the pseudo-Dionysus — Scriabin's music, for instance, or Swinburne's poetry. It is precisely his strident belief in the actual Revolution that enabled Scriabin's contemporary, Aleksandr Blok, to transcend the gaseous dissolution of consciousness that is so disgusting in the "Poem of Ecstasy" and the "Prometheus" Symphony. Without his socialism, Blok would be dangerously close to Scriabin. In fact, his whole poetic, which is based upon what he calls the "spirit of music", is the best example we have of the influence of Nietzsche on later writers, and, again, makes the best possible contrast to Yeats. Blok diagnosed the sickness of the West in true Nietzschean spirit as a decaying Apollonian dream, the dream of bourgeois humanism, which must be swept away by the great revolutionary movement of the repressed energies of mankind: "Man's entire being is in revolt; he has risen from a century-long stupor of civilization. Spirit, soul and body have been caught by the storm and, in the turmoil of the spiritual, political and social revolutions which have their causes in the cosmos, there takes place a transformation — the birth of the new man." Here are all the elements of Nietzschean Romanticism: the vision of the spirit of the Cosmos, with which man must get in tune; the idea of the transfiguration of man and of the new birth to follow. The "spirit of music, which, opposed and persecuted by civilization with such zeal, will endure forever" — is plainly Blok's equivalent of Nietzsche's Dionysiac energy. The entire essay from which these quotations come, *The Decline of Humanism*,[21] bears Nietzsche's imprint at every turn. What saves Blok from the orgiastic formlessness of Scriabin's stupefying dissolutions ("I shall not die, I shall dissolve") is the manifest sincerity and conviction with which he awaited the coming of the actual revolution.

For it is Blok who takes the important step of identifying the Dionysiac spirit with the repressed energies of "the People". The People are "closer to the soil and in touch with the rhythms of nature" and they "dream and create legends about the earth". For "the earth is at one with them and they are one with the earth, indistinguishable from it". If this is Blok's conception of the "People", his view of the bourgeoisie is, like Nietzsche's, that of a class besotted with the dream of culture: "they work, they sing; they conduct world dances — as if in a dream, in self-oblivion, in intoxication. It is the same great dream and the same intoxication as that of infinite culture. In the words of Nietzsche, it is the 'dream of Apollo'." Just how complete was Blok's dismissal of bourgeois culture — that culture of which his own poetry had been a fine late flower — can be gathered from the words which follow a little later: "The flower of the intelligentsia, the flower of culture, lives in an eternal Apollonian dream, or in the dream of an ant."[22]

This essay was written after the Revolution — the Revolution which killed off Blok's poetry as effectively as cholera killed the man, but it is entirely in the spirit of the essays he had written a decade before and consistent with the spirit of "The Twelve", the great Dionysiac masterpiece of Revolution which he had written a year earlier. As a whole, Blok's thought represents the Dionysiac opposite of everything Yeats believed in. The vision of an ultimately released, transfigured man whose innate goodness finally coincides with his Will in a dissolution of all structural constraints, was absent from Yeats from the first. The few examples we have noted of his vision of some ultimate transfiguration of man are either unconvinced or alarmed. "Easter 1916" views the Dionysiac transformation almost entirely as deterioration. He had early rejected the "wild god Dionysus". It is now perfectly clear that his rejection of Dionysus, and implicitly of the Dionysiac philosophy of Nietzsche, is no mere intellectual disagreement, and that it extended not only to the sphere of politics but to every area of his thought. Yeats took no joy whatever in the prospect of revolution. No less aware than Blok of the "dream of civilization", he grew to value its appurtenances as passionately as Blok to despise them. It is fashionable nowadays to "explain" this conservatism of Yeats in terms of his Anglo-Irish snobbishness. This is a crude misapprehension: his political conservatism, his high valuation of "culture" and his aesthetic procedures are all remarkably consistent, and collectively display an inexorable progression towards the essentially tragic philosophy and poetry of these years (roughly from 1916 to 1923). There is indeed an impressive consistency of attitude and poetry in both Yeats and Blok: Blok, the Dionysiac poet, urges revolution in a disruption of the rhythms of societal consciousness, a union with the "One" and a victory of the "spirit of music". Yeats, the Apollonian, imposes control over the Dionysiac disturbances in his poetry, and proclaims the necessity of an ordered and strengthened Culture based upon inheritance and hierarchy.

Consistent with his generally Apollonian stance, Yeats regarded that essentially Dionysiac notion of an intimate relationship with the Earth or The One, which Blok praised in "the People", with deep mistrust. Nowhere does he celebrate man's oneness with the universe; there is no expression in his verse of that dithyrambic rejoicing which is so magnificently expressed in the Ninth Symphony. His attitude towards the union-with-the-One is, like his attitude towards Dionysiac disturbance, hostile. Yet he was a profoundly rhythmical poet, deeply responsive to tremors within himself that must come, if from anywhere, from the earth, or the collective memory of the race. (Some quasi-Jungian conception of the Great Mind was important to Yeats later.) His rhythmic susceptibility afforded him evidence of some profound mystic connection at least once. A sense of union with the Godhead-cosmos is powerfully felt in "A Meditation in Time of War". It is, in the first place, significant that the thought should have come to Yeats "in time of war". There is nothing consoling about it:

For one throb of the artery,
While on that old grey stone I sat

Under the old wind-broken tree,
I knew that One is animate,
Mankind inanimate fantasy.

The oneness with the universe that comes so powerfully through the poem does not elate Yeats, though it surprises him: the poem transmits "knowledge", but without any cause for joy. The momentary feeling of being in tune with the natural world merely convinces Yeats of man's general incapacity for such experience, of his unalterable alienation. The idea of nature itself being a "fantasy" is roughly parallel to Blok's concept of the "spirit of music". The fantasy which is nature — according to Yeats — is "animate": whole and alive. The dream or fantasy which man both is and acts is "inanimate": man is broken off, fragmentary and therefore alienated from things. It is a Hegelian, rather than a Nietzschean view.

We learn much about Yeats from this grim little poem. Rhythm, in the first place, seems increasingly important: the deep rhythmic responsiveness is an organ of knowledge in Yeats as well as an expressive instrument. Yet although his rhythmic susceptibility put Yeats in touch with deeper, precivilized strata of existence, he refuses the myth of a beautiful, necessary and inevitable barbarism disrupting the facade of civilized life. Technically, this means that he never indulges rhythm for its own sake, as Swinburne did so often. Certainly, rhythm originates in "the body", the nervous system; it seems to be rooted, through the heart and the feet, in the earth. Rhythm is the signal omission from neo-classic theories of poetry. Yeats's susceptibility to rhythmic messages and disturbances means that he was all too conscious of the reality of the barbarous strain in civilized man. Yet nowhere in the whole of his poetry (with a notable exception which we shall come to in due course) shall we find Yeats letting rhythm have its head: his diction, and the general sturdiness with which his stanzas rock around their rhythmic fulcra alert us to the attentive vigilance with which Yeats regards those matters that do often seem to transmit their presence through rhythm. We can see this mirrored also in the increasingly conservative social philosophy. Although this tendency led him to favour the rise of Mussolini in Italy, it is plain that what Yeats thought the Italian dictator stood for was not the unleashing of popular passions — which is what fascism was if it was anything — but authority and control: "It is impossible not to ask ourselves", he said in 1924, "to what great task of the nations we have been called in this transformed world, where there is so much that is obscure and terrible. The world can never be the same. The stream has turned backwards, and generations to come will have for their task, not the widening of liberty, but recovery from its errors — the building up of authority, the restoration of discipline, the discovery of a life sufficiently heroic to live without the opium dream."[23]

When he uses the first person pronoun in the plural here, Yeats is speaking as a Senator. The context in which he spoke — the meeting of the Royal Irish Academy to confer honours on men who have brought "honour and dignity to Ireland" — makes it clear that Yeats assumed the task of restoration and discipline to lie in the hands of an élite of enlightenment and culture: the last thing Yeats had in mind was the imposition of the will of a maniacal demagogue. His naïvety in political matters may have made it hard for him to tell the one thing from the other, but we must at least be clear about what he envisaged. The nominated part of the Senate in the Irish Free State was a remarkable body of men, and its atmosphere of learned concern must be taken into account when Yeats's politics are discussed. He was for order and distinction, not for brute force and repression. He was élitist and patristic; he was not reactionary. Thus, the Liberty whose curtailment he recommended in his address to the Irish Academy, represented not the enlightened emancipation of all men which the great Dionysiac artists — Beethoven, Shelley, Nietzsche — had intended. It was rather the unleashing of the violence, envy and barbarism he discerned just beneath the surface of civilized man. It was his experiences of the last ten years which had moved him towards this conservative position. If he was naïve in respect of Mussolini and

the *fascisti,* he was no less naïve than many believers in
the Socialist Revolution which was to liberate all men but
only enslaved them more efficiently.

The key to his particular fear of the dark underside of
the human mind may, again, be found in his own persistent interest in magic and the occult. Strangely enough, his
politics and his occulterie were closely related. Yeats was,
I have suggested, something of a double agent, one whose
real function in occult and magic circles was as an observer
out for information. This perhaps requires a further
qualification. Yeats's perpetual vigilance was exercised not
only on the magic lore that lay outside, but upon himself:
he was himself the source of his inside knowledge on these
matters. He regarded himself as a medium. This may have
led him to some pretty silly episodes in life (rubbing his
hands and thinking the room full of the smell of roses as a
result, for instance), but as regards his poetry and its
deepest registers, his mediumistic view of himself assumes
considerable importance.

Rhythm addresses the body; it also possesses the
nervous system, but its primary drummings come through
the limbs. Yeats is a curiously physical poet. States of
mind, emotions, thoughts even, are registered and felt with
deep physical reverberation. This is not the "having the
senses at the finger-tips" which Eliot praised in the Metaphysical poets. We are concerned with the blood, the
marrow, the bone. His root-words mediate between mind
and body, cognition and impulse, darkness and light,
reason and unreason. The catching of the breath, the
impulse of the heart, the leaping of the pulse — these
sensations provide the sutures of Yeats's poetry, they are
its irruptions and its revelations. It is by means of them
that he came to knowledge of himself and of the world he
lived in. The knowledge thus achieved both encouraged
and alarmed him. If he continued to haunt the threshold
of the under-world, to dabble in that magic which, as
Joseph Hone observed,[24] is always black, was it not
because he wanted to *know,* to acquire power and control
over the darkness which he always feared lay at the heart

of things? If the Dionysiac artist without the vision of a transfigured man becomes the sensation-monger whose "spirituality" is more materialistic than the bourgeois himself, so the Apollonian without the sense of darkness at the heart becomes the one-dimensional dreamer ridiculed by Aleksandr Blok and Nietzsche. The characteristic tension of Yeats's verse — its buoyancy of rhythm — surely expresses the intersection of two forces — disturbance and control. Technically, his rhythms grew subtler as his knowledge increased. He possessed a natural sense of rhythm, but his development of this rhythmic responsiveness also represents a growing depth in his philosophy.

(v) "A Prayer for my Daughter"

There is a perceptible increase in the disturbing force of the Dionysiac rhythms in the poetry Yeats wrote between "The Magi" (1913) and "Meditations in Time of Civil War" (1923). This corresponds to a deepening of Yeats's "antithetical" vision, and this, in turn accompanies the increasing momentum of nationalist agitation and the disintegration of civilized order in Europe over the course of the Great War. It also accompanies Yeats's gradual understanding that the roots of this disorder are in ourselves. This self-knowledge is essential to Yeats's understanding of the political world. He despised "objective" men — men who claimed to be able to regard the world critically, as if they were not part of it and therefore a source of distortion. In the poem "Demon and Beast", published in the same volume as contained "Easter 1916", Yeats identifies two drives within himself:

> For certain minutes at the least
> That crafty demon and that loud beast
> That plague me day and night
> Ran out of my sight;

The substance of the poem concerns the achievement of a peace, a sweetness supervening when these two creatures, demon and beast, cease their conflict. This was the period when Yeats was most concerned with the theory of the *daimon,* incidentally, when he was most aware of the identities living side by side within the same breast.[25] "Demon and Beast" is characteristically sceptical about "the natural man":

> . . . every natural victory
> Belongs to beast or demon,
> That never yet had freeman
> Right mastery of natural things,

"Right mastery" is what we strive for when we seek for peace and sweetness — what, presumably, Yeats took Wordsworth to be seeking in *The Excursion.* Yeats's view is that eternal vigilance is required for man to sustain civilization. The natural man hardly exists. Man is actually possessed by two inner identities, the demon and the beast; that is to say, the side of him that dreams, and the side that is unleashed by these dreams into action. There are very few angels in Yeats: he has no equivalent of Rilke's concept of the Angel, and his dreams are beginning to turn more persistently into nightmares. No wonder he had no faith in a renewal of man through Dionysiac disintegration! Between "crafty demon" and "loud beast" man now runs his course. It is the collaboration of demon and beast that explains the action of the Yeats dialectic, that paradox of enchantment, with the stillness of the dreamer on one hand, and the wild abandonment of the unleashed beast on the other. This grim preoccupation with the paradox of enchantment receives its most intensely demonic, yet most stringently Apollonian, expression in "The second coming", "A Prayer for my Daughter", "Nineteen Hundred and Nineteen" and "Meditations in Time of Civil War".

The tense relationship between the forces of Dionysiac disturbance and those values early elected by Yeats for Ireland (in "To Ireland and the Coming Times") can be seen with especial clarity in "A Prayer for my Daughter". Yeats wrote the poem at a time of relative calm: the Rising

was done and down, and the Black and Tans not yet
unleashed upon Ireland. Yet he never evoked with greater
power the destructiveness of the dark forces. The poem
also reveals with great clarity — almost as if for demonstration — the difference between Yeats's regular, Apollonian
rhythm and the Dionysiac disturbances:

> I have walked and prayed for this young child an hour
> And heard the sea-wind scream upon the tower,
> And under the arches of the bridge, and scream
> In the elms above the flooded stream;
> Imagining in excited reverie
> That the future years had come,
> Dancing to a frenzied drum,
> Out of the murderous innocence of the sea.

In the first four lines, we see Yeats at his craft, deploying
the elements of his versification with workmanlike guile.
The repeat of "scream", for instance, is adroit: we read the
first occurrence of the word — "scream upon the tower"
— in a different way from the way in which we read the
second, where the pause at the end of the line forces us to
hold the and hear it again. By breaking up the otherwise
dangerously steady play of the iambics, moreover (more
lines after the pattern of the first two would have been
monotonous), Yeats sees to it that we are interested in a
scene that has itself no detail that is especially interesting.
Once again we have to take note of the paradox that Yeats
lacks almost entirely the gift of "exquisite particularity",
yet habitually works through visual scenes. It is an
important part of Yeats's effect as a poet that his
characteristic introversion of temperament, making him
less interested in what was going on around him than in
the "inner" processes of the mind — to say nothing of his
poor eyesight itself — did not stop him being a clear, if
simple presenter of those scenes. Rhythm predominates in
Yeats, but it does not result in blurred or imprecise
imagery. It is simply that the work done by the scene is
not as important as it is in the poems of those poets who
preyed upon Nature for clues of immanence. Although
Yeats claimed to scour the world for symbols, he really

sought for them in books or in some inner reach of his own mind.

Thus, Yeats makes sure that we see the flooded stream now not by illuminating it for us by some perception into its reality, but by placing it at the end of the line and the paragraph. We are almost too conscious here of the hand of the craftsman, guaranteeing that his stanza will have the familiar sturdy buoyancy — a verse-effect imitated by so many later poets, and consciously avowed by at least one, Theodore Roethke, whose own imitation perhaps throws light on the nature of the original: "I take this cadence from a man named Yeats."[26] That is a subtle enough combination of dactylic and iambic disturbances to come from the master himself. But then, such things are copyable. What is less easily copyable is what Yeats engineers with this rhythmic instrument of his. There is a price to pay for the kind of carefulness displayed in the quatrain of "A Prayer for my Daughter": if it is not redeemed by some more interesting kind of *aktualizatsia*, it can appear to exist for its own sake. In fact, the craftsmanship is not only redeemed by what follows, it is seen in retrospect to have been an important and indispensable part of the total effect. For the fifth line of the stanza immediately serves notice of more urgent matter than the paternal concern which had seemed to satisfy itself in the carpentry of the opening lines. A deeper tremor sets in than the rhythm had earlier created. Yet the new urgency of the verse is related to that parental concern by more than the requirements of structural contrast. The first quatrain is dominated by a sense of expressionist foreboding, the clear dark lines of the scene reminding us of those overcast city-scapes of Vlaminck, where also a competent technique is well in control of a sombre imagination. But from the moment that the first person pronoun that has opened the stanza is given a present participle, "Imagining", in line 5, we understand that the parent's concern is justified by his knowledge of some violence transmitted through the verse.

Now this construction is one we have had reason to

notice more than once already. Yeats had long been in
the habit of exploiting the suspensive effect of the present
participle. In particular, we remember the rocking rhythm
of "The Magi" — "Being by Calvary's turbulence
unsatisfied". There, too, the rhythmic disturbance was
both grammatical and lexical: the device indeed was taken
to new extremes of disruptiveness. Here, the present
participle, "Imagining", not only suspends the meaning of
the sentence, it disrupts the rhythm just as the excitement
it describes disturbs the poet's consciousness. The sturdy
iambic movement of the first quatrain (underlined as it
was by its occasional deviations from the metric norm, as
in the first line, for instance) is completely destroyed. If
the effect of rhythm in English poetry is obtained, as
Hopkins said it was,[27] by the counterppointing of deviations from the metric grid, this line of Yeats goes as far
as it is possible to go in the direction of deviation without
actually ceasing to be metrical within the paragraph. No
syllable, except for the second syllable of "Imagining"
occupies a conceivably "correct" metrical place. Taken in
isolation indeed, the line can hardly be scanned or read as
poetry at all:

Imagining in excited reverie.

The line has three units: (1) "Imagining in" (2) "excited"
and (3) "reverie". Each insists on being taken indepen-
dently: if we wrote out their rhythms in code, with *dah*
for stressed, and *di* for unstressed syllables, we would see
more clearly that each measure has a strong rhythmic
inscape of its own: (1) di-dah-di-di-di, (2) di-dah-di, and
(3) dah-di-di. It is not merely the stress position that is
changed, but the number of slack syllables. The extra *di,*
for instance, given by including "in" with "imagining" in
(1) is an important part of its rhythmic effect. Alternatively, "in" can be read with "excited" in (2) as common
usage enjoins: this speech-habit yields a more flowing
pattern, joining "excited" and "reverie" in one bumpily
flowing unit. Yet the verse-pattern does not easily let us
pause at the end of "Imagining": the stress in "imág-" is

too strong to let the preposition escape its orbit. There is, therefore, a tension between verse-logic, requiring us to continue the metric unit beyond "-ing" and the demands of sense. We therefore use "in" as a pivot, which is probably what happens when we read the line first. Whatever conclusion we reach, there can be no doubt either that we have here a prime example of Yeats's rhythmic intelligence, or that the effect of the line depends considerably upon the meanings of the three characteristic Yeats words, "imagining", "excited" and "reverie". Taken together here, the three words in meaning, in rhythmic inscape and in their relations to the staid measures of the first quatrain, set up a powerful cross-current that merges into the stamping rhythm of the next lines:

That the future years had come,
Dancing to a frenzied drum,

It is the influence of this frenzied drum that the poet wishes to ward off from his daughter; all the more interesting, then, that Yeats "evokes" the drum more by an act of possession than of mimesis. Nowhere does Yeats summon up those powers of possession — violence, darkness, barbarism — more powerfully than he does here. Nowhere does he place more finally and unarguably those Dionysiac forces which Blok called "the spirit of music". Yeats has little rapture, and in this he stands apart from his admired Shelley, whose vision most lambently destroyed the forms and orders upon which traditional society had rested.

Yet he knew the Dionysiac forces from the inside: this perhaps explains the difference between a genuine conservatism and an ugly reactionary prejudice. To observe the forces of violence and disruption outside oneself — merely in other classes of society, for instance — generates by opposition the full hegemonic reaction: a will to dominate and oppress other classes born of self-interest, out of fear. The reactionary fear is purely fear *of*, though it may dress itself up as fear *for*: "I'm doing this for your own good", much as the headmaster claims to be more hurt than hurting when he canes the boy. To have felt the forces of disruption and violence within oneself, on the other hand, can generate the political philosophy of conservatism. The fear — of disorder, anarchy, intense hatred — is grounded in the poet's knowledge of himself. It is not "I'm going to save you from yourselves", but "Let us choose *that* rather than *this*", where *this* is known by experience within the self. Thus the difference between reaction and conservatism, manifesting itself in different political positions. The one, reaction, is a choice made for others, and it is inherently different from the choice made for oneself also, and for others only out of the common ground is established not by an abstract theory of man, but upon the poet's self-knowledge. The image of Yeatsian man is arrived at in this way — by inspection of his dreams (the activities of the demon) and the knowledge of the beast's potentialities.

At any rate, the beat of the rhythm tells us that the "frenzied drum" of which Yeats speaks is known by personal acquaintance, not by political theory. The image reminds us that a problematic, Platonist conception of music as disruptive influence, the antithesis of the Nietzschean afflatus, in general underlies Yeats's poetry. We shall come to this in dealing with "Nineteen Hundred and Nineteen". Now the "future years" come "out of the murderous innocence of the sea". The symbol of the sea is of too wide a reference and too general an application for one to locate a precise significance for it here. Yeats's phrase interprets itself. It is clear that the future is black, and that it surrounds the island of the present, as the dark ocean surrounds the land. That it is "murderous" we can understand in terms of Yeats's general feeling about the shape of the world to come. What of its "innocence"? What is the meaning of this brilliant oxymoron? Yeats has said enough already about the dangers of unlettered ambition to give us a reasonable guide to interpretation here, I think. The rest of his poem recommends order, cultivation and civilization against anarchy, disorder and illiterate politicking. The sea may, therefore, stand for that barbarous mass of mankind likely to be unleashed into power before it has had time to civilize itself: it is innocent because it knows nothing, and murderous for the same reason. Once more, Yeats intimates his mistrust of the Rousseauesque idealization of the natural man.

The axis of the poem, therefore, is essentially political, though Yeats transcends it, by setting the political in a context greater than itself. It is here that Yeats speaks most fiercely and contemptuously of Maud Gonne: "An intellectual hatred is the worst", he begins — worst because the mind, fixed in its opinion, will not let the blood forget when nature would have it forget. This part of the poem is deeply significant for Ireland in general. Maud-Helen is associated early in the poem with the "horn of plenty". She was born "out of the mouth of plenty's horn", but would

> Because of her opinionated mind
> Barter that horn and every good
> By quiet natures understood
> For an old bellows full of angry wind . . .
>   "A Prayer for my Daughter"

In dialectical response to this, Yeats arrives at the idea of a more "radical innocence", which is "self-delighting,/Self-appeasing, self-affrighting", and which would, free of obsession and evil influence, put man in harmony with the universe: "its own sweet will is Heaven's will". We note that the thought here rests upon a point outside a pantheistic conception of a cosmic harmony in which man is willy-nilly either a discord or a concord. The "innocence" which Yeats postulates here is different from that intimated in "A Meditation in Time of War", where the throb of "the artery" apprises the poet of his unity with all things in a disturbing way. The "self-delighting" joy in "A Prayer for my Daughter" stands apart from any such predestinarian or pantheistic theory of creation. It is specifically modern: an inexplicable and otherwise underivable value is positted.

The pre-condition of joy, in this context at least, is that

"all hatred" be "driven hence". At the end of the poem, Yeats returns to the attack on the "opinionated mind":

> For arrogance and hatred are the wares
> Peddled in the thoroughfares.

This finally establishes the dialectical antithesis that lies at the heart of the poem. We may feel that Yeats defines his symbols too clearly in this poem. When he concludes, as if supplying the key to a riddle,

> Ceremony's a name for the rich horn,
> And custom for the spreading laurel tree.

we have the feeling that nothing has been added to what has gone before:

> O may she live like some green laurel
> Rooted in one dear perpetual place.

These lines tell us why the poet values what he says he values by means of the images he uses and the emotive words he uses to define them. To call this "custom" later is to tell us nothing new and to drag Yeats's own poem into the empiricist "thoroughfares" where words have clear definitions and the business of language is to supply them unequivocally. His analogy — "may she live *like* some green laurel" — is closer to true poetic practice — not a statement but a desire.

(vi) "The Second Coming"

It was to be some years before Yeats fully understood the concept of joy arrived at in "A Prayer for my Daughter". He was at this stage more concerned with the ungoverned ocean. The increasing anarchy of twentieth century life is most forcibly expressed in "The Second Coming". Here Yeats draws upon metaphors of control to underline the futility of man's attempts to exercise mastery over his own twin creations — society and himself. Yeats derives much of his imagery and inspiration here from a passage from

The Prelude. The derivation of Yeats's classically conservative poem from a great "radical" text, is surely significant. *The Prelude* constitutes a reversal of radical thought, while never quite relinquishing the radical hope. In Book X of his poem, Wordsworth describes the crisis of the radical intellectual, so convinced of the rightness of history, that he undergoes mental torture to justify to himself the horrors unleashed by that history. He has withdrawn to his high room in Paris, his mind full of the September massacres. He has tried to rationalize them to himself, intelligently and plausibly, much as left-wing intellectuals in the West justified the horrors of Stalinism, by invoking the myth of historical inevitability. Shut up in his room, Wordsworth works upon himself, until, at a frenzied pitch of excitement, his imagination is delivered up, not to nightmare, but to an apothegmatic visionariness. He sees "into the life of things", as the poet of "Tintern Abbey" would scarcely have dreamed possible:

> The horse is taught his manage, and no star
> Of wildest course but treads back his own steps;
> For the spent hurricane the air provides
> As fierce a successor; the tide retreats
> But to return out of its hiding-place
> In the great deep; all things have second birth;
> The earthquake is not satisfied at once; . . .
> Wordsworth, *The Prelude,* Book X

It is these seven lines which transmit the oracular trance. The lines leading up to it provide setting and context, winching the passage into position so that its delphic utterance will have maximum force. The lines following them resume the level of psychological history:

> And in this way I wrought upon myself,
> Until I seemed to hear a voice that cried,
> To the whole city, 'Sleep no more.' The trance
> Fled with the voice to which it had given birth;
> But vainly comments of a calmer mind
> Promised soft peace and sweet forgetfulness.

Dramatically, we notice, it is the voice shouting "Sleep no

more" that is the most effective element. Yet poetically
the force has already been spent in the apothegms of the
oracular pronouncement: we experience in these seven
lines the excitement and the certitude of great poetry.
Here is that quality Arnold tried to isolate in *Culture and
Anarchy* as constituting the greatness of great poetry –
that clean classical quality that seems to sum up human
existence, that seems to offer "truth", at the same time
representing the utmost mastery of the poet's medium
– language. Our excitement is an amalgam of pleasure in
the mastery of the poetic performance and an exhilaration
in the sense of revelation: here is that mystery at the heart
of existence, that "eternal core of things" in Nietzsche's
phrase.

It is significant that Wordsworth should have used the
word "trance" to describe his state of mind: for he stands
high among the supreme European poets precisely in virtue
of his Apollonian susceptibility to the trance state in
which "truth" is revealed. The artist's control – his
mastery – is what distinguishes his visions from, say, the
schizoid utterances of a Christopher Smart, who is like the
Delphic oracle without Apollo: fragments of revelation
come up as from a punctured volcano, jumbled together
with nonsense from the poet's private personal history.
The relations between art and neurosis that have exercised
so many distinguished minds in this century could hardly
be better illustrated than from the poetry of Wordsworth:
his dedication of himself to the "unknown" is complete,
yet he retains the ability to transmit its message back – to
himself in the first instance, then to the rest of us.

In the lines from Book X of *The Prelude*, the mastery
manifests itself at a number of levels: we note, above all,
the powerful mesh of repeated vowel sounds: *horse-taught-
course; back-manage; treads-spent; provides-tide-hiding;
birth-earthquake.* The sense of uncontrollable forces
derives substantially from the strength of these
"inexorable" sound-echoes. There is also the strange
ambiguity of control in the passage: the impression created
is of frightening "possession" – of titanic forces

unleashed. Yet Wordsworth really describes a universe of tyrannical order: the horse is "taught his manage". The tide comes out of "the great deep" (a terrifying phrase in the context), and re-emerges at the behest of some still greater power. It has a hiding-place, like a horrible monster, and it is the monster hidden in these words that produces the idea of the second birth and the further notion of the earthquake, which has an appetite like a monster in a fairy-story.

It is not only the notion of the "second birth" that Yeats took from Wordsworth. He took also the schema of a universe terrifying in its disregard of human scale, yet the more terrifying in its own evident tutelage to a still greater master. Finally he also borrowed certain of Wordsworth's metaphors. Like Wordsworth, he begins with an image of the human domination of animals: Wordsworth's horse "taught his manage" becomes Yeats's "falcon". Yeats has no equivalent of Wordsworth's star, his hurricane or his earthquake. But the dominant image of his opening paragraph is that of the tide, also borrowed from Wordsworth. As significant as these parallels of image is the apothegmatic mode – poetry as revelation by generalization in the present tense, a description of a state of affairs by means of general images proffered as "universally" true. Yet Yeats's purpose is ultimately different: he – wisely – does not try to compete with Wordsworth's utterances. Instead he translates its oracular manner into a more local, historically limited "relevance". The excitement of Wordsworth's passage is that it shows the poet bursting through a contemporary situation to arrive at a revelation of "the eternal core of things", so that the September Massacres – and with them the whole drama of political life itself – are revealed to be in the grip of a far greater drama, one of which we can comprehend no *régisseur*.

Yeats in one sense diminishes the scale of Wordsworth's imagery. Instead of placing contemporary political madness in a relation of unwitting player in greater drama, he describes it in terms of a strictly human system of ritual

which has simply "got out of hand." Thus, his falcon bears
obedience not to the greater, vaster forces revealed to
Wordsworth, but to the human falconer — civilization,
ordered values, the past. Yeats's poem, in fact, reserves its
greatest power for the revelation in its second section, here
confining itself to a brooding, monitory shaking of the
head. Its apothegms, though less exhilaratingly absolute
than Wordsworth's, are more trenchantly local:

> The best lack all conviction, while the worst
> Are full of passionate intensity.

This remains true of our own time, and it does so for
reasons Yeats has defined again and again in the poetry of
his middle period. The best, being civilized, have learned
that their own desires must be muzzled, sublimated, while
the worst are the worst by a natural process of selection:
if energy and egotism (the egotism "natural" to man as to
all animals) are given their head, the most destructively
powerful will gain mastery. Yeats's opposition of best and
worst in this poem must be understood within a context in
which a confrontation of enlightened order and ignorant
barbarism was being engineered by socio-political
evolution. (This of course is to present the case in Yeatsian
terms. Obviously, to a different political persuasion, the
confrontation would be presented rather as that between
entrenched privilege and righteously aspiring oppressed
masses.)

The "revelation" itself defies critical comment. It is the
naked image itself we are impressed by, not any
"meaning" it might have. It is introduced by a characteristic rhythmic disturbance mediated by the root-word
"Troubles", and the verse that follows reels about the
image itself as the desert-birds do in the actual picture
Yeats presents. Finally, when the curtain drops back, the
poet "knows" something he did not know at the end of
"The Magi". "The Second Coming" is deeply related to
the earlier poem. Here, too, is the stoniness, the "rocking"
disturbance, and the vexation — all, again, associated with
the Christian advent. What the poem *says* is that the

Christian era, presented as a period of "stony sleep", has been "vexed to nightmare" by the rocking cradle — of the infant Christ himself, of course. As to the nature of the "beast" whose hour has come round at last, Yeats leaves us with only the epithet "rough" for clue, and the fact that it "slouches". Circularly, the question that ends the poem leads us back to the "mere anarchy" that is evoked at the beginning. Like Wordsworth, Yeats sensed the coming of an age of disorder and violence, and he saw that it was really already beyond man's power to control.

It is surely this characteristic disabusement that distinguishes Yeats's image from the Nietzschean beast that might be supposed its prototype. At the end of *Also sprach Zarathustra,* Zarathustra leaps from his cave in the morning after the evening on which he has taught to the "Higher men" — his disciples — the meaning of his teaching, the Dionysiac joy of the "Drunken song":

> Ye Higher Men, for yourselves pineth joy,
> the unrestrainable, the blessed — for your woe, ye
> that have failed! For eternal joy ever pineth after failures.
> For joy ever seeketh itself, and therefore it seeketh grief![28]

As the tone of this suggests, things have not gone too well at the orgy: the Higher Men in effect resurrect the old religion, superseded by Zarathustra's religion of joy, and worship the brayings of the Ass. Now, in the new morning afterwards, Zarathustra, disciple-free, emerges into the clean air outside his cave and "unawares . . . laid hold of thick warm shaggy hair, and at the same time there went up a roaring, a gentle prolonged lion-roar." This is the visionary, apocalyptic beast (the "mighty yellow beast" of the desert) that frightens off the Higher Men, and finally releases Zarathustra into his freedom of *work.* "Do I strive for happiness? I strive for my *work!*" Renewed, he issues forth from the cave, "glowing and strong as the sun at dawn coming from dark mountains." The general structure of this somewhat laboured allegory was, of course, already familiar to Yeats from his early apprenticeship in Blake. Yeats knew of Blake's Rintrah, "roaring and shaking his fires in the burden'd air"; he knew also that "the roaring of lions" was one of the "portions of eternity". I doubt if Nietzsche really added much to Yeats's knowledge of these matters. It is wholly characteristic of Yeats to transform Blake's and Nieztsche's lions into a slouching, mindless omen of disaster.

(vii) "Nineteen Hundred and Nineteen"

That the poetry of this period, the early and middle nineteen-twenties, represents a particularly intense and tragic phase of the poet's total *oeuvre* is attested by Yeats's own somewhat surprised reflections on the volume in which they appeared. "Re-reading *The Tower*", he wrote in 1928 to Olivia Shakespeare, "I was astonished at its bitterness, and long to live out of Ireland that I may find some new vintage. Yet that bitterness gave the book its power and it is the best book I have written."[29] It is hard not to agree. The thrust of the bitterness that produced "The Second Coming" is continued, with undiminished force in the two sequences Yeats wrote in direct response to the events associated with the creation of the Free State in 1922, "Nineteen Hundred and Nineteen" and "Meditations in Time of Civil War". The two sequences were written four years apart, as the events that inspired them took place. We must bear in mind that Yeats was out of Ireland both for the Easter Rising and for the Black and Tans period. If he had been astonished by the Rising, he was outraged by Lady Gregory's accounts of the incidents she had witnessed involving the Irregulars. Paradoxically, the earlier poem is more sombre and violent than the later, even though Yeats was resident in Galway during the Civil War.

"Nineteen Hundred and Nineteen" begins with a lament on the passing of the appurtenances of civilization:

Many ingenious lovely things are gone
That seemed sheer miracle to the multitude,

> Protected from the circle of the moon
> That pitches common things about.

"We" who were civilized — Yeats speaks here very much as a member of the Protestant Ascendancy — dreamed that "the worst rogues and rascals had died out". What is most interesting here is the contrast between the tenor of this opening section of the sequence, and indeed the sequence as a whole, and the strength of Yeats's actual feelings about the Black and Tans. Yeats was invited to speak at the Oxford Union about the troubles in Ireland; the accounts that come down of the poet's behaviour on this occasion show a man possessed, insensate with rage. He "strode up and down the aisle between the Ayes and the Noes, waving his arms and shaking his fists at the audience, pouring out a sustained flow of eloquence".[30] We could wish for no better illustration of the relations between a poet's poetry and his personal opinions than the contrast between this oratorical rage and the controlled sombre power of "Nineteen Hundred and Nineteen". In the poem, the bestiality of the Irregulars is treated as an illustration of a general fault in man: the political incidents are subsumed in a tragic context that transcends them in giving them their most powerful expression. In the opening section of the sequence, Yeats dams up the power until the fourth stanza, when the dramatic present tense discloses "the facts":

> Now days are dragon-ridden, the nightmare
> Rides upon sleep: a drunken soldiery
> Can leave the mother, murdered at her door,
> To crawl in her own blood, and go scot-free;

Again, the rhythm and prosody collaborate to give us the movement of disturbance. Here, it is the metaphor of the nightmare which affords Yeats his structure: he exploits its literal meaning, and powerfully evokes the feeling of riding by placing the word "nightmare" at the end of the line, so that it flares off into space. The half-rhyme with "door" is also of great power; "scot-free" makes a sardonic reference to the national origin of the Irregulars (mainly drawn from the Black Watch Regiment). The direct and powerful image of the mother crawling in her own blood is unique in Yeats: nowhere else does he exploit in such a naked way the emotional power of sheer image. There is nothing arcane here: this is "passive suffering", surrounded by the poet's anger, much as we see it in the poems of Owen and Rosenberg, though Yeats, with an inconsistency we shall have cause to note again, chose to disapprove of it in them.

The overt dramatic image of the mother is followed by what is perhaps Yeats's most powerfully generalized statement on "the human condition":

> The night can sweat with terror as before
> We pieced our thoughts into philosophy,
> And planned to bring the world under a rule,
> Who are but weasels fighting in a hole.

It is difficult not to associate the pronoun "we" with the English, the people who, most obviously, had tried to "bring the world under a rule". Of course, Yeats means all men, mankind; but this is hardly the response an Irish nationalist could have been expected to make. The truth is that Yeats does not write as a nationalist in these poems of his greatest period. It was only later, in those jaunty jingles of *A Full Moon in March,* that he writes as a nationalist. He shows his distinction of mind in withholding from his most serious poetic statements the kind of emotional colour we know — from Mr Collis's account of the debate at the Oxford Union, and from many other testimonies — that he actually felt at the political events of the time. A nationalist would be quick to point out that the image of weasels fighting in a hole is hardly appropriate to a situation in which a powerful nation is oppressing a less powerful one. That "more sinned against than sinning" tone which is so common (and so inevitable) in Irish writing, finds little room in Yeats, and none at all at this period. The political events give evidence of some much deeper human malady.

The opening section of "Nineteen Hundred and Nineteen" in fact goes on to suggest ways in which "He

who can read the signs" without being cowed into
accepting some panacea proffered by "shallow wits" might
derive comfort, though of a cold order: it seems that the
man who *can* read the signs aright also knows that nothing
worthwhile can stand. By the same token, however, he
knows that any wordly triumph would "break upon his
ghostly solitude". This is a bleak enough prospect: it is
no less so than the idea that the horrors of the weasels
fighting in a hole are mere *signs* − portents of what unimaginable dereliction? The conclusion is simply that "Man
is in love and loves what vanishes". Thus, the political
events are reduced to symbols: those who carry out the
horrible violence are "Incendiary and bigot" who would,
if opportunity arose, destroy civilization itself − "burn
that stump on the Acropolis,/Or break in bits the famous
ivories/Or traffic in the grasshoppers or bees". What is
remarkable about this is that the men burning and pillaging
Ireland during the year 1919 are cast in the same role as
those passionate patriots of "Easter 1916": there is a
direct continuity from "The Magi", through "Easter
1916" to "The Second Coming" and "Nineteen Hundred
and Nineteen". Man is threatened by his own destructiveness and passion. There is a direct link between the
"frenzied drum" of "A Prayer for my Daughter" and the
black nightmare of "Nineteen Hundred and Nineteen".

Mention of the "frenzied drum" reminds us again of
that problematic, Platonist conception of music underlying
Yeats's poetry. The second poem in "Nineteen Hundred
and Nineteen" returns to the image of music as essentially
dangerous. Yet Loie Fuller's dancers, who appear on the
scene now, are described as the very essence of grace and
loveliness, hardly materialized: when they glided in and
out of their "floating ribbon of cloth", it seemed "that a
dragon of air/Had fallen among dancers". The days
described in the first part of the sequence were "dragon-
ridden", and the recurrence of the word now cannot be
fortuitous. It is not: the mythic creature becomes an
impalpable yet irresistible force that takes control of the
troupe and so becomes an image of some world-spirit, or

historicistic force that governs man's movements. It is as if it

> ... whirled them round
> Or hurried them off on its own furious path;
> So the Platonic Year
> Whirls out new right and wrong,
> Whirls in the old instead;

It does not matter particularly that the year (or Year) is Platonic: we must be careful to take Yeats's arcane dabblings neither too seriously, by inquiring too closely into their precise denotations, nor too lightly, by dismissing them as irrelevant to a poetic truth. What matters is that Yeats has rendered in verse a strong image of a dictatorial force whose behests man perforce obeys: the spirit behind the "dragon of air" is a reality, and one we must take seriously. Yeats punches home his highly ambiguous image of dance with a sardonic apothegm:

> All men are dancers and their tread
> Goes to the barbarous clangour of a gong.

We may note that "tread" (with all its grammatical variants) is an important Yeats word; it carries a fatalistic force, rather as the word *track* does in Dickens. The "tread" of the dancers is as it were enchanted to the measures of the dance, not liberated by it. In *tread,* Yeats found a word capable of bearing and at the same time distributing a heavy rhythmic stress: it comes down hard on its own meaning, yet achieves a paradoxical weightlessness by appearing to withhold stress. Its function is typical of Yeats's use of rhyme in general, and is akin to that of the flying buttress in mediaeval architecture. Here it is exploited to suggest feet beating, and pressing, and of time passing in the enchained dance of life, drawn on in spite of itself.

Yeats's use of images of dance and music makes a stark contrast with T. S. Eliot's conceptions of them as paradigmatic of civilized values. In Eliot's later verse, the dance stands for a Dantesque order, the heightening of mere existence out of the fragmentary material state into the realm of significance and art. Eliot wants existence to share the quality of art — order, music, formal significance. Yeats wants for nothing but to retain "ghostly solitude". The difference is fundamental. For Eliot the greatest evils were meaninglessness and ugliness, so that he defined value in terms of the opposites of these things: the grace of dance and the delicate "handling" of the skilled lover. Eliot is the poet of anomie, ennui, pointlessness. These things do not appear to have worried Yeats much at any time. For him, the enemy to civilization was violence, fixation, the transfiguring intensity of hatred and fanaticism. Yeats was able to conceive — as Eliot never was — of the happy peasant, the lower unit of the social order who plays his part in the dream of sweetness and heroic peace. Thus, we shall look in vain for those flutes of Eliot's, the "antique flute" that "enchanted the may-time". The enchantment Eliot evokes is not like Yeats's. Rather it expresses the innocence of freely chosen discipline — *"En la sua voluntade e nostra pace."* Instead of these antique flutes and the grace of discipline, we get the "frenzied drum" and the "barbarous clangour of the gong". Instead of "fear in a handful of dust", correspondingly, we find the poet's belief that

> . . . to be choked with hate
> May well be of all evil chances chief.
>   "A Prayer for my Daughter"

It is not a heap of broken images, therefore, that Yeats offers us at this, the most intensely tragic phase of his life, but the vision of life and history as being at the mercy of, and in the grip of, powers that dictate and direct what we are doing without our being aware of it. Yeats gives these powers various names — the "Primum Mobile" that makes "the very owls in circles move"; the "Platonic Year", the Gyres, the Phases of the Moon. What is important is the intensity of Yeats's dread that we are in its grip, and his fear that the barbarousness within us seems to emerge involuntarily out of "the murderous innocence of the sea", when we least expect it. Yeats characterizes our relationship to this greater force in various ways — as master to slave, as dancer to dance-master, as circus animal to ring-master. In "Nineteen Hundred and Nineteen" the per-ception of this human powerlessness leads Yeats to conceive of civilization as itself simply another dream. We have touched on this already in referring to the vanity of the belief that "we" have brought the world under a rule. In the third section of the sequence, Yeats returns to this idea from a different angle. Aligning himself, as arcane ruminator and dabbler, with the rulers of mankind, he observes that

> A man in his own secret meditation
> Is lost amid the labyrinth that he has made
> In art or politics;

He recurs also to that Hindu idea that if a man really succeeded completely in his life, he would vanish without trace, suggesting that man's monuments and relics are but signs of his failure. The section ends with a pessimistic reflection on the dream of civilization:

> O but we dreamed to mend
> Whatever mischief seemed
> To afflict mankind, but now
> That winds of winter blow
> Learn that we were crack-pated when we dreamed.

There is perhaps a conscious acknowledgement here of the poet's indebtedness to *King Lear*. At any rate, in diction and vision, Yeats moves closer to Shakespeare than he had ever been hitherto. The following section — the bitterly Irish song on Mockers — closes with another approxima-tion to the storm-scene in *Lear*:

> Mock mockers after that
> That would not lift a hand maybe
> To help good, wise or great
> To bar that goul storm out, for we
> Traffic in mockery.

The sequence as a whole reaches some kind of climax in Section VI — the frenzied vision of nightmare in the

Witches' procession on St John the Baptist's Eve. This procession is itself a monstrous parody of order, almost like Loie Fuller's dancers stripped of their phoney grace and delivered up to a foul femaleness. The poison felt at the core of things throughout the sequence comes to the surface at the end of the first paragraph:

> Violence upon the roads: violence of horses;
> Some few have handsome riders, are garlanded
> On delicate sensitive ear or tossing mane,
> But wearied running round and round in their courses
> All break and vanish, and evil gathers head:

Helen of Troy becomes Herodias's daughter, Salome, a declension into foulness and obscenity, a sick triumph both of the power of dance, and of the power of the beautiful woman over the male:

> Herodias' daughters have returned again,
> A sudden blast of dusty wind and after
> Thunder of feet, tumult of images,
> Their purpose in the labyrinth of the wind;

This is the evil incarnation of all the images of the enchained mind, released by trance only into violence, "for all are blind". The vision then fades, much like the revelation in "The Second Coming", to be followed by one of Yeats's most solemn incomprehensibilities: how, after this frenzied Witches' Sabbath, we should be expected to be interested in "that insolent fiend Robert Artisson", or why someone called Lady Kyteler should have brought him "Bronzed peacock feathers", I cannot fathom. At any rate, the poem peters out.

(viii) "Meditations in Time of Civil War"

It is difficult not to feel that Yeats's inability to find poetic form for the violent emotion that "gathers head" at the end of "Nineteen Hundred and Nineteen" is crucially significant in our evaluation of the poet's final status. There is no equilibrium of Dionysiac and

Apollonian here — the verse eddies and spirals, suggests labyrinthine imprisonment in the line "... wearied running round and round in their courses", but fails to master whatever it is that is forcing itself upon the poet's consciousness, and so gives all up to the esoteric. Certainly, there is none of the Shakespearean power here. Neither is there any serious approach to it in the sister sequence, "Meditations in Time of Civil War". This is not, by the way, to erect an irrelevant yardstick by which to measure a different kind of poet. Shakespeare is more than a kind of artist in these matters: he is the ultimate test by which we judge the achievement of European poets, and it is a sign of Yeats's power that he obliges us to look to the Shakespearean yardstick. He seems to have felt something of the sort himself, for Shakespeare was principal among the poets Yeats re-read at this time of his life.[31] At a time when things were falling apart, in the poet's mind as in the world, it was natural for him to turn to the great tragic poet.

Initially, the "Meditations" recur to the antithesis of "A Prayer for my Daughter". That poem had postulated two forms of opposition to the "frenzied drum" whose beating threatened to destroy civilization: first, an ideal mode of civilized living symbolized in the custom and ceremony of the great house; second, a certain inward joy, which, "self-delighting", derived from the "radical innocence", which, in turn, is recovered by the soul when "all hatred" is driven hence. It is important to note that the social ideal — the great house with all its gracious appurtenances — is proffered alongside the personal one, without which, indeed, the desire for the house must appear the most superficial social opportunism — a desire that the daughter be numbered among the Haves rather than the Have-nots. The "way of life" is valued because of spiritual values it makes possible — values which in turn may be farmed back into society at large, so that the whole state of man is leavened. This, at any rate, is the heart of a conservatism which must be heartless indeed without such a commitment to "joy", and "radical innocence". We must feel this radical innocence to be under threat from the "opinionated mind" and the "murderous innocence" it unleashes, for the poem as a whole to stand up. Whether "A Prayer for my Daughter" does stand up is a moot question: its descent to overt equivalences and identifications betrays a certain deterioration in organization, I think. (It is questionable indeed whether Yeats ever succeeded in organizing a poem on a large scale without recourse to narrative or dramatic means: his constant recourse to the suite or sequence form suggests that his imaginative span was shorter than, say, that of Eliot.) Such, at any rate, is the mechanism of the poem. By the time that he came to write the "Meditations", Yeats had absorbed the new dialectical terms of his poetic thinking well enough to be able to throw them into definition at once ironic and supportive:

> Surely among a rich man's flowering lawns,
> Amid the rustle of his planted hills,
> Life overflows without ambitious pains;
> And rains down life until the basin spills,
> And mounts more dizzy high and more it rains
> As though to choose whatever shape it wills
> And never stoop to a mechanical
> Or servile shape, at others' beck and call.
>   I, "Ancestral Houses"

This is more effective than the overt definitions of "A Prayer for my Daughter" for at least two reasons. First, because it throws up its key-metaphor, that of the spontaneous fountain of life, without naming it; second, because it in fact asserts nothing, but entertains a hypothesis ("Surely . . . "), and yet succeeds in getting our assent to a proposition, that the existence of the great houses and their way of life is necessary to the defiance of the "mechanical/Or servile".

There is no doubt that we are meant to answer Yeats's implicit question in the affirmative: yes, Life does — or should — overflow there; if it fails there, where can it succeed? Yet this cautious, but formidable speculation — far truer to Yeats's genius than either the hysteria of

"Violence upon the roads" or the dogmaticism of "A Prayer for my Daughter" — prepares us for a difficult journey. For the force of that "Surely" is in fact to undermine the certainty of the expectation it is meant to arouse. Sure enough, the first words of the second stanza dismiss the hypothesis out of hand — "Mere dreams, mere dreams!" Civilization itself — of which the first stanza has given us a beautiful if generalized evocation — is as much the product of dream as the brutal violence of fanaticism. The awareness of this fact is surely crucial here: whatever the poem says, it does not advocate an *un*-ironical acceptance of the rich as a class. The airy dismissal — "Mere dreams" — is, however, in turn itself instantly qualified:

> . . .   Yet Homer had not sung
> Had he not found it certain beyond dreams
> That out of life's own self-delight had sprung
> The abounding glittering jet; . . .

Perhaps we need to know the relevant lines from "A Prayer for my Daughter" to get the full significance of these lines. The "self-delight", we note, is not identified with the fountain of joy; it is a condition of that "abounding glittering jet", not the jet itself. Technically, the lines from the later poem surpass anything from the earlier in the way that the qualifying "Yet" is governed from below by the irruption of that symbol which was unnamed in the first stanza: what made life "overflow without ambitious pains" is the "abounding glittering jet", and this, in turn, is born out of "life's own self-delight".

At this point, moreover, the image of the fountain, which had qualified the dismissive scepticism of "Mere dreams", is itself counter-qualified. As a symbol of "the inherited glory of the rich" Yeats now suggests, instead of the "abounding glittering jet", the image of the seashell. This shell is "marvellous", but "empty". It is, moreover, flung "Out of the obscure dark of the rich streams". "Obscure dark" seems anomalous, whichever way we look at it — it is pleonasm of a curious sort. The word "rich" picks up the quality of the black water powerfully, anyway. This is a retreat to a different symbolic order. Previously, civilization was seen as overflowing from the "abounding glittering jet" which came out of man's capacity for self-delight. Now, Yeats proposes the image of a powerful subterranean force tossing up civilization as contemptuously and unintentionally as the river in "Kubla Khan" which generated the stately pleasure dome and hurled "huge fragments" about as easily as "rebounding hail". Coleridge's poem, with its beautifully evoked image of civilization as a mirage-like palace dancing in the air, and its subsequent disclosure of a subterranean river of life, would seem to have provided Yeats with his structure here.

Nevertheless, Yeats has committed himself to saying that it is "certain beyond dreams" that something valuable − life's own self-delight − exists within man and nature, and this idea provides him with his foothold on the last stage of his dialectical climb. He does not delude himself that this force (whatever it is) can be striven after, much less constructed by method or discipline. Still it is there, that new quality, joy or self-delight; it is quintessentially, definingly human, and it resists disintegration by dream; it resists also *in*tegration into nature. It runs necessarily counter to any drift in nature, is essentially artificial. Civilization itself is disintegrated, we note: civilization is the product of man's capacity for self-delight; it is also a dream, though a benevolent one. What is not a dream is the "abounding glittering jet", the "obscure dark of the rich streams", something inexplicable, outside itself, but an irrefutable fact in man. Thus, Yeats is − for the first time − postulating a radical difference between man's dreaming function and some capacity (no abstraction, but a reality as vibrant and palpable as the "rich stream") that neither exhausts itself nor wholly identifies itself in the dreams which are as natural to his nature yet also as non-natural as consciousness itself. As we shall see in "Ego Dominus Tuus", Yeats is coming to believe that the poet's task is to mediate between these two human functions, his

capacity for self-delight and his actual dreaming. As the
expression "self-delight" itself suggests, moreover, there is
an implicit reliance upon a mirror-image here, and this may
ultimately prove to be central to all Yeats's thinking about
consciousness, culture and civilization.

The nature of civilization is investigated further in the
third stanza of "Ancestral Houses", where two important
strands of Yeats's thought for the first time coalesce:
the idea of all human concept-formation as dream-like,
and that of all activity as being antithetical in nature. It
is interesting that Yeats began to formulate the notion of a
kind of compensation-theory of creativity (in *Per amica
silentiae lunae*) as early as 1915.[32] In the poem under
discussion, the already heavily qualified notion of the great
house and its civilization is now overtly described in terms
of its opposites. Though they express and epitomize the
ideal of human culture, they were brought into being not
by tranquillity and wisdom but on the contrary through
the exasperated dreaming of "Some violent bitter man",
who "called architect and artist in", who being "violent
and bitter men" also, might

> . . .   rear in stone
> The sweetness that all longed for night and day,
> The gentleness none there had ever known;

The artistic and cultural magnificence, then, is the result of
an idealism frustrated in life: it is, in a word, compensation.
For, having suggested that the creators of this magnificence had only bitterness to fuel their endeavour, Yeats
goes on to raise the troubling question that underlies the
whole poem. What if these things — which not only we
ourselves but "the greatest of mankind" consider to be the
things which "most . . . magnify, or . . . bless" mankind —
what if these "take our greatness with our bitterness" —
with our violence? The thought is clear: the verb "take"
here means "absorb", or, to use another favourite
Yeatsianism, "consume" — to sublimate, in another idiom,
so that we are left with nothing of those qualities which,
along with the bitter violence of our minds and hearts,

went to the creation of the magnificence. In other words, man becomes great out of his bitter exasperation in life. Man's greatness, as expressed in civilization and great works of art, exhausts itself in fulfilling itself in the images of the desired greatness (peace, ease, magnificence). In slaking his frustration in creation, man also loses his greatness, leaving a "slippered" generation to muse away life in the leisure afforded by the strenuous and often violent efforts of the predecessors.

The sequence of ideas in the poem, then, is as follows. Civilization is a dream that exhausts the dreamer. The negative energies of man in a sense remain negative. They are the source of violence and misery, but also the tokens of our greatness, so that the "inherited glory" of the rich (in which life is allowed to overflow without those ambitious pains that make the bourgeoisie so ugly), must necessarily be an idle, somewhat absurd thing, set apart from the workings of those "rich streams" which generate man's destructive, along with his constructive, energies. Constant at the heart of man is "an aching heart" — the lack, the hunger for something: "only an aching heart/ Conceives a changeless work of art". Civilization consists in the process whereby generations of men and their business take on the "soul's unchanging look". But as the third section of the sequence, "My Table", suggests, "the most rich inheritor" (the apogeum of the privilege evoked in "Ancestral Houses") has himself just such an aching heart. Because he knows that

> . . . none could pass Heaven's door
> That loved inferior art,

he too had "waking wits". The discontent, that is to say, is central to the whole process of civilization itself. Thus, the well-dressed epitome of civilization is the peacock whose piercing screams express the inner hunger of the rich man. So it goes on.

What we have here in "Meditations in Time of Civil War" is obviously a continuation of a thought-process that began a quarter of a century earlier in poems like "The

Song of the Happy Shepherd" and "The Rose of Battle":
man dreams because he is both greater and less than the
animals. Animals, as Yeats's short poem "Death" tells us,
neither dream nor suffer, and therefore do not know
death. To know death is not to die simply, but to have
"invented death". By the time he came to write the
"Meditations", Yeats had extended his thinking on these
matters to embrace a theory, which if not particularly
clear, is nevertheless genuinely historical. His thinking on
the process of civilization no doubt owed much to his
awareness of his own antecedents. The Yeatses more or
less consciously opted out of the trade cycle late in the
eighteenth century, when the will of Benjamin Yeats
disposed "of the small remains of his property that may
be saved from the wreck of disappointments and the
unforeseen misfortunes of this world".[33] Thereafter, they
were rectors and scholars and artists — people aspiring to
the state of the gentry, in other words. Those old
commercial fathers gave Yeats the "vigorous mind" he
boasts of in "My Descendants". Yet because of this,
the poet feels he must "nourish dreams": without a certain
squandering violence making the torn petals "strew the
garden plot", there is only decline — the natural declension
of the soul — and "common greenness". I take this latter
phrase to be a reference to ordinary Catholic Irishness; the
whole poem is arrogantly Anglo-Irish. Yet this somewhat
tedious recitation of the need to build through ambition,
through a sense of greatness, is lifted by the only reference
to the historical theory that Yeats was constructing in
A Vision:

> The Primum Mobile that fashioned us
> Has made the very owls in circles move;

The theory as a whole is undoubtedly well characterized
by F. P. Sturm as a dead system, "parts of a machine that
was thrown on the scrap". Sturm was almost the only man
who told Yeats the truth about his theorizing without
appearing negative: "the Primum Mobile no longer moves,
the even planetary spheres are dull as a steamy cookshop

window ... "[34] This is undoubtedly true of most of *A Vision* itself. Yet when we read poems like "The Cat and the Moon" and these lines in "My Descendants", it does not seem possible to deny that Yeats has intuited, and presented in verse, a real process: there is a force of disturbance and control behind these lines. It is no accident that here, once again, even in a tired piece of Ptolemaic jargon, those favourite syllables and letters recur — "mobile". Here again is the *bl*-sound, the liquid syllables, the dactylic disturbance. And the word-order in the second line guarantees that we *feel* "the very owls in circles move". Never was that pedantic "very" made to work more effectively.

This sense of human behaviour as being governed from below, from without, or from within — at any rate governed — dominates the next three sections of the poem. The following two — V and VI — maintain a subdued tone: the incidents of the Civil War are retailed with none of the intensity of "Nineteen Hundred and Nineteen". It was a case of Irishman killing Irishman, of course, and there was no convenient enemy to rail at. Moreover, Yeats was there during the Civil War, whereas he was away in England during the Black and Tans disturbances. The fourth and fifth lyrics of the "Meditations" are accordingly personalized, almost anecdotal. Yet the fourth builds to a remarkable moment: the poet, envious of the men of action passing his door, catches himself off-guard:

> ... (I) turn towards my chamber, caught
> In the cold snows of a dream.

I am at a loss to account for the power of these lines. The entire poem has been dream-like, a set of meditations on various sorts of dreaming. Rarely has the quality of abstractedness been captured so precisely as Yeats has captured it here. What are those "cold snows" exactly? Of course, we cannot say; to produce such verbal equivalents of thought and sensation is the purpose of poetry. The poet has "caught" himself adrift on that stream which flows through the whole sequence of poems.

In the fifth section, "The Stare's Nest by My Window", the underlying trend of this current is revealed in a couplet which in a sense expresses the heart of Yeats's political thinking more pungently than anything else he wrote. The first three stanzas, written in a very low key, build up an image of a world in which masonry is crumbling, walls are loosening, yet in which "We are closed in, and the key is turned/On our uncertainty". (What the relationship is between these lines and Eliot's more famous ones at the end of *The Waste Land,* if any, I do not know.) The land is in turmoil, men are killed, houses burned, yet there is "no clear fact to be discerned". Yeats invites the bees to bind these crumbling fragments together, and "build in the house of the stare" — that is, in the abandoned starling's nest outside his window. He cannot have been unaware of the double meaning of the old word "stare": at any rate, the refrain emphasizes the dazed human world in a subtly unemphatic way. The point of this slow build-up only begins to emerge towards the end of the third stanza, with the skilfully plangent half-rhyme on "wood": the young soldier "in his blood" is "trundled" down the road almost carelessly as if he were drunk. How powerful is the generalizing apothegm that opens the fourth and last stanza of the poem:

> We had fed the heart on fantasies,
> The heart's grown brutal from the fare;

The whole drift of Yeats's poetry, from "Easter 1916" onwards, has been to extend the territory of his reference until it includes man as a whole. This is not merely Irishmen, or Englishmen and Irishmen, but all men shown here at work of hatred and violence. The couplet that lies at the root of the "Meditations" nevertheless has a specifically Irish as well as a general human application. We had accepted without demur that the Celtic Twilight grew naturally out of the ruminations of a people long oppressed and unused to self-governance, and that the process of emerging into nation-hood would involve the explosion of this dream in favour of the reality. And, as we have seen already more than once, Yeats was aware of the guilt of his own class — the Anglo-Irish ascendancy — in having refused to take Irish politics seriously enough. It is nevertheless something of a shock to be told now that not only had Ireland nourished a tendency to substitute fantasy for reality, and charm for praxis, but that this long history of illusion-making (the dream of independence and the nostalgia for a mythical lost greatness) should have *brutalized* the Irish. This thought comes as a shock. Yet that is what Yeats says. It is, of course, wholly in line with the consistent attitude he maintained towards Maud Gonne and her friends, and towards the Easter Rising. Nowhere does Yeats express more pithily the relationship between his first period and his second: the antithetical violence is bred by opposition out of the fantasy. As a result, there is, he now says, "more substance in our enmities/Than in our love". When the refrain now returns, it is with a fully justified intensity:

> . . .   O honey-bees,
> Come build in the empty house of the stare.

What had been a rhetorical request becomes a deeply-felt plea.

Consistently with the anecdotal structure of the entire sequence, the sixth and last section of "Meditations in Time of Civil War" follows the progress of the poet up the stairs of the tower to behold "Phantoms of Hatred and of the Heart's Fullness and of the Coming Emptiness". We must remember that "Ancestral Houses" had described no actual house, made no recommendations, advocated no social philosophy. Its underlying drift is plain: the writer clearly holds order and ceremony in high esteem. Yet it is a hypothesis the poet tenders, and one that, as I have tried to show, is fraught with qualifications, doubts and counter-qualifications. It also adumbrated a theory of culture and behaviour which made any overt conservatism merely descriptive. Such a state may be preferable, but it is not unequivocally "the good": it derives from the bitterness and violence against which it now seems to provide the only bulwark in a world which has, by social and political evolution, released the demons of bitterness into political orthodoxy.

It is important to hold this highly qualified, somewhat pessimistic view of human activity in mind when we consider Yeats's conservatism in general, and the visions of disruption which erupt in the last section of the "Meditations" in particular. We know now that the Primum Mobile is dictating our actions. We know also that the relationship between our exasperation and our noblest actions is counterpointed by a sinister relationship between our tendency to dream (seemingly pleasant and harmless) and our brutality in action. These themes are all taken up and given their head in this last section of the sequence. The symbols and images of the earlier lyrics — the snow, the mist, the sword, the moon — sweep by, "white glimmering fragments of the mist". It is a *résumée* not merely of the preceding six lyrics, but of human action and politics themselves seen as mist and dream ("Mad as the mist and snow", as Yeats put it rather nuttily in a later poem). Everything is confused and confusing, so that

> Frenzies bewilder, reveries perturb the mind;

This is, of course, a festival of Yeats's root-words. It would indeed be impossible to find a single line that better illustrates the nature of Yeats's poetic philosophy. Both in rhythm and denotation the four principal words "Frenzies", "bewilder", "reveries" and "perturb" enact that Dionysiac disturbance which is, in a sense, Yeats's real subject-matter. Once again, it is next to impossible to scan the line with any kind of confidence: "Frénzies bewílder,/réveries pertúrb/the mínd;" the last three words form an apparently orthodox iambic rump. But they swim loose in a void created by "reveries", which in turn tremble in the wake of "bewilder", one of the most important elements Yeats had added to his vocabulary over the previous ten years. Once more the mind is — bewildered: we can only go back to Yeats's own word. And what bewilders it is frenzy. The experience of the

whole line refuses to be summed up either through an
account of its rhythm or of its meanings: both co-operate
to create the complex disturbance that is the life of the
line.

It is in the wake of this profound, complex disturbance
that the "monstrous familiar images swim to the mind's
eye". What follows surpasses even the tragic disclosure of
"Nineteen Hundred and Nineteen" in its powerfully
labouring intensity. The violence is heralded by a skilful
exploitation of that meaningless esotericism which mars
the end of the earlier poem. Where that "insolent fiend
Robert Artisson" remains a sinister but unexplained
reference beyond the poem's texture, the "murderers of
Jacques Molay" depend for their effectiveness in the verse
precisely upon their obscurity. We neither know nor care
who Jacques Molay was, or why there should be vengeance
upon his murderers. The point is just that the poet wishes
to capture the effect of being "carried away". What more
effective way of dramatizing the vortex of violence that
has gripped society than this hysterical shrieking of a
rallying-cry the poet does not really understand? At the
end he still keeps his head, he had only *"all but* cried/
For vengeance on the murderers of Jacques Molay". We
can do no better than quote Yeats's Note at this point:
"A cry for vengeance because of the murder of the Grand
Master of the Templars seems to me fit symbol for those
who labour from hatred, and so for sterility in various
kinds."[35] Yeats does not always seem to have known so
clearly what he was doing in his best poetry. Certainly the
lines describing the "labour from hatred" take his explor-
ation into rhythmic disturbance and, indeed, his entire
investigation of the evil gathering head in man to a point
from which it could only decline:

> . . . In cloud-pale rags, or in lace,
> The rage-driven, rage-tormented, and rage-hungry troop,
> Trooper belabouring trooper, biting at arm or at face,
> Plunges towards nothing, arms and fingers spreading wide
> For the embrace of nothing; and I, my wits astray
> Because of all that senseless tumult, all but cried
> For vengeance on the murderers of Jacques Molay.

Over the first three lines here, the dominant element is the
sound of the long "a" (*pale, lace, rage-, rage-, rage-,*
be*la*bouring, *face*). But it is a triumph also of repetition —
of *rage,* and *troop-* in particular, mimetic of the horrible
pounding of blow upon blow. If we return for comparison
to the passage in the "Three Beggars" we shall see by how
much Yeats has advanced not only in technical precision,
but in the tenacious seriousness with which he pursues —
with an Anglo-Saxon doggedness oddly at variance with
the aura of Irish charm he laboured to conjure around his
work so often — the core of his meaning.

This sickeningly powerful evocation of physical violence
is followed by a still more extraordinary evocation of the
nausea of nothingness. Again, it is a triumph of versification and sound: the verse plunges us towards "nothing",
then, as if in horror, attempting to stop, stiffens out onto
"spreading wide". Again, as in "Nineteen Hundred and
Nineteeen", Yeats exploits the line-end to create a gulf
which we as readers must experience before we close on
"a phantasm" — "For the embrace of nothing". This is the
nausea of nothingness that lies within the possession of
violence. The phrase Yeats uses in the next line to sum up
this *horreur du vide,* draws upon another of Yeats's
favourite words: "senseless tumult". "Tumult" occurs
again and again at important moments in Yeats's poetry to
evoke a variety of states. It can be joyous, as in that
"lonely impulse of delight" which sent the Irish airman in
search of the "tumult above the clouds". Alternatively, it
can join "frenzy" and "bewilderment" in the attempt to
define human madness. Whatever way Yeats uses the word,
he invariably exploits its rich properties (the *-mu* suggests
swelling, the *-lt* liquid disturbance) with strategic skill.
Again, the rhythmic inscape of the word — its two even
stresses ride the metric grid of the verse — also indicates
Yeats's reasons for being so fond of it.

The opening stanza of the section had prepared us for a
series of phantoms, of visions; and that is what we get. The
troopers belabouring each other gives way without preface
or explanation to the procession of exquisite ladies,

Their legs long, delicate and slender, aquamarine their eyes,
Magical unicorns bear ladies on their backs.

— Whose minds "are but a pool/Where even longing drowns under its own excess". We need no acquaintance with *A Vision,* or any other source external to the poem, to understand the point of this vision: Yeats has taught us to read his symbols over the preceding six poems that make up the sequence. So that when he says of the ladies that

Nothing but stillness can remain when hearts are full
Of their own sweetness, bodies of their own loveliness . . .

we know that he is drawing upon the theory of culture and behaviour in terms of antithetical compensation. Just as the making of the great house and its attendant culture demanded the strenuous effort of "the aching heart", and as the "slippered contemplation" that enjoyed its fruits necessarily lacked the greatness that went into the making, so, here, we know that these exquisite ladies represent the satiety of a complacently fulfilled civilization. The fact that they have been set in juxtaposition to the evil fanatic hatred of the troopers belabouring each other emphasizes the general point: these are opposed images, the phantoms of hatred and of the heart's fullness for which the poem's title has prepared us. They give way to that terrifying "Coming Emptiness" that must succeed to the complacent fullness of the achieved civilization. Here is the foul synthesis of the dialectic Yeats has constructed in the poem. The progression reads: thesis-hatred of deprivation; antithesis-satiety of achievement; synthesis-violence proceeding out of the emptiness after fullness.

Yeats now gives us what was to remain his most powerful and frightening image of the future, those "brazen hawks" that inevitably suggest Goehring's Stukas:

Nothing but grip of claw, and the eye's complacency,
The innumerable clanging wings that have put out the moon.

From this terrifying vision, the poet, understandably, retreats:

I turn away and shut the door, . . .

As well he might. For, whatever we might in general think
of Yeats's somewhat eclectic ways of putting together
symbols, there can be no doubt that in reading this
sequence of stanzas, we experience that familiarity with
the unfamiliar which is poetry's *raison d'être*. This is our
time, with its sated civilization "lacking all conviction",
and its "worst full of passionate intensity". It is notable
that Yeats only ever found marginal use for that truer
"passion" which sometimes seem to lie at the heart of his
conception of the heroic and the transcendant. Here, as
so often elsewhere, sanity is served by resignation, widsom
by accepting that we must make the best of the bad job
human life is. He wonders, as he turns aside from the
palpable evidences of human passion in action, how many
times he might himself have "proved (his) worth". But
even had he succeeded in doing this (how, he has no idea),
the result would have been but another instance of that
general law of human consciousness: success makes us
"pine the more". The poem has already argued that this
is what constitutes the heart of civilization: civilization is a
set of images of what we want. Success here clearly means
success in action, by the way. For what he turns "away"
to is "The abstract joy". This turns out to mean the "half-
read wisdom of daemonic images". This may refer to the
poet's own lack of any formal intellectual education:
Yeats confessed himself to the end a "smatterer",
dependent more or less on chance to throw his way what
books it chose. Or it may refer to the fact that we can only
ever half-comprehend what images we do inspect. At any
rate, he is happy to conclude with a line which both in
cadence and in diction recalls the great Romantic poet he
had been re-reading, though with scant acknowledgement
of his influence upon himself: these "daemonic images",
he says, "Suffice the ageing man as once the growing
boy."[36] Something of Wordsworth's serenity and strength
informs the close of the poem, but it is a bitter after-taste.

At the very heart of Yeats's view of civilization,
therefore, there is a profound paradox. He believes in a
fountain within man, a capacity for spontaneous joy,

inexplicable, all-enabling, and bred out of "self-delight". Yet his image of man remains that of a hungry dreamer, and his civilization that of a sad ruin. This being so, it is questionable whether we can even call Yeats a political conservative. He sees through his own conservatism, wholly and sadly, and remains conservative only in the sense of harbouring a trenchant dislike of the drift of twentieth century civilization and its levelling technological barbarities. Once again, being Irish helped Yeats here. The Georgian mansions and Norman keeps and Celtic towers that litter the desolate countryside of Ireland serve as a model for his essentially despairing view of civilization better than the well-kept-up stately homes of England or the châteaux of the Loire. Civilization for Yeats is a mere dream, and its ruins confirm the suspicion.

(ix) Role, mask, and the "vision of reality"

The two great poem-sequences of the early twenties, "Nineteen Hundred and Nineteen" and "Meditations in Time of Civil War", attain a sustained intensity which Yeats was never again to equal. We are justified, I think, in regarding them as the climacteric of Yeats's second, tragic or antithetical phase. Thereafter, we shall mark a slackening of tension, a broadening of vision, or both. Both poems, however, set more questions than they answer, and before going on to examine what we might call Yeats's last period, we must pause to look at some of the theoretical attempts Yeats made around this time, either in verse or in expository prose, to provide himself with a conceptual framework for his findings.

These efforts followed directions already indicated in the poetry: it is important to bear this in mind. The unanswered questions posed by the great tragic poems derive from the thoroughness of Yeats's investigations of his own poetic preoccupations. Principal among these are the notions of human behaviour as dream-like, and of art as being concerned with the interpretation of dream. What is the nature of the poet's commitment, exactly? How does it differ from the ordinary man's situation? If culture is a dream itself, is it based on quicksand? What, finally, is the nature of human personality itself?

Yeats addresses some of these questions directly in a number of poems of the early twenties. These are generally below Yeats's best as poetry: they are too excessively concerned with theories and ideas not themselves realized within the texts to be satisfactory poetry. Despite this, however, or because of it, these are fascinating and important works. "Ego Dominus Tuus", to begin with, examines the creative process in terms equivalent to the general cultural theory we have seen emerging from earlier poems: it is an account of creativity in terms of compensation. The poem takes the form of a dialogue between two voices, *Hic* and *Ille*. *Hic* begins by chiding *Ille* for choosing to remain under the vassalage of certain projects:

> . . . you . . . still trace,
> Enthralled by the unconquerable delusion,
> Magical shapes.

This is a thoroughly Yeatsian accusation, couched in classically Yeatsian terms: Yeatsian man, as we have noted repeatedly, is habitually "enthralled", under the domination of some idea. The adjective "unconquerable", too, shares the quality of disturbance we note in "Calvary's" and "uncontrollable" in "The Magi"; "delusions", finally, joins "fantasy" and "dream" as a root-word for man's characteristic mental imprisonment. Here is Yeatsian man, then, mirrored in his own self-awareness.

Ille doesn't reject the charge: what he is doing, in his search for arcane images, is, he says, seeking his own opposite. This introduces a new idea into Yeats's poetry: what does it mean — to look for one's opposite? What might one's "opposite" be? We shall see later. Meanwhile, *Hic* replies that *he* is looking not for an image, but for himself. Obviously, this is a reasonable piece of self-doubt on Yeats's part. He was well aware that he was out of step with the drift of modern writing, and the very existence of these manifesto-poems testifies to the uncertainty he seems to have experienced. What *Hic* proposes is simply the introspective mode natural to most modern writers: what the writer does in this view is annotate his inner experience in making a self-portrait, much as the prose naturalist holds a mirror up to contemporary mores.

Ille's response is considered and trenchant. Such introspective self-portraiture, he says, is "our modern hope":

> . . .   and by its light
> We have it upon the gentle, sensitive mind
> And lost the old nonchalance of the hand;

Shrewdly, Yeats observes that the modern writer is less a creator than a critic who can "but half create,/Timid, entangled, empty and abashed". This is Yeats's most cogent definition and criticism of the limitations of modern writing, and it is a powerful attack. *Hic* returns with the example of Dante: if what *Ille* says is true, and modern self-portraiture has robbed the artist of the old craftsman's skills, why is it that we know the face of Dante so well? Surely this is a tribute to the power and necessity of realistic self-representation? *Ille* answers in the negative, though using rhetorical questions instead of straight denial:

> And did he find himself
> Or was the hunger that had made it hollow
> A hunger for the apple on the bough
> Most out of reach? . . .

It was not honest positive "presence", psychological realism of the modern sort, then, that made Dante etch his portrait so fiercely, but need, hunger, lack. Dante's image was "fashioned from his opposite"; he ate "that bitter bread" in life.

On this view, all art, like civilization itself, is tragic: deriving from man's sense of lack, from the piteous disparity between his own highest imaginings and what he must settle for in daily existence. Yeats's conception is severely consistent: *Ille* resists *Hic*'s counter-examples.

When *Hic* wants to suggest that *some* writers are "lovers of life", and "sing when they have found" happiness, *Ille*'s answer is that those that love the world "serve it in action". And the writer who thinks he can enter into "action", will be like a fly in marmalade. The successful realist novelist would make a good example, with his often reformist social stance. According to Yeats's view, such writers are caught in illusion: they are not real artists, but frustrated men of action, rather like Oscar Wilde, as Yeats had noted in *Autobiographies*.[37] *Hic's* final attempt to get back into the argument through the example of Keats (the great yea-sayer among modern poets) is swatted down with lordly disdain. Yeats relies excessively here on Matthew Arnold's snobbish and ill-founded view of Keats as an ignoramus longing for the goodies of bourgeois enlightenment. Yet who, reading the Nightingale Ode or the "Bright Star" sonnet, can deny that Keats "sank into his grave/His senses and his heart unsatisfied", or that his "leaden-eyed despair" is indeed related by antithesis, as Yeats suggests it is, to his "luxuriant song"? Yeats is not so far off the mark here.

What then is the artist's role — to sing unhappiness? Yeats has provided an answer to this question already in the poem, yet it is an answer that raises more questions than it satisfies. In rejecting both the reformist's fly-in-marmalade role, and the "impulsive" happiness-seeker's song of joy, *Ille* is moved to define the poet's function in terms that seem forthright and unequivocal:

> The rhetorician would deceive his neighbours,
> The sentimentalist himself; while art
> Is but a vision of reality.
> What portion in the world can the artist have
> Who has awakened from the common dream
> But dissipation and despair?

The latter lines certainly cohere with the general tragic conception of art, explaining the egress into dissipation of those decadents (Lionel Johnson *et alia*) among whom the young Yeats had learned his craft. According to this view, dissipation and despair are reasonable options for the poet, who knows precisely that happiness is the "apple on the bough/Most out of reach". But what are we to make of "the common dream" from which the poet has awakened? Does this bring Yeats into line with the view of cultural empiricism — that poets merely see reality more often and more disabusedly than other men? Is this what Yeats means by calling art "a vision of reality"? The phrase rolls glibly enough off the tongue: it is, roughly speaking, the man in the street's view of art. But surely it runs counter to Yeats's whole Apollonian stance? Didn't *Ille* earlier in the poem reject *Hic*'s realist claims, those claims which sought to base art precisely on a "vision of reality"? Wasn't he prepared to accept being "Enthralled by the unconquerable delusion", knowing that the realist dawdling down a lane with a mirror was fooling himself in believing that he was able to capture reality? Isn't it just this mirror-like view of naturalist art that Yeats had always found so unsatisfactory? What then is the nature of the "reality" of which the poet is supposed to have his vision? And what is the nature of the vision? These are the questions we must try to answer.

It is characteristic of Yeats, F. R. Leavis observed, to have had no centre of unity.[38] Yeats would seem to have little in common with Shakespeare, and Shakespeare was Keats's prime instance of the poet of "Negative Capability". Yet Yeats seems to have derived much of his conception of himself from Keats's theory of the poetic personality. "A poet", Keats remarked, "is the most unpoetical of anything in existence . . . ".[39] Whatever Keats actually meant by his observation, there is no doubt that the description of the poet that follows closely resembles Yeats himself: "he has no Identity — he is continually in(forming) and filling some other Body. . . ." Yeats was early aware of this somewhat centreless, over-affective nature of his. In *Autobiographies,* he describes himself as "a gregarious man, going hither and thither looking for conversation, and ready to deny from fear or favour his dearest conviction. . . ."[40]

When, therefore, *Ille*, in "Ego Dominus Tuus", says that
the poet must "seek an image, not a book", and when he
says that he seeks not himself but his own "opposite",
he is exploring lines of thought long familiar to the poet.
Inevitably, this way of thinking led him to formulate a
theory of masks. There is no doubt that the example and
articulations of Oscar Wilde had early etched the notion of
the mask in Yeats's mind. *The Decay of Lying* is one of
the important early influences on Yeats, and Wilde's
manner itself was an early demonstration of the way in
which character is forged out of its opposite. As he was
vilified and abused in public, Wilde's "manner had
hardened to meet opposition and at times he allowed one
to see an unpardonable insolence. His charm was acquired
and systematized, a mask which he wore only when it
pleased him . . . . "[41] Yeats sensed, too, that there was
something definingly Irish about Wilde's cult of the mask.
"We Irish", Wilde had remarked to Yeats, "are too poetical
to be poets; we are a nation of brilliant failures. . . ".[42]
It is clear how such a conception of the mask coheres
with Yeats's general view of culture itself as antithetical,
as compensatory. *Ille*'s statement that he seeks his own
"opposite" is to be taken more literally than may at first
sight appear necessary. He rejects modern introspective
realism because the writer is not "there" in his work, but
underlying this view is the more fundamental one that
perhaps man himself is not "there" in what he does. It
is a view which many modern sociologists and social
psychologists have espoused: Erwin Goffman, for instance,
states unequivocally that man reduces without remainder
to the role he chooses to play.[43] It is difficult — for the
present writer at least — not to feel that such theories
simply leave something out of account: the idea of the
mask or the role remains a metaphor, a metaphor pre-
supposing a player within the mask. Yeats touches on this
question at many points. A good instance is that supple
little lyric, "The Mask". The beloved bids the lover take
off his mask, that she may know "love or deceit". The
lover replies that it was the mask which "engaged (her)

mind" not "what's behind". But he might be her enemy, she persists. What does it matter, the lover answers:

> . . . so there is but fire
> In you, in me?

In this conception, the actor cannot be known from the part he plays. Significantly enough, Yeats's lovers are seen as being controlled by their love: they are "engaged", their hearts are "set to beat"; there is "fire" in them. This brings us again to that central problem in Yeats: the relations between the passion that transfigures a man and the passion which destroys and dehumanizes him. Keats, in a famous passage that certainly influenced Yeats, observes that "Though a quarrel in the streets is a thing to be hated, the energies displayed in it are fine; the commonest Man shows a grace in his quarrel . . . ."[44] Blake, moreover had distinguished between being *in* a passion (good and positive), and having a passion in you (bad and negative). That is, the "passion" that is in a man spoils or poisons him; only when he is transformed or translated out of himself, is he god-like. But Blake's poetry is held together by the notion that "Everything that lives is holy"; a similar faith informs the poetry and letters of Keats. There is no such binding element in Yeats. To the contrary, he is filled with a sense of evil at the heart of things. Possession, as we have had occasion to note several times, is generally identified with destructiveness and hatred by Yeats.

Considerations of this kind make it impossible to accept, without crippling reservations, Yeats's attempts to derive his own conception of masks from the greatest classical exponent of role-theory, Plotinus. In the third *Ennead,* Plotinus makes his extended parallel between human life and an actual drama:

> In the dramas of human art, the poet provides words but the actors add their own quality, good or bad — for they have more to do than merely repeat the author's words: in the truer drama which dramatic genius imitates in its degree, the Soul displays itself in a part assigned by the creator of the piece.[45]

For Plotinus, the actor may or may not have charm; he may muff his lines or say them with spirit, but the drama remains "as good a work as ever". The idea has influenced many writers since Plotinus wrote these words. Calderon — a writer important to Yeats at this time — adapted it in his play *El Gran Teatro del Mundo*, in which the great "autor" reveals his rationale to the poor man who has complained at being given a drudge's role: you can play your role well or badly; you can be a good beggar or a bad one.[46] The notion is found also in Sartrean existentialism with its notion of authenticity as defined in terms of a responsibly chosen and accepted role.

It is clear that Yeats lacked the central philosophical vision required to legitimize such a theory of role. Plotinus conceived of three kinds of role-playing: on the lowest level is individual anarchy, devoid of any knowledge of role; next, is the bondage of social role-acceptance, in which man has an antlike part; third, and noblest, is the heroic freedom-within role. It is in this way that Plotinus redeems his plan from being a merciless blue-print, laid down in heaven: man's freedom is exercised through intelligence, yet he is secure within the great plan. Plotinus conceives of the "good" man fighting his way free of mere accident to find his true role — the one laid down for him from the start — in the great drama of existence. Yeats's very attempt to preserve these categories illuminates with callous clarity the inadequacy of the philosophy behind the theory. The heroic struggle of Plotinus's good man degenerates, in Yeats, into mere assertive egotism: the hero fights his way out of "mere accident" (the hindering condition of being a social animal in the world of the industrial revolution), and is entitled to dispense with the obligations of being a good neighbour. Such a conception is dangerous in a world from which the sanctioning condition of Plotinus's intellectual scheme no longer obtains. If we do not believe in the Great Design or the Great Designer, we cannot authentically conceive of any "proper" role for man. We cannot know our role because, properly speaking, we do not have one. There is no

symphony, no cosmic drama with invisible but omni-
present *régisseur*. If we try to behave as if there were, we
end up not with beauty, but with ugliness: the State-as-
work-of-Art becomes the *Tausend-jährigesreich*.

Yeats was, as is now notorious, eventually to flirt with,
and more than flirt with, Fascism as an answer to modern
man's dilemma. At about the time he was writing the
poetry we are now concerned with, he found powerful
support for his view of things in a writer who was actually
to give personal advice to the squalid Führer of the Reich.
Oswald Spengler's *Untergang des Abendlandes* presented a
theory of history which came close to the ideas Yeats himself was botching together. Here was a theoretical
framework for that sense Yeats had always had of some
greater force or reality lying *beyond* the things men do in
their daily affairs. If there is no cosmic *régisseur* benignly
ordaining significant roles for good men, there was at least
a serpentine Something twisting and convoluting its way
through Time. And unless we understand that this is so,
we cannot understand the things we do. Our acts are not
individual responses made, in full knowledge of facts, to
given unique situations; they are blind performances,
obeying the behest of the great serpent of history.

Yeats availed himself of an astrological structure to
body forth his own sense of this serpentine force – the
nearest thing to a God in Yeats's work. Again and again,
the sense of lunar change is transmitted powerfully onto
the page through rhythm and syntax. In "The Phases of
the Moon", there are two speakers, Robartes and Aherne.
Aherne in fact is a mere acolyte, who prompts Robartes to
rehearse the details of "the changes of the moon once
more". (The poet himself, incidentally, is present "Off"
throughout the poem with "His sleepless candle and
laborious pen" – the image of dream-wasted man.)
Robartes describes history as moving towards certain
climaxes: when a society is on the wax, man seeks himself,
as *Ille* had, and produces more and more detailed and
splendid images of himself. At the full of the moon, this
process reaches a zenith, at which man ceases to move

forward and rests inert in self-contemplation. We have seen
this already in those ladies with aquamarine eyes in
"Nineteen Hundred and Nineteen". Historically, this
means the High Renaissance with its magnificent
iconography and its conception of the "State as work of
art". Thereafter, as society wanes, and man seeks the
world, like *Hic,* this magnificent iconography declines into
mere realism. The decline of Europe from the high noon of
its own humanist magnificence proceeds eventually to the
reformist realism of the nineteenth century:

> . . .   all is changed,
> It would be the world's servant, and as it serves,
> Choosing whatever task's most difficult
> Among tasks not impossible, it takes
> Upon the body and upon the soul
> The coarseness of the drudge.

The only consistent philosophy of role modern man has
been able to come up with is the Christian-Socialist one,
with its distinction of good self-effacement and bad self-
interest. Nietzsche had already dismissed this alternative as
the "morality of slaves". Yeats's repugnance finds strong
expression in the lines just cited. Yet Christian socialism is
still the most dignified of modern man's philosophies, and
to reject it is likely to lead a man into inconsistency and
ugliness. It is this fact, we have seen, which emerges from
a comparison of Yeats's and Plotinian role-theory: Yeats's
hero is no good man struggling to find the role laid down
for him, but an assertive egotist, much like Nietzsche himself. Yet the development of modern civilization had lent
strong support to Yeats's vision: modern reformist realism
had set free — in the years following Nietzsche's death —
a shapeless horde crying to one another like bats:

> . . . having no desire they cannot tell
> What's good or bad, or what it is to triumph
> At the perfection of one's own obedience;
> And yet they speak what's blown into the mind;
> Deformed beyond deformity, unformed,
> Insipid as the dough before it is baked,
> They change their bodies at a word.

This is surely an astute characterization of the "half-baked" multitude released by modern mass-education – a population which, denied the ancient authorities of a sure culture and a spiritual establishment, can speak only "what's blown into the mind" by the media. Propaganda was to become a vast agency in human culture for the first time in the very decade in which Yeats wrote this poetry.

In "Meditations in Time of Civil War" this battish insipidity leaves the sphere of human affairs wide open to the persuasions of "the worst", and the now-moonless darkness fills with the clanging wings of war. In "The Phases of the Moon", the image of the unbaked dough is continued in Robartes's next speech: it is kneaded, as the minds are manipulated by advertisers and propagandists, by "cook Nature". Then, "the first thin crescent is wheeled round once more". At this point, the poem's symbolism – to me at least – seems to become arcane and hermetic: the Hunchback and Saint and Fool do not hold the objective cogency of the historicistic thesis Yeats has been outlining.

This thesis is wholly consistent, and profoundly coherent with Yeats's gradually evolving conceptions of dream, and of human consciousness. He has already articulated his fear of human energy in the paradox of enchantment. Cynical as he was about socialist reformism, therefore, he was not taken in by the attractions of the demonic: there is no flirtation with anarchy or abandonment. Instead of distinguishing between repression and freedom, therefore, as have so many modern thinkers, basing themselves upon a quasi-Freudian or Blakean model, Yeats distinguishes between different sorts of dreaming. He admits that civilized order, grace and beauty are the products of conquest and effort, which were, in turn, merely the instruments of a particular kind of dream-project. The historicism which created *A Vision,* and poems such as "The Phases of the Moon", starts to make human sense when we view it as the pulsations of a great supernal dream.

Nothing makes this clearer than Yeats's famous alter-

cation with Sturge Moore about modern philosophy.[47]
Yeats attacked the empiricism of Moore's brother, G. E.
Moore, on the grounds that it reduced the world to a
"reality", which the human mind merely recorded. He
found his own basic postulates — that, to the contrary,
the mind *creates* reality — confirmed within the corpus of
Idealist philosophy, from Bishop Berkeley, through Kant
to Croce and Gentile. Now on the strict philosophical
level, Yeats's arguments have no interest. He simply did
not understand Berkeleyan idealism. He took the Bishop
to have suggested that "reality" is a creation of the human
mind, and therefore

> That this pragmatical, preposterous pig of a world,
> > its farrow that so solid seem,
> Must vanish on the instant if the mind but change its theme;
> > "Blood and the Moon"

This is perhaps what certain German Idealists thought
Berkeley meant. From the empiricist point of view,
Berkeley was a thoroughgoing empiricist who, far from
showing that nothing existed outside man's consciousness,
demonstrated that there was no difference between the
primary and secondary qualities of matter because everything that was real could be sensed. This is why G. E.
Moore spoke of things as bundles of possible sensations:
a thing is merely the basis of possible sensations, not a
mystic entity underlying what we see, but a linguistic convention. Thus, Berkeley's philosophy is primarily
linguistic, the foundation of the modern school of
phenomenalism. No sane man has ever really thought the
world would disappear if "the mind but change its theme".
Berkeley's so-called solipsism (which became the basis for
that Idealism Yeats praised in Schopenhauer) is a critique
of language, rather than an ontology.

Yet if Yeats failed to understand Berkeley's philosophy,
there is something valid in Yeats's acceptance of the
Bishop's conception of a God whose never-failing
consciousness guarantees the perpetuity of the world.
During his debate with Sturge Moore, Yeats made

significant reference to Calderon: "I return to Calderon", he wrote, "not only things, but dreams themselves are a dream".[48] Disorganized as it appears to be, there is a profound consistency in Yeats's thinking: precisely because he never forced himself to make the discrete elements of his thinking consistent with their neighbours, perhaps, Yeats remained free of the vice of trapping himself with logic, and therefore retained a deeper consistency than that of the systematic logician. The lynch-pin of his thinking is the notion of dream: according to Yeats, empiricism is wrong because it thinks we can "know" the truth or know reality, by introspection (false subjectivity) or by observation (false objectivity). The truth is, Yeats believed, that life never escapes the vassalage of dream. Metaphysically, this emerges in his conception of existence as the dream of a great dreamer (History or Time or whatever). Culturally, it emerges in the vision of consciousness as something we inherit from our "Race" — the symbols and systems of thought Yeats scrutinized so tenaciously. We are not given new on earth: we inherit these symbols with our consciousness. When we discover ourselves through self-awareness, we are already embarked upon a dream or series of dreams:

> Many times man lives and dies
> Between his two eternities,
> That of race and that of soul,
>   "Under Ben Bulben"

Modern individualism, we have seen, is nothing but a particular configuration of dream, composed of a conflicting amalgam of egalitarianism and trust in an ultimate affluence. If we are given in our language when we are born, it follows that we can never really "know" ourselves, or our essential nature. All that introspection can yield us is traces of the dream that is dreaming us; or, in less Yeatsian terms, the cultural traces deposited in language by our Race.

Only our images, our symbols, occasionally give us knowledge of ourselves, of the universe, of the greater dream whose figment we are. Thus our selves are not to be known so much as interpreted. And since what we know ourselves is an interpretation already of "reality", and the poet deals in interpretations of dreams, we may say that the poet's task is to interpret interpretations. It is in this light surely that we are to view Yeats's at some times foolish indifference to the external world, to "things that seem"; and his attentiveness to arcane interpretations of symbols in order that they may reveal the "Real". If the fool would persist in his folly, said Blake, he would become wise. Yeats became wise precisely through the "foolishness" into which his thoroughgoing idealism led him.

It was in man's essential nature, Yeats believed, to be enthralled, dominated, driven, by some dream or other. Within this susceptibility lay the secret of man's humanity. Only by knowing man's dreams can we know man himself: it is not introspection or observation that enable us to understand man, but interpretation. And this, finally, is what Yeats meant by describing the poet as one who had "awakened from the common dream": this is his "vision of reality". It is for these reasons that Yeats's greatest poetry concerned Ireland. For Ireland was the very embodiment of the theory that nations live through dreams. Deprived of actual political history, apart from the fact of being oppressed, what could Ireland do but dream? Politics itself is a series of dreams, far-off goals which are striven for, no matter what actually exists in the present. Irish political deprivation surely explains the vague yet tangible sense of "soul" attaching to Ireland itself and the Irish. In Ireland one encounters nothing but the past, yet the countryside seems empty. It is devoid of history — whole ages of architecture are un-represented in Ireland — yet, as if waiting for History to come into being, it is full of unconsumed dream. (Yeats was fond of this verb in this sense: "The painter's brush consumes his dreams".) By comparison with Ireland, England is dense with history, yet it is difficult to find anywhere in England — certain parts of Cornwall possibly excepted — that presence so commonly met with in Ireland: at Cashel, at Glendalough (where it survives a battering tourism), a presence we can only call soul. No matter how beautiful the landscape of England is — and it is the more beautiful island — it breathes a sense of completeness, as of a history done-with and fulfilled. It is the exhaustion of the dream, and a certain stoniness attends the aftermath of success.

Yet the soul of Ireland — its residue of unconsumed dream — is, like that of the American negro, troubled. Is it not significant that the initial reaction to the removal of British overlordship in 1922 was not a joyous peace but the paroxysm of Civil War? It is as if the objective focus were replaced by one chosen from within the subject — from within Ireland itself, in other words. Ireland turned upon itself, its hatred of England unslaked by any act of vengeance. The need to avenge the long insult persists today in Ireland's pursuit of England to the courts of Strasbourg and in the horrible campaigns of the Irish Republican Army, strenuously and successfully procuring fresh injuries to be avenged. These are things W. B. Yeats would have understood all too well.

PART THREE

Synthesis: Gaiety

Introduction

The basic ground-plan of the present book suggests a division into three more or less neatly defined phases of an *oeuvre* which is of its very essence overlapping and reptitious. It is only for philosophers and literary historians that life packages itself so tidily. The last period of a great writer often seems to be chracterized by a certain detachment from the materialities of Life — those of body, time and society. There is a characteristic deepening of perspective, a feeling of the religious: tragedy is habitually de-intensified. Death, which had dominated the tragic period of the great writer, assumes, now that it has come closer, a less terrible aspect. The writer begins to mull over the possibilities of Resurrection. We think of Racine's Christian plays, of Shakespeare's Romances, of Dickens's late otherworldliness, of Ibsen's unearthly mountains, of the serenity of the late Beethoven quartets. These qualities appear often enough in the works of the greatest writers to seem characteristic. Serenity in general, in the sense of a reconciliation with the fact of human existence, can be offered as the lynch-pin of "the" third-period style. Yet we must remember that the last works of great artists also comprehend much bitterness and ' exasperation: Prospero is paranoid, the older Beethoven knew his rages, Rembrandt's later self-portraits show a wizened, pathetic little man.

Synthesis, with its suggestion of an assured and tidy resolution of all irreconcileables, is an inappropriate term to apply to Yeats's later poetry. *The Winding Stair, Last Poems* and *A Full Moon in March* contain little that is serene in any conventional sense, and much that is strident, morose and bitter. There are indeed, as I shall try to show, good reasons for accepting F. R. Leavis's judgement that in much of the last poetry, there is "striking loss and the organization is significantly less rich".[1] There are also, however, excellent reasons for persisting with the language of dialectic to describe Yeats's later poetry: if there is little genuine synthesis, and less serenity, there are qualities and ideas which are derived from the work of the preceding decade by dialectical opposition. There are also properties we could identify simply as "last period", with or without the support of any such theoretical framework.

The volume in which these ideas and motifs are first seen is *The Tower* of 1928, in which, as we have already observed, some of Yeats's most powerful tragic work is to be found. *The Tower* contains work from about six years. Once again, the order in which Yeats chose to present the poems amounts to a creative act in itself, but confuses any attempt to follow Yeats's development. It opens with "Sailing to Byzantium", which appears to launch Yeats onto a last voyage towards death, yet in fact post-dates a number of important poems which already establish last-period motifs and emotions. This is especially relevant to "The Tower" itself, which comes next in the collection, yet obviously precedes it in theme and meaning. There follow the poems we have analyzed above as constituting Yeat's most intensely tragic phase, "Nineteen Hundred and Nineteeen" and "Meditations in Time of Civil War". The first thing we must do, therefore, in attempting the analysis of Yeats's later evolution as a poet, is to disregard the interesting but fictitious "poem" created by Yeats's own ordering of his work.

There are of course no definite watersheds in a poet's evolution any more than in a man's life. Yet Yeats's life ran roughly parallel to that of the modern Irish nation, from its beginnings in the agitations of the late eighteen-nineties, through the Easter Rising, the Black and Tans years, finally to the establishment of the Irish Free State in 1922. To understand Yeats's poetic evolution, we must take account of the immense importance these events had in his life. All in all, 1922 is as good a candiate for the role of watershed year as any we could bring forward: Ireland, at last, was an independent nation. The event created more turmoil than assurance. It made 1922 a year of crisis in poet and nation, and guaranteed, if anything did, that Yeats's last years would not be tranquil.

(i) "Leda and the Swan", "Among School Children"

Perhaps the best illustration of the nature of the break that occurs between the most intense of the "tragic" poems and those of a period which if not more serene, is less intense and broader in vision, is the contrast between two poems contained in *The Tower,* "Leda and the Swan" (1923) and "Among School Children", written in 1926. The striking thematic continuity of the poems only intensifies our sense of a radical change having taken place in the years intervening between their composition.

Both are Maud-Helen poems, and both treat the subject with a certain breadth of vision. The sonnet initiates the slightly brutal sexuality common in many of Yeats's later poems: in this it anticipates the nineteen-thirties. Yet it makes a strenuous effort to sustain the tragic intensity of the preceding decade, and it is this quality of strain that marks it off both from those genuinely intense poems, and from the less intense writing of "Among School Children". The seduction of Leda is a rape which begets Helen: it is therefore the first cause in a chain of consequences which ends in the burning of Troy. Yeats had been preoccupied with such chains, as we have seen, for most of his creative life. Here he pushes the sequence of events back beyond the effect of Helen's beauty upon Paris, thus creating the image of humanity trapped in processes beyond its control. This plainly relates the poem to *A Vision* and to "The Second Coming", to the tragic phase in general. The "burning roof" and Tower "And Agamemnon dead" are all "engendered" in the begetting of Helen, who has therefore shrunk to the level of an unknowing instrument in a process much greater than herself. All this makes the poem both central and interesting in Yeats's *oeuvre.*

Yet there seems something sensational in Yeats's treatment of the theme. In the first place, there are the anaphoric definite articles which have themselves engendered one eminent stylisticist account of the work:[2] Yeats says "*the* great wings", "*the* staggering girl", where normal usage would demand the indefinite article. This device is more common now than it was when Yeats wrote his poem: it still smacks of artifice, heightening the dramatic element in the incident by playing off the "unexplained" references against the associations the poet knows the reader will bring to it. There is something specious, something of the Victorian narrative painting about it, as if G. F. Watts had sketched it all first. The rape itself is "done" with undeniable power, but it has an air of relishing its forbidden content: there is a too-conscious attempt to make us feel the heat of the impropriety, so that the mythic event is reduced to the level of the historical novelette. This impression is surely heightened by the spurious profundity of the rhetorical question with which Yeats ends his sonnet: "Did she put on his knowledge with his power?" Does Yeats expect an answer here? What difference after all would either an affirmative or a negative answer make? Ranging back over the poem — "terrified vague fingers . . . feathered glory . . . brute blood of the air" — it is difficult not to feel that the poem itself is something of a rape.

It is because of this slightly forced, overdone violence that "Leda and the Swan" makes such an excellent contrast with "Among School Children", which was written three important years later. In the later poem, the scene is "set", very consciously and with slightly slumsy realism. In place of the hectic heroics of "Leda and the Swan" there is the studied ordinariness of the "sixty-year-old smiling public man". At once, having given us this setting, Yeats launches into the historico-mythological reverie that makes up the body of the poem. The source of the reverie is the crowd of little girls in the room who remind the affable inspector of schools of his beloved Helen: here, too, Maud Gonne is "Ledaean", her begetter a "paddler". Yet the framework of the poem — we are still conscious of being in the school-room — gives its reverie infinitely greater pathos than the dramatic gestures of the sonnet. How much more real — and at the same time more mature — than the almost prurient fascination with Zeus's virility, is the old man's admission that merely to see Maud

in the little girls (she must have been like that, had that
colour hair or complexion) robs him of his calmness:

> And thereupon my heart is driven wild:
> She stands before me as a living child.

He then thinks of her as she is now, old and ravaged:

> Did Quattrocento finger fashion it
> Hollow of cheek as though it drank the wind
> And took a mess of shadows for its meat?

We shall find this vision of the neurotic agitator in other
poems of this period. Here, it makes the poet think of his
own physical degeneration. But there is a certain sanity
about the alternative he proffers to her ravaged hollowness
— "There is a comfortable kind of old scarecrow." Would
the mother with her child on her lap think it all worth it,
he next wonders, "did she but see that shape/With sixty
or more winters on its head?". The real content — of the
philosophies of Plato, Aristotle and Pythagoras — is, in
the last analysis, just this fact of age — "Old clothes upon
old sticks to scare a bird". The two sorts of female
protectress the poem has referred to — nuns and mothers
— are now brought together. Both worship images, the
images the nuns worship — those of the hanging Christ —
are different from those of the mother. Yet both sorts of
image — the marble or bronze icons of the nuns and the
fantasy-heroes of the mother's "reveries" — break hearts.
Why do the images of the nuns break hearts? These are the
Presences

> That passion, piety or affection knows,

and they symbolize "all heavenly glory": these are "self-
born mockers of man's enterprise". Again, why? The
answer is because

> Labour is blossoming or dancing where
> The body is not bruised to pleasure soul,
> Nor beauty born out of its own despair,
> Nor blear-eyed wisdom out of midnight oil.

The poem has been about the relationship between human

hopes (the ambitions of motherhood, the worship of nuns) and human tissue. Age is merely a visible representation of that process of worsening and punishing that is at work all the time as the mind, with its ceaselessly active aspirations and reveries, takes its toll of the body's beauty. This has been a central theme of Yeats's for many years. He never surpassed the depth and tenderness of his treatment of it here. The body suffers for the soul's pleasure (its endless schemes and dreams): beauty and wisdom similarly are antithetically related to despair and midnight toil. Finally man himself, or at least his identity as a fixed being, disappears under scrutiny. Something is working through all our various selves and realizations: as inveterate role-players, we cast ourselves variously (Young Hero, Blushing Bride, Suffering Martyr, Wise Savant) yet fail to see that "Labour is blossoming or dancing" only in the absence of our intellectual and mental schemings. It is finally impossible to say that the chestnut-tree is either its leaf, its blossom or its bole, or that the dancer is distinct from the dance — the player from the role he plays. We exist at all times, in all our forms and guises: there are no fixed points in time, as our images suggest there are.

The line, "Labour is blossoming or dancing where" is of course magnificently ambiguous. What is the tense of the verb here? Is it a present continuous, meaning that Labour is blossoming now, at this moment? Or is it the "is" of equivalence or definition, making "blossoming" and "dancing" verb-nouns? The difference in sense does not seem great whichever way we read it, since the ensuing lines clearly oppose the "pleasures" of the soul-mind-intellect to the beauty of the body. Yet the ambiguity seems to play a considerable part in the effect of the lines: "labour" after all is not something we generally approve of, especially in poetry. Early in life, though, Yeats had shown himself "labouring in ecstasy":[3] the peculiar strenuous joy so often achieved in his poetry is more eloquent for his theory of culture and cultural creation than any amount of theorizing could be. When we turn to those "monuments of unageing intellect" that have proved troublesome to some critics of "Sailing to Byzantium", we shall have to bear in mind the kind of profound meaningfulness human effort could have for Yeats.

(ii) "The Tower"

"Man", Yeats observed in a little poem from his next collection "Death", "has created death". Such an insight might be thought of as the defining property of the tragic vision: it concedes not merely that man must admit that he will die, but that his awareness of this fact itself creates "death". Yet the truth is that such an awareness is really post-tragic. The essentially tragic rhythm of Yeats's antithetical phase had passed, never to return, by the time he came to write "Among School Children". The overt concern with the tragic condition of man testifies to the passing of the tragic consciousness itself. For the essence of tragedy is its refusal of the condition which it must endure, and which it articulates in its struggling. *Antony and Cleopatra,* for instance, is not a tragedy because it implicitly accepts the essential state against which Lear raged and Hamlet complained. Yeats begins to "describe" the conditions of man's tragic state only when the intensity of tragic revolt is past.

It is in "The Tower" that Yeats gives strongest expression to the humiliations of old age. It unites awareness of the ageing process with meditation on the end of age itself. Initially, the poet protests against his state:

> What shall I do with this absurdity —
> O heart, O troubled heart — this caricature,
> Decrepit age that has been tied to me
> As to a dog's tail?

Yet his irritability assumes acceptance: he must resign himself to its exactions, "bid the Muse go pack", and

> Choose Plato and Plotinus for a friend
> Until imagination, ear and eye
> Can be content with argument and deal

In abstract things; or be derided by
A sort of battered kettle at the heel.

How subtle Yeats's rhythmic sense has now become can
be gauged by the gap Yeats allows between the image of
the age that has been tied to him "as to a dog's tail" in the
first lines of the section and this clattering music in the
last. (Certainly there is no musical effect in poetry more
subtle and precise than the impression of battered metal
created in the juddering d's of these latter lines.)

The long central section of the poem takes the by-now
familiar form of the concitation of old stories or friends.
Yet the list of incidents brought to mind is not so random
or casual as might seem at first. The dominant motif
is of the irrational behaviour of men "maddened" or
driven wild. First, a serving-man brings his mistress (Mrs.
French) a farmer's ear, because of some hint dropped by
the lady. Next, there is the story of the countrymen who
"maddened by those rhymes" about the beauty of a girl,
went out at night and got lost so that "one was drowned in
the great bog of Cloone". The reflection that the man who
sang the song that told this tale was blind leads the poet
inevitably to his beloved Homer:

> . . .   the tragedy began
> With Homer that was a blind man,
> And Helen has all living hearts betrayed.

But Yeats, too, "must make men mad" if he is to succeed.
The poet thinks next of his own most lively creation, Red
Hanrahan, who also "drunk or sober" was "driven" (by
his creator):

> Caught by an old man's juggleries
> He stumbled, tumbled, fumbled to and fro
> And had but broken knees for hire
> And horrible splendour of desire;

The juggleries of the old man in the story bewitched the
pack of cards they were playing with into a "pack of
hounds" — all except one card, "And that he changed into
a hare." This is a truly Celtic transmogrification: the

"bewitching" power of the old man's hands is superbly rendered through Yeats's twinkling rhythms. *Shuffling, twinkling, bewitching* — the subtle movements of Yeats's later poetry have now replaced the powerful dactylic disturbances of his tragic period.

Hanrahan follows the pack of hounds created by the old ruffian's magic, as bewitched as the serving-man in the story about Mrs. Frnech and the farmer drowned in the great bog of Cloone. But Yeats abruptly halts this progress of maddened and bewitched men —

O towards I have forgotten what — enough!

This is merely to replace these mythical characters with the real though misty one of the earlier owner of the tower, "An ancient bankrupt master of this house." This harried man and his men-at-arms are to be asked whether they too have found old age as repellent as Yeats himself finds it. Hanrahan, finally, is retained, the others having answered Yeats's question with their "impatient" eyes. Hanraham is questioned as to the repository of the images stored in "that deep considering mind", the "Great Memory" in which the ghosts of the men-at-arms were stored — death, the country surrounding us at all times and permanently possessed of all the images that have ever existed. Hanrahan is chosen because he too would have known what it was to make the "unforeknown, unseeing/ Plunge, lured by a softening eye,/Or by a touch or a sigh,/ Into the labyrinth of another being".

This, then, is the thread that connects all the episodes and incidents recounted in this section of the poem: the poet too has been "lured", bewitched, bemused — but not, it appears, far enough. He admits that the great love of his life — it is of course Maud Gonne who is referred to here — was rejected by him. Out of pride, or cowardice, or "some silly over-subtle thought", he has turned aside "from a great labyrinth". It appears, then, that the poet envies those foolish men whose enchantment he has been cataloguing with such roguish amusement. The poem constitutes, we slowly understand, a great confession on

Yeats's part (the greatest, perhaps, he was ever to make). He had turned aside from the great labyrinth of the woman's being, just as he always turned aside from the dark regions of magic whose threshold he had haunted for so long. He had irked the members of the Golden Dawn by suggesting tests of a medium's probity: he had stood against the republicans in their revolt. At every point, a dogged refusal of the Dionysiac forces has stamped the quality of his verse — in its plated technicality (its refusal of the *vers libre* of the modernists, Pound and Eliot), its distancing, judgemental diction, its marvellous rocking rhythms that yet never quite "take off". Do we not see in "The Tower" the confession of the Apollonian poet who resists the powers of darkness even at the risk of his own life? Still, he will be susceptible to the thought: if he should but think of her again:

> . . .   the sun's
> Under eclipse and the day blotted out.

We have noted more than once that Yeats sustains an active vigilance on the powers of darkness at the same time as he regarded it as necessary to risk arcane dabblings. Now he wonders if he had not lost by refusing to enter that darkness, that "great labyrinth" to which he had never given himself up.

It is only when he has made this admission that he can make his will. The verse-form alters, interestingly, from the meditative pentameters of the second section to the brisker more decided short line (it varies from six to eight syllables) he is later to use in his more overt confessions, "The Man and the Echo" and "Under Ben Bulben". The will he makes takes the form initially of an asseveration of his Anglo-Irishness. He pronounces himself bound

> . . . neither to Cause nor to State,
> Neither to slaves that were spat on,
> Nor to the tyrants that spat,

This is significant in the context, for the Anglo-Irish represented, among other things, principles of rationality and dominance as opposed to the mysticism traditionally associated with Irish culture. When the poem finally floats downstream, the decision to commit himself to a spiritual life different in quality from what he had known is already made:

> Now shall I make my soul,
> Compelling it to study
> In a learned school
> Till the wreck of body,
> Slow decay of blood,
> Testy delirium
> Or dull decrepitude,
> Or what worse evil come —

Once again, as at the end of the first section of the poem, it is the sequence of *d*-sounds that gives the verse its tonality and unifies it, suggesting kinship of the ageing process and the "learned school". *Study-learned-body-decay-blood-testy-delirium-dull decrepitude*: it is a remarkable piece of musical organization. (Naturally, I do not suggest that there is anything inherently "age-like", or battered kettle-like, in the letter d. The music, as ever, is in no approximation, to a natural phenomenon — what could possible provide an analogy for "age"? — but in the collaboration of sound and meaning. That Yeats should have been able to suggest the harsh, dry sound of clattering metal by the subtle use of the d-sound, and, later, exploit the same sound to evoke the process of ageing, certainly does not prove analysis foolish. We might, in both cases, point to the underlying preoccupation of age. But it is enough simply to point at the effective functioning of ordered patterns of sound.)

The goal of studying in the "learned school" was to make all those evils charted above seem

> . . . but the clouds of the sky
> When the horizon fades;
> Or a bird's sleepy cry
> Among the deepening shades.

(iii) "Sailing to Byzantium"

Yeats's crafty shuffling of his poems once again obscures a crucial inter-relationship. "The Tower" was written in 1926, the year before "Sailing to Byzantium". "Sailing to Byzantium" launches *The Tower,* and its presentation first in the book is a strategic master-stroke. Yet the poem in fact dramatizes the decision reached at the end of "The Tower". What Yeats gained from launching his book with an overt *poème de voyage* is lost in the reversal of the actual relations between the two poems: "The Tower" floats downstream in its final section, and "Sailing to Byzantium", as it were, catches the tide.

Apparently, "Sailing to Byzantium" confirms the decision made in the previous poem to commit himself to the "learned school": it is "about" the poet's preference for "monuments of unageing intellect". Or is it? The poem has become the subject of controversy. It is compact of an unusual complexity of emotion and expression. By general consent, it is among Yeats's most satisfactory poems. Yet there are wide divergences even among its admirers. The focus of these differences of opinion is the poem's irony: does Yeats really say that he prefers "monuments of unageing intellect" (sculptures, poems, cathedrals) to the "sensual music" of life? Does he really express a desire, at the end of the poem, to be a tin bird, as W. H. Auden acidly said?[4] Where precisely does Yeats's emphasis come down? Is it the poem's unique virtue that it is impossible to say?

These questions assume particular importance when we wish to describe Yeats's development as a whole. It will be obvious to the reader of the present book that I regard a respect for the early and middle Yeats as indispensable to a proper view of the poet as a whole. To set too high a store by "Sailing to Byzantium" can easily threaten such a view, can easily lead to a denigration of Yeats's *oeuvre* as a whole. F. R. Leavis was the first critic, probably, to suggest that Yeats achieved a new kind of writing in *The Tower,* a poetry that allowed the serious reader of poetry to consider him with Gerard Manley Hopkins, Ezra Pound and T. S. Eliot as a significant figure in the modern scene. Leavis followed his early assessment of *The Tower* (in *New Bearings in English Poetry,* published in 1932) with a number of essays all tending to substantiate the view expressed there.[5] This view — which was enormously influential — was that Yeats had been a peacocking Irishman, an aesthete bred under Morris's wing, who at last, in "Sailing to Byzantium" and one or two other poems, broke through to a "modern" self-awareness by means of an accommodating irony. Such a view necessarily means holding a largely contemptuous view of the vast majority of Yeats's poems. In particular, it commits us to a rejection of what Leavis calls "the vatic stance" — Yeats's frequently expressed sense of himself as a Poet. For the "vatic stance" — the poet's sense of role, as it appears in Wordsworth, Byron, Baudelaire, and in almost every important poet of the past two hundred years — exalts certain contents and emotions at the same time as it denigrates others. In particular, it tends to place too high a value (too high for Leavis, that is) on certain orders of sacerdotal meditation, and, in consequence, to scorn or neglect the demands of Life — ordinary human emotion in its richest and most positive aspect.

Now this rough description of the critical problem here can serve also to describe a problem which Yeats himself engaged himself with in many of the poems of his last twenty years. At the end of "The Tower", he had dedicated himself to the "learned school", having sensed that old age had got him in its grip. "Sailing to Byzantium" sets off, metaphorically, upon the journey to which this dedication implicitly committed him. The poem therefore weighs the emotions and experiences forsaken against those embraced, and it is Yeats's emphases that have caused the differences in critical interpretation. Leavis characterized the poem in a series of fine phrases, all of which express the same view of the poem as containing a particularly significant balance: it has "poise" and tension, offering a complexity of meaning "corresponding to" an often complex and contradictory experience.[6] (We may note here by the way a classic instance of cultural empiricism: in Leavis, the poem "corresponds to" the emotions it represents; in Yeats, it is, on the contrary, a compensation for emotions the poet lacks.)

Leavis wishes to say, in these judicious and sensitive appraisals of the poem, that it has the recalcitrance of great art. On Leavis's view, as on I. A. Richards's, great art precisely sustains itself upon such complexities: irony is merely the outward sign of them. The poise and tension of "Sailing to Byzantium" are understood to derive from the competing claims of two principal drives. On the one hand, there is the "sensual music" — the full life of emotional and physical man uncomplicated by hankerings after eternity or spiritual Absolutes: this is that "ordinary life", the equivalent of what Leavis analyzed so beautifully in those writers he loved — Lawrence and Shakespeare, Keats and Hopkins, Tolstoy and Dickens. On the other hand there is the life of "the spirit", lived under the shadow of those upper-case abstractions — Absolute, Infinite, Eternal, Ideal — dedication to which entails the impoverishment of that ordinary life celebrated in the poem as "sensual music".

The "poise" of Yeats's poem therefore represents the poet's success in transmitting his own dividedness: the life of the poet, with all its formless devotions and prohibitions, vitiates the ordinary responsible life; the poet regrets the fact, and writes his poem out of the acknowledgement. Leavis praises Yeats for having "realized" both poles of the opposition: this is important. Not only is the "sensual music" beautifully and poignantly realized (to parody Leavis himself), but the "monuments of unageing intellect" themselves, if full of "ironic potentialities", are felt in the poem not as bloodless abstractions, but as "positive presences". Yet Leavis cannot accept these presences at Yeats's evaluation: they are "placed" (in Leavis's word) by a "sardonic irony".[7] At a stroke the poem's deep regret is transmuted into a destructive irony. Thus when Yeats at the end of the poem asks to be gathered "into the artifice of eternity", Leavis loads "artifice" with a powerful charge of irony.[8]

We must object here. For Leavis, the phrase "artifice of eternity" may be readable only as an absurdity, a delusion incompatible with intellectual honesty and maturity. But there is nothing in "Sailing to Byzantium" to show that it was so for Yeats. The dilemma (and there is one) is tragic, and inescapably so: it is not any avoidable past error that Yeats is regretting, but the nature of modern existence itself. In the same way, when Yeats – apparently – asserts that he would like to take the form of a mechanical bird (as W. H. Auden sarcastically observed), Leavis can make sense of the verse only by positting "duplicity":

> The duplicity of the last line gives the completing touch to the irony: "Of what is past, or passing, or to come".[9]

Many, I fancy, share Auden's and Leavis's discomfort with Yeat's expressed desire. But is the remedy to posit an irony which reverses the apparent intention of the poem? Leavis himself seems to sense a strain here. He becomes concessive about the *actual* (as opposed to the ironical) impact of the line: "This retains, inevitably, something of the solemn vatic suggestion that emanates from the foregoing poem."[10] Why "inevitably", we might ask? Is the "solemn vatic suggestion" (noted with characteristic sarcasm by Leavis) that emanates from the poem part of it or not? If it is (and obviously it is since it must emanate from something), how does it retain its identity without being destroyed by the "sardonic irony"? If it is not, on the other hand, how does it emanate from the poem at all? We accept that Yeats's poem is complex, and even tentative in the poise of its conclusion. But it is not confused, and the truth is that a reading such as Leavis's can only be sustained at the cost of diminishing and distorting Yeats's last lines. To strive after, to take seriously, such spiritual goals as are expressed in those "monuments of unageing intellect" – so Leavis's argument runs – is necessarily to end up with triviality. So that Yeats's desire to be turned into a tin bird must be read as

an ironical *reductio ad absurdum* of the futility of the
Byzantine aspiration altogether. The final line, accordingly,
tells us that the only proper activity of such a cultural
aspiration is to enjoy the superficialities of aristocratic
small-talk:

> . . .   to sing
> To lords and ladies of Byzantium
> Of what is past, or passing, or to come.

Yeats is therefore understood to be ironically placing these
words. But *is* this the effect of Yeats's line? and what
would be the point of the poem if it were? Surely the line
— like the whole foregoing poem — has a more positive
function than that of showing us the futility of the poet's
cultural ambitions? Mention of court gossip, of course,
reminds us of Yeats's debt here to Shakespeare:

> so we'll live,
> And pray, and sing, and tell old tales, and laugh
> At gilded butterflies, and hear poor rogues
> Talk of court news; and we'll talk with them too —
> Who loses and who wins; who's in, who's out —
> And take upon's the mystery of things
> As if we were God's spies; and we'll wear out
> In a wall'd prison packs and sects of great ones
> That ebb and flow by th'moon.
>   *King Lear*, V.3, 11–19

"Tormenting complexity of experience"? Surely. But
there is as little of that "sardonic irony" in Lear's words
as there is in Yeats's: Yeats too produces an effect of
exalted tenderness. Like Lear, the poet-speaker feels himself outside, beyond the turmoil of "life". It is not only
the stress of spiritual effort which has dominated his
creative life for more than forty years that is being
distanced. Yeats's clear and never-abandoned estimate
of the value of the Byzantine ethos and the "monuments
of unageing intellect" is precisely what cannot be
sacrificed if the real import of these final lines is to be
understood. If our conception of the "tormenting
complexity of experience" in the poem has been reached
at the expense of the "monuments", — if, that is, the

ironies attaching to them are allowed too great a destructive power, much more has been lost than has been gained: the tension of the poem vanishes with the loss of one of its poles. What has been lost, ironically, is just that complexity Leavis wants to reveal in the poem: the tender regret loses much of its pathos, the intensity is slackened, if the spiritual ambitions represented in the "monuments" is belittled as Leavis suggests it should be. Of course Yeats regrets the "sensual music": the thought of the "young in one another's arms" torments as much as it enchants him. This surely accounts for the poem's curious magic: it is the nostalgia of the pilgrim turning his back finally on "the world", and setting out. For "Sailing to Byzantium" is, as its title suggests, a *poème de voyage*; it is Yeats's "Marina", his "Ship of Death". In each of these poems we may say that the renunciation enacted would interest us less than it does if the poet's response to life − his sense of the sheer beauty of the ordinary − were less strong and intense than it was.

Yeats's poem, then, does not say that art is better than life, or that philosophy is more rewarding than music, or timeless realms of thought more interesting than "what is past, or passing, or to come". It is a poetry of age, in which the beauty of youth and the life of the body − the magic of the ordinary − are fondly regretted; and the poem's richness derives from the depth of the poet's involvement. Seen in the light of the admissions made in the second section of "The Tower", the commitment expressed in "Sailing to Byzantium" assumes especial importance.

(iv) "The Choice"

If, in Freudian terms, the Dionysiac worships the id, and the Apollonian the ego, Yeats in "Sailing to Byzantium" expresses acceptance of the super-ego − the final subjugation of self to the higher power imitated, feebly but authentically, in our most exalted artefacts. In Yeat's

personal life, the poem plays a crucial part as signalling a
new attitude taken towards the facts of ageing and dying.
But it also articulates a problem with which Yeats had
been wrestling, consciously and unconsciously, for most of
his adult life: his resignation to the fact of age here should
not blind us to the deeper dilemma he had always been
caught in. From the very beginning of his creative life,
Yeats had put a particular emphasis on certain symbols of
unchanging value: one could call him a Symbolist in fact,
not because of some vague attachment to the unsayable
or the mystical, but in virtue of his immediate apprehension of the symbolic properties of certain ideas. The
literary symbol, from this point of view, is best defined as
an expression in common use which the poet uses to stand
for ideas rather than to evoke emotion by association.
For this kind of Symbolist, the symbol will have no associations but its own meaning: it stands hard and clear, and
resists being drawn into a web of associations all vaguely
but precisely collaborating to form an emotional symbol
greater than any of the constituent parts. In Yeats, the
inner life is transmuted into form by means of such
symbolism, not by means of the finding of associative
correlatives in ordinary language. Already in early pieces
such as "The Madness of King Goll", many of Yeats's
permanently valid symbols are present: the "keen stars"
already betoken the eternal and the immortal. The poem
as a whole is not tightly controlled, and there is an
ultimate vagueness at the heart ("Of some inhuman
misery/Our married voices wildly trolled"). Yet Yeats had
already scented his subject-matter and his manner. Already
moonlight, starlight, and the night itself are marked out as
the proper field for man's central endeavour — the spirit,
fire, eternity. Manner and matter are interrelated: the birds
in "The White Birds" are symbolic, not merely evocative
or pathetic. So it is with Yeats's constant preoccupation
with the sea, the moon, the stars: they are not merely
decorative Romantic effects, but are already symbolic —
though of what, Yeats is not yet sure. The symbolic propensity emerges as a way with words and ideas long before

it finds satisfaction in particular identifications. What Yeats was concerned with in his first few volumes of verse was the task of building a symbol, not, as the soaked Romantic diction might suggest, the finding of subtle objective correlatives for emotional states.

We have seen this propensity assert itself in the thorough and oddly persistent pursuit of certain motifs and correlations. In these later poems we now see Yeats becoming conscious of the cost, in human terms, which this apparently haphazard, actually near-monomaniacal, concentration has entailed. Thus, the regret in "Sailing to Byzantium" is not merely the regret of an old man no longer able to enjoy the joys of youth, but, still more poignantly, that of a man who feels that he has sacrificed them all his life. It is the professional dilemma of the poet which Yeats is articulating here. He gave succinct expression to it in a trim couplet:

The intellect of man is forced to choose
Perfection of the life or of the work.
                    "The Choice"

Now we shall find this conflict of incompatibilities not only in Yeats but in all the major Symbolist and post-Symbolist writers — Valéry, Joyce, Eliot, Proust, Thomas Mann, Rilke, Hart Crane. Is the poet to risk everything on one throw of the dice, and commit himself to poetry, or is he to throw in his lot with marriage, responsibility, relationship — the option offered by "ordinary life" and the world of organized work? That, crudely expressed, is the dilemma not only of Symbolism but of Romanticism, and perhaps of all poets at all times. It is the theme dramatized by Thomas Mann in the Faust myth, and by Joyce in that of Icarus.

It is no use being sensible about it all, and telling the poet to snap out of it, get married, live the "full life". We are confronted here with a fundamental dilemma, which the greatest creative writers of our time have failed to resolve satisfactorily. Yeats's statement of the problem in "The Choice" is aphoristically glib, certainly, and drew the fire of W. H. Auden, who commented on it, "This is untrue; perfection is possible in neither."[11] In point of fact, Yeats's couplet hardly suggests that it is. It defines fairly enough the dilemma most of Yeats's contemporaries found themselves in: there is a terrible price to pay for the kind of insistent direction of attention necessary to the creation of a body of literary work. This does not mean Yeats thought you ever got perfection. On the contrary, you get neither; but life exacts commitment to the pursuit of one of the two: you choose the end. Such a choice is demanded by life, and Yeats's later poetry shows the strain of it. We find him more and more often debating the dual claims of "world" (political, emotional, sexual life) and that more abstract spiritual realm symbolized by the art of Byzantium in that particular poem, and, throughout his life, by stars, heavens and darkness. The power and tension of Yeats's later poetry derive substantially from the strength with which these conflicting claims are sustained in polarity: there is no easy victory, no easy choice.

There is a natural progression from "The Tower" to "Sailing to Byzantium" and from "Sailing to Byzantium" to "A Dialogue of Self and Soul", written a year afterwards, in 1927. Here Yeats's naturally dialectical way of thinking provides natural personae for the two poles: *Soul* will stand for the claims of the Absolute, *Self* for the natural man. The poem begins with the *Soul*'s imperious summons, dramatized in a marvellous series of gradations, moving the eye from one point of the ascent to the next above with strategic naturalness:

> I summon to the winding ancient stair;
> Set all your mind upon the steep ascent,
> Upon the broken, crumbling battlement,
> Upon the breathless starlit air,
> Upon the star that marks the hidden pole;
> Fix every wandering thought upon
> That quarter where all thought is done:
> Who can distinguish darkness from the soul?

All thought is done, of course, in the quarter that resolves intellectual discriminations and differences in the greater

knowledge of mysticism, or, simply, religious as opposed
to philosophical thinking. There the mind will cease to
"wander" (the wandering habits of mind were well-known
to Yeats, and, while they kept him from ever being a systematic thinker, yielded immense poetic profit). There,
surely, World will disappear in the darkness of the "soul".
The winding stair is that of age, the same perhaps as draws
Eliot upwards in "Ash Wednesday", and Yeats is being his
own Sarastro here. But what is particularly interesting in
Yeats's self-examination is that, urgent as the *Soul*'s
summons is felt to be, *Self*'s counts more. His initial
response to the summons in the second stanza of the
poem, to be sure, is a weary *non sequitur,* and there is a
touch of absurdity in his fondness for Sato's ancient blade.
Yet, triumphantly as *Soul* dismisses *Self*'s stumbling justi-
fications of "human action" (the naked blade of Sato
symbolizes politics and an involvement in the sordid
human enterprise), still *Self* has the long last word — the
whole second half of the poem in fact, which might easily
have been proffered as a poem in its own right.

The formal model of this poem is no less than that old
banality, "If I could have my life over again . . . ." Here is
any human life with all its humilitations and embarrass-
ments [Yeats was quite as expert as Eliot in the
psychology of humiliation] — "the finished man among
his enemies". The "finished man", we note, is finished by
the opinion of those he lives and suffers among: these are
his "enemies", and the mechanism of growth, self-
awareness and even of consciousness itself is no less than
that of the mirror placed by Jacques Lacan at the origin
(and growth) of self-consciousness.[12] You can't win, Yeats
says:

> How in the name of Heaven can he escape
> That defiling and disfigured shape
> The mirror of malicious eyes
> Casts upon his eyes until at last
> He thinks that shape must be his shape?

And if you do — somehow — "escape", some undeludable
part of yourself will find you out:

And what's the good of an escape
If honour find him in the wintry blast?

We tend to think of Yeats as an arrogant, somewhat ego-
centric man — a Hero. We should do well to remember
how much self-awareness and frankness, and how much
humiliation and suffering of the day-to-day kind, was
comprehended in that Olympian stance. In point of fact,
Yeats's conception of the nature and importance of the
poetic role was probably shaped by his awareness of
himself as personally an inadequate man. Maud Gonne, of
course, inflicted more wounds on him than anyone else,
and was more responsible than anyone else for the
formation of Yeats's self through the mirroring action of
her scorn. Hence, the poet's ambivalence towards her —
the resentment of her own rough treatment of himself, and
an obscure sense of gratitude for the knowledge of himself
this afforded.

The "wintry blast" of the knowledge now gives way to
the resolving synthesis: "I am content to live it all again".
This might itself be regarded as significant evidence enough
for placing the poem as "third period". But this is no easy,
complacent review — gaining some kind of prestige from
appearing to dare sufferings which he knows full well
he is safe in fact from re-experiencing. The poem is more
precise and exploratory than this. What happens in fact is
that the intense tragic involvement of the poetry of the
previous ten years, with its actual physical violence and its
fixities of hatred and vengeance, has separated out into
two elements. On the one hand there is the new spiritual
hauteur of the *Soul*; on the other, the acceptance of the
Self, which itself, fascinatingly, turns out to be compact of
two elements. First there is the "ditch", with all its
associations of filth and degradation. (The heroic grandeur,
we notice, has gone entirely into the austere detachment
of the *Soul*'s summons.) In a strange way, the *Soul*'s
disdain of the *Self*'s clutching onto the things
"Emblematical of love and war" is justified by the abjectness of the *Self*'s obstinate refusal to renounce what he
concedes to be disgusting — the "frog-spawn of a blind

man's ditch". Blindness is still there — it will always be — as Yeats's verdict on human aspiration: dreams make us blind. And the old violence still re-echoes, though more wearily, "A blind man battering blind men". And the blindness of action is still intimately associated with Love.

The human condition, therefore, is now accepted as "filthy". Love has returned with something of the "Leda" tone:

> ...   that most fecund ditch of all,
> The folly that man does
> Or must suffer, if he woos
> A proud woman not kindred of his soul.

Yeats had always kept Maud-Helen carefully separate from the idea of sex, but he comes close to associating her with it here. That "most fecund ditch of all" is clearly the vulva, and it is in this richly erotic — even foully erotic — guise that Love re-enters Yeats's poetry in its last transformation.

But just as we are prepared for a synthesis based upon the acceptance of a certain foulness in reality and a separation of this foulness from the "higher" reaches of the mind, Yeats surprises us. The last stanza of the "Dialogue" expresses the poet's determination to "follow to its source/Every event in action or in thought". Honesty is the best policy here, because it leaves you unsurprisable, so that having measured "the lot", you can forgive yourself "the lot". This candour towards his own past experience is important in Yeats. Messy, rambling and full of absurdities as it is, his life acquires its own completeness, provided only that it is all acknowledged. A determination to bring all his past experience to mind was a vital part of Yeats's poetic enterprise: "being a poet" for him meant not capering in "pretty plumage" but, as he will say later, seeing that "all's arranged in one clear view".

The consequence, in the "Dialogue", is the upsurge of that joy which appeared as inexplicable yet decidedly human in "A Prayer for my Daughter":

When such as I cast out remorse
So great a sweetness flows into the breast
We must laugh and we must sing,
We are blest by everything,
Everything we look upon is blest.

In the "Prayer", the soul discovered its "radical innocence
only when all hatred was driven out: it learned to enjoy its
own reflection in the glass — that essential glass of
consciousness — and to understand that it is self-appeasing,
self-affrighting". In the "Dialogue", too, joy is attained
through the use of the mirror, for the sweetness flows into
the breast only when remorse is cast out, and remorse can
be cast out only when "it all" (the whole of past life) is
re-lived, and the man faces up to that image he cannot
escape in the mirror created for him by his friends and
enemies.

Thus, Yeats arrives at the idea that brooks no reduction,
the synthesis of his long dialectic: the idea of joy, or, in a
later version, gaiety, which is the source of emotional
power inexplicable except in terms of man's essential
nature. It is by means of joy that Yeatsian man escapes
the wheel of determination and dream upon which he has
been stretched. The idea is profoundly integral to
Romantic art. The role of joy in Coleridge's "Dejection:
an Ode" (which is directly influential upon Yeats) and
in other Romantic works, most notably the Ninth
Symphony of Beethoven, is related to the general spiritual
and cultural predicament of Western Europe at the end of
the eighteenth century. It is not a concept which
would have occurred to an age sure of its religious beliefs:
it is specifically designed to refute a mechanistic
psychology and a utilitarian ethic. In Yeats, it springs
inexplicably, miraculously from the tortuous background
of dream-obsession and hatred: it can therefore validly
stand as a dialectical synthesis, the final term in the
fantasy-brutality progression.

Once again, Yeats's grouping of his poems obscures the
interconnections between them. The "Dialogue" was
written a year after "Sailing to Byzantium", yet appeared

only in *The Winding Stair* (1933). Yet of course the joy
derived from the man's recollection of all his life,
absurdities and all, follows naturally on from that
key-motif of the earlier poem:

> An aged man is but a paltry thing,
> A tattered coat upon a stick, unless
> Soul clap its hands and sing, and louder sing
> For every tatter in its mortal dress,

What is here entertained as a hypothesis, almost stumbled
upon as a strangely unhandleable thought, is explored to
the full in the Wordsworthian explorations of "A Dialogue
of Self and Soul". Less thorough than that poem, but
building upon it, in its aphoristic way, is "Vacillation",
another dialectical poem, composed several years later, in
1932.

The opening section of the poem presents the dialectic
of man's "extremities" — the night-and-day, light-and-dark
polarities continually exerting their conflicting pressures
upon man. These end in either physical death or moral
remorse, but "if these be right", the poet asks, "What is
joy?" It is a good, unanswerable question.

The subsequent sections of the poem will systematically
(too systematically, perhaps) contrast two different states
of being (the extremities of the poem's first line). There is
the world of the natural man — "Get all the gold and silver
that you can, . . animate/Trivial days and ram them with
the sun" — and that of the spiritual man:

> My body of a sudden blazed;
> And twenty minutes more or less
> It seemed, so great my happiness,
> That I was blessed and could bless.

Yeats wisely does not make this rather commonplace
epiphany carry too much weight. The next section
describes him as too weighed down by responsibility to
look at the beauty of a nocturnal scene that should
transport the natural man. The burden of what is
commonly called conscience is what weighs him down, and

this is an account Yeats will bring himself to face later, in "The Man and the Echo".

But it is not for these somewhat inconclusive annotations that "Vacillation" is remarkable. It is rather for its meditations upon the modern writer's peculiar dilemma. The poet's labour is useless, Yeats states, if it produce works

> That are not suited for such men as come
> Proud, open-eyed and laughing to the tomb.

The joy-motif here carries Yeats beyond the death-consciousness encouraged in so many modern writers by Kierkegaard and Dostoievsky. Yeats has given notice that he is beginning the preparation for his death in the poem: but the association of death and joy brilliantly surpasses mere death-consciousness.

The meticulous articulation of the "eternal" states of being, and the consistently pointed contrasting of these states with the "trivial" side of experience, makes "Vacillation", though unsatisfactory, an important stage in Yeats's confessional poetry. The evil that had gathered head in the tragic poems seems to have generated the detachment of the poem, such as it is. For Yeats makes no clear decision: he "vacillates". The point is of some importance, since it affects our interpretation of Yeats in general, especially as regards Dr. Leavis's view of Yeats as a poet over-addicted to the Absolute at the expense of a proper life-enchancing ordinariness.

Yeats's self-division on the point emerges most richly in the dialogue that makes up the seventh section of "Vacillation". Here the two claims are symbolized simply as *Heart* and *Soul*. The poem declares itself now as specifically addressed to the modern poet's thematic problem. *Soul* starkly urges the poet to "Seek out reality". This is that hidden reality we have seen Yeats constantly preoccupied with, not the so-called objective reality of "things that seem". *Heart* refuses *Soul's* persuasions: the "fire" of the Absolute may be simple but it would leave the poet as dumb as a mystic. Yeats gives *Heart* the last word: "What theme had Homer but original sin?" Here then is the poet's terrain: man's ordinary behaviour, love, war, art. Or is it?

As in "A Dialogue of Self and Soul", Yeats leaves us in no doubt that the man holding the pen is a real man, and that all real men are in the end "ordinary". But the poet remains torn by his dual obligation to an absolute realm of discourse and a more ordinary human one. We note again that Yeats always gives the ordinary earthly man meshed in blood and emotion the last word. The exception to this rule is the one genuinely Dionysiac poem that Yeats wrote, "Byzantium". It is here that Yeats writes most contemptuously of "All mere complexities,/The fury and the mire of human veins". The cocks of Hades in the poem crow scornfully and the "miracle, bird or golden handiwork"

> . . .   scorn aloud
> In glory of changeless metal
> Common bird or petal
> And all complexities of mire or blood.

It was presumably the contrast offered between this poem and "Sailing to Byzantium" which prompted F. R. Leavis to speak of a "striking loss", and "organization significantly less rich". Instead of the subtly realised regrets and tendernesses of the earlier poems, there is now an orgiastic fantasy, driven from rhythm to rhythm, image to image. No scene is realized, no stable floor offered. For the first and last time in Yeats, the Apollonian diction fails to hold the Dionysiac rhythms in check:

> . . . blood-begotten spirits come
> And all complexities of fury leave,
> Dying into a dance,
> An agony of trance,
> An agony of flame that cannot singe a sleeve.

This is Dionysiac poetry all right, but unlike the poetry of the real Dionysiac poet (Shelley or Blok or Swinburne),

Yeats fails to re-integrate his disintegrations in a greater whole. The poem ends with chaos:

> Astraddle on the dolphin's mire and blood,
> Spirit after spirit! The smithies break the flood,
> The golden smithies of the Emperor!
> Marbles of the dancing floor
> Break bitter furies of complexity,
> These images that yet
> Fresh images beget,
> The dolphin-torn, that gong-tormented sea.

The well-armed scholar and exegete can hunt down Yeat's bizarre imagery to its sources in arcane lore easily enough. What he cannot do is show that this is good poetry. What use does Yeats make of his sources here? He has, I suggest, produced a sick-bed poem, which may have had therapeutic value, as Yeats himself says in his Note to the poem,[13] but which amounts to no more than a series of hallucinations that testify impotently to a craving for release. This is psychologically interesting, but does not make for real poetry.

The decline from the high pitch of "Sailing to Byzantium" is surely related, as Leavis implies, to Yeats's loss of organization, to his lack of grasp on complexities he had honoured so finely. There is no dedication to the Absolute in "A Dialogue of Self and Soul" or "Sailing to Byzantium" or "Vacillation", no opting for a spirituality or intellectuality cutting the poet off from "mere complexities" of "mire or blood". Yeats does not choose the eternal, the starlit dome, at the expense of the full human life. He never made any unequivocal commitment to that dome. We find in the poetry evidence of a profound conflict within man and poet, one that remained unsolved until the end of his life. The personal struggle, of the man of late middle age trying to reconcile himself to age and debility, takes on the general cultural dimension, that of the poet unable to find a public theme to structure large-scale poetic projects.

(v) "Quarrel in Old Age", "The Results of Thought", "Remorse for Intemperate Speech"

The dialectical oppositions of "Vacillation" and "A Dialogue of Self and Soul" separate certain elements, but retain their grip on a real complexity. The dialectical disjunction, in fact, is also a conjunction: Yeats unites what he appears to separate. The poems do not make things easier for us, but shuttle back and forth endlessly, from one position to its contradictory. In considering the poetry that follows, we must try to decide whether this grip on complexity is maintained. We must also try to locate the source of Yeats's hold on these complex matters. "A Dialogue of Self and Soul" and "Vacillation" have already made clear that a great deal of the power of these later poems derives from the poet's sheer candour — a kind of common sense which accompanies the more obviously Irish of his qualities. This is especially true in his treatment of his more nationalistic friends, whose sad progress the *Collected Poems* incidentally documents. The notion of joy first erupted in "A Prayer for my Daughter": it did so in direct response to the anger and exasperation Yeats witnessed in the figure of his beloved Helen, the woman who had "trod so sweetly as t'were on a cloud" become "an old bellows full of angry wind". A beautiful and significant image of Maud-Helen occurs in "Among School Children", where it was

Hollow of cheek as though it drank the wind
And took a mess of shadows for its meat.

The antithesis to this obsessive idealism was given in that poem in the image of the "comfortable kind of old scarecrow", the poet himself, beyond that fanatical fixatedness. In the fiercely objective, yet sympathetically regretful poem that opens *The Winding Stair,* "In Memory of Eva Gore-Booth and Con Markiewicz", Yeats returns to the shadow-image. The two women are political extremists; the elder

> . . .   condemned to death,
> Pardoned, drags out lonely years
> Conspiring among the ignorant.

Still more pertinently, the younger is

> . . .   withered old and skeleton-gaunt,
> An image of such politics.

It is such wastedness that the joy-motif sprang into existence to oppose.

Yeats brings a new common sense — acrid, bitter, yet roughly sympathetic — to his consideration of fanaticism in the best of the short poems in *The Winding Stair*, "Quarrel in Old Age", "The Results of Thought" and "Remorse for Intemperate Speech". Instead of the rhythmical upheavals of the past, there is a rueful acceptance of the poet's own participation in the common condition. Maud is referred to in the first two poems. "Where is her Sweetness Gone?" he asks, and answers with a succinct sketch of political Dublin:

> What fanatics invent
> In this blind bitter town,
> Fantasy or incident
> Not worth thinking of,
> Put her in a rage.

It was in "Among School Children" that Yeats offered his most powerful vision of Time. Here he is able to summon up all his past images of Maud, hold them together, and see beyond the "curtain/Of distorting days"

> . . .   that lonely thing
> That shone before these eyes
> Targeted, trod like spring.
>   "Quarrel in Old Age"

As in "The Cat and the Moon" and "Meditations in Time of Civil War", the movement of the verse tells us that the reality beyond the curtain has been felt and seen by the poet and, indeed, that the image of the curtain is no casually "wise" metaphor of the type easily culled from

Mallarmé or Theosophy. Precisely what the last line means I do not know. "Targeted" — as one of Yeats's correspondents guessed[14] — means covered by a shield (or target). So, presumably, the target with which the eyes cover themselves is the distortion of "days" — projects, defences, deceits, lies. But "trod" could either be a past participle, in apposition with "targeted", or a main verb governed by the conjunction "eyes". "To tread", as I have pointed out before, is an important verb in Yeats and generally carries fatalistic connotations. The ambiguity is surely part of the poem's effect. If "trod" is a participle, the eyes are trod*den* as the earth is in spring. If it is a main verb, the eyes themselves assume the remorseless vigour of the incoming season. The eyes are those of the woman referred to in the poem's first line, where they had "sweetness". The sweetness has gone with time, yet the lonely shining thing is there still, within the present reality. The question raised at the end of "Among School Children" has been given its answer.

In "The Results of Thought", the "dear brilliant woman" is included with "the best-endowed, the elect" (the Anglo-Irish intelligentsia) as being "undone" — "by that inhuman/Bitter glory wrecked". Here is the central paradox of Yeatsian man again — undone by his strengths, wrecked by his glory, inhuman in his ideals. Once more, Yeats penetrates to a deeper vision of political and social history. He differentiates himself clearly from his contemporaries ("But I have straightened out/Ruin, wreck and wrack") with that clear-sighted honesty that was always a vital part of his poetry. We accept fully his statement of his findings:

> I toiled long years and at length
> Came to so deep a thought
> I can summon back
> All their wholesome strength.

This is that wholesomeness that lay in the "elect" initially, before their "inhuman bitter glory" wrecked them: it is everlasting, like the shining thing that existed once in

Maud Gonne. Yet with an unmediated transition that shocks us as much as it surprises him, Yeats comes upon foulness again:

> What images are these
> That turn dull-eyed away,
> Or shift Time's filthy load,
> Straighten aged knees,
> Hesitate or stay?
> What heads shake or nod?

"Time's filthy load": there remained something foul at the core of Yeats's vision of the world and of time, and he is a fundamentally tragic poet because of the candour with which he faces it.

If all things exist all the time — which is the meaning we can least refrain from drawing from "Among School Children" and a number of other poems of the same period — it is plain in what way a cyclical theory of history should have appealed to Yeats and in what way Christianity, with its essentially dramatic, onward-moving conception of time and history, remained alien to him. There is to be no redemption for Yeats, none of the Dionysiac artist's deliverance through rhythm and disintegration. "All things" shall not be well. What we have in its place is the Apollonian candour, the dignity and grace of control and open-eyed laughter. Perhaps the last poem in which this clear generosity of spirit is applied to a specifically Irish political subject is in the brilliant little lyric "Remorse for Intemperate Speech". Yeats surely speaks here for all Irishmen when he admits that he cannot rule his "fanatic heart":

> Our of Ireland have we come.
> Great hatred, little room,
> Maimed us at the start.
> I carry from my mother's womb
> A fanatic heart.

We shall soon enough find ourselves longing for this candour.

(vi) "Coole Park, 1929", "Coole Park and Ballylee, 1931"

It has become abundantly clear already that to speak of "a" last period in Yeats, as if all the work produced after a particular date shared a common set of qualities, is more or less absurd. There are, at least, two separate periods within the "final period" I have suggested above. I have suggested that the year 1922, in which the Irish Free State was founded, was a particularly important one for Yeats, not only personally, but for his social caste, the Anglo-Irish ascendancy as a whole. The ensuing ten years were extremely turbulent ones for Ireland: I have already suggested reasons why it should have been so for Yeats. His attitude towards the nationalist cause had always been tempered with reservations and misgivings, ending in a more or less complete break with it. This was not merely because Yeats loathed and mistrusted the kind of single-minded zealotry created by political activism, but because he felt somewhat alienated from the end itself. He wanted Ireland to be free, but he did not relish the prospect of a sudden end to the Anglo-Irish hegemony.

The "whirlpool of hate" which Yeats found in Dublin on his return there from Oxford in March 1922 found expression, as we have seen, in "Meditations in Time of Civil War". He had been appalled at the narrow fanaticism he encountered everywhere in that segment of the nation which clearly regarded itself as the "real" Irish: the Catholics with Irish names who had no stake in the culture established by the British. Yeats felt everywhere a powerful hostility to his own caste, and he gave this sense powerful poetic expression in "The Tower". Did the entire class feel in these years a crisis of identity – a need to affirm its own apartness, yet also at a deeper level, to make irrevocable the choice between Ireland and England? Before and during the First World War, there were hundreds of thousands of Loyalists, who voted Unionist at election-time and supported Great Britain passionately in the conflict with Germany. These Loyalists wanted to preserve the old association with England, and were horrified at the treasonableness of the Easter Rising. What happened to all these Anglo-Irish Loyalists? They cannot all have been turned into nationalist zealots overnight by the execution of the sixteen men after the Rising.[15] The human conscience is far more resilient than that.

That Yeats, at least, experienced a profound disturbance is evident not only from "The Tower", but from the speech he made to the Irish Senate in June 1925. The immediate issue was divorce. But Yeats obviously felt that the move to ban divorce in the Free State merely masked the desire of the Catholic majority to repress the Anglo-Irish. At any rate he made a passionate and magnificent apologia for the class:

> We against whom you have done this thing are no petty people. We are one of the great stocks of Europe. We are the people of Burke; we are the people of Grattan; we are the people of Swift, the people of Emmett, the people of Parnell. We have created the most of the modern literature of this country. We have created the best of its political intelligence.[16]

Yeats's speech was felt to be excessive in its anger, and divisive in spirit. This was certainly true of the article he later contributed to the *Irish Statesman*: "Ireland is not more theirs than ours," he wrote, "We must glory in our difference, be as proud of it as they are of theirs."[17] Yet within less than a decade, the Anglo-Irish ceased effectively to exist as a caste. For although the Protestant Ascendancy remains, it lost its character with its name, and its sense of identity with its character. The choice was made, the class effectively buried with its name. When Yeats writes of "the Ascendancy" later, it is not only with regret, but with the conviction that Ireland's chance of becoming a civilized nation as well as a free one, has been thrown away: "our upper class", he wrote in *Poetry,* as commentary to "The Three Songs" of 1934, "cares nothing for Ireland except as a place for sport, . . . the rest of the population is drowned in religious and political fanaticism."[18]

Granted that the dates of demarcation in a poet's life must be more fictitious than actual, we can, I think, assign

the year 1932 the same kind of significance as 1922. For
it was the death of Lady Augusta Gregory in that year
which signalled the last profound inner change in Yeats's
life — the last change, that is, to be reflected in the poetry.
It is after this date that we begin to see the really serious
signs of that "loss of organization" which Leavis
diagnosed: Yeats's ability to hold contradictory elements
of experience together in one view seriously weakens. He
had always been the poet of influence and domination.
What was more natural than that, with the withdrawal of a
profound source of personal control and influence over
himself, he should slacken within? After the death of Lady
Gregory, Joseph Hone observed that "Yeats began to ask
himself whether the subconscious drama which was his
imaginative life had closed with Coole."[19]

Yeats's two elegies on the Gregory House and its
cultural life, "Coole Park, 1929" and "Coole Park and
Ballylee, 1931", are included in *The Winding Stair*. They
command such a weight of gravity and appear so
trenchantly to sum up an age that it is easy to believe that
Hone was right, and that with the end of the Anglo-Irish
civilization, Yeats felt himself, too, ready to die. That
spring and thrust of the mind, buttressing stanza and
paragraph with sturdy lightness, receive in these two
poems what is arguably their last satisfactory expression. It
is hard to find the quality of this poetry, generously lucid,
fine, yet firmly anchored in the real, in any of the poems
Yeats later wrote.

The relationship between the two poems is something
like that existing between "Nineteen Hundred and Nineteen" and "Meditations in Time of Civil War": the second
is generally more bitter and more final than the first.

"Coole Park" celebrates with infinite sadness the values
of civilization, and the beneficent power of a woman over
men. *Was* it the withdrawal of this particular woman's
power that left Yeats emptier and less directed than he had
thought possible? Lady Gregory represents a necessary
antithesis to the destructive blinding power of
Helen-Maud. Unlike Loie Fuller's dancers driven by the

"barbarous clangour of a gong", the scholars and poets associated with Augusta Gregory are dominated into harmony, so that their thoughts are "knitted into a single thought", and a "dance-like glory that those walls begot". The poem begins with a "swallow's flight", but the connection between this and the civilized patterns celebrated thereafter is revealed only in the third stanza:

> They came like swallows and like swallows went,
> And yet a woman's powerful character
> Could keep a swallow to its first intent;

Once again, then, human behaviour is defined in terms of domination and subjugation, only here, as in "At Galway Races", it is positive and beautiful, not negative and destructive. And again civilization itself is defined in terms of dream; the intellectuals dominated by Lady Gregory "found certainty upon the dreaming air". The rewards of culture and spiritual achievement are conceived as a deliberate transcending of the natural: "the intellectual sweetness of those lives" (those of the poet and painter) "That cut through time or cross it wither-shins." Time is natural; culture cuts across it, or transcends it, as we sometimes say.

The poem ends proleptically with a vision of the house destroyed by time — the natural enemy — and a request to the passing scholar of the future to dedicate

> A moment's memory to that laurelled head.

The poem here justly appropriates the diction and gesture of the great elegies in English and Classical literature. The glories celebrated are as they always are in Yeats — located in the past. The final vision of the great house ruined where "nettles wave upon a shapeless mound" places house and civilization itself in a greater context of time.

"Coole Park and Ballylee", written two years later, is, from first to last, darker and less serene. It is disturbed from within, and the image of the swallow that held the earlier poem together with its suggestion of a unity of wayward liberty and ordered control, is replaced by an evocation of the dark streams that are seen as underlying civilization itself. Here is Coleridge's fountain again, but equivocal, running underground fitfully, resurfacing finally in a somewhat artfully amenable way within "Coole demesne" itself — "there to finish up/Spread to a lake and drop into a hole". This sombre river of life is finally characterized as "the generated soul". "Who can distinguish darkness from the soul?" Years had asked ten years earlier, in "A Dialogue of Self and Soul". Whatever he means by these things, the dark stream that drops into Raftery's cellar by no means harmonizes with the civilized ethos the poem is to celebrate. Something of its sullenness is borrowed by Nature itself — its "rant" is like the mirror of the poet's soul, and eventually discloses, as an appropriate correlate, the swan like "a concentration of the sky". The evanescence of the swan is taken to typify the ephemerality of human life itself, but in an unconvinced, rhetorical way: "it sails into the sight/And in the morning's gone, no man knows why". This is on its own but a poor re-hash of "The Wild Swans at Coole", in which the questions raised by the poet are generated naturally by the behaviour of a family of swans. Yet the rather hollow rhetoric of Yeats's questions in "Coole Park and Ballylee" is curiously effective in bringing to the surface the uncertainty that has shed an equivocal light on the whole poem. When the swan is first seen, it is noted by the poet almost absent-mindedly, as if it has broken in upon his musings: "Another emblem there!" he cries, almost parodying himself. The symbol, too honestly acclaimed to be tendentious, rises and falls from consciousness, with exactly the premonitory ominousness the context requires. For the poem's true subject is not the "generated soul" of water, nor the ephemerality of life — these would be comfortably classical themes. What is far more disturbing is the image of the owner of the House, Lady Gregory herself, the controller and inspirer of talented men in the earlier poem, reduced to the "Sound of a stick upon the floor, a sound/From somebody that toils from chair to chair". The simple "realistic" sound-effect penetrates at once to the centre of the issue, as the earlier grandiose rhetorical questions had failed to (as, indeed, they were meant to fail). The impact of the lines is arguably greater if we have just read "Coole Park", where we witness the effective glories of the woman's power. Whether we have or not, they generate, with that subterranean subtlety that is the hall-mark of Yeats's best poetry, the generalized metaphor of the stanza that follows:

> We shift about – all that great glory spent –
> Like some poor Arab tribesman and his tent.

The shifting movement of the nomad beautifully parallels the stick-assisted movement of the old lady from chair to chair. As she is now no controller of men, but an old lady with a stick, so "we" are no longer the swallows in gay captivity but the subjects of "fashion or mere fantasy". This is swapping one form of dream for another: civilization, no longer fit to animate and energize great movements, is reduced to nomadic shiftings that leave no trace. The poem ends with its famous epitaph – "We were the last Romantics", who "chose for theme/Traditional sanctity and loveliness". Once again Yeats hammers home his central belief: culture does not concern itself with "truth" in the empiricist sense. It takes as its "theme" the already generated "values": it embraces certain dreams at the expense of others. The degradation of the modern world reflects the abjectness of its dreams, and that "high horse" that Oisin rode, is now without a rider.

Yeats documented the various stages of Maud Gonne's decline for thirty years. Yet no poem he wrote to her expresses so deep a sense of loss and final sundering as the poems that mourn the approaching end of Augusta Gregory. Without her profoundly sane influence, Yeats seems to have lost a proper sense of balance within himself. Balance had always been the essential quality of his political thinking and of his poetic thought: without it, he easily degenerated into a ranting bigot. The process was accelerated by illness and old age, of course, as he often enough admits in the poems. Suffice it to say, that the

badness of much of this late poetry is paralleled by
incidents in his actual life which could hardly have been
invented, so extreme and absurd are they. There is, for
instance, the appalling incident concerning Osip Ossietsky,
a Jewish prisoner of the Nazi Government (what Joseph
Hone, with really extraordinary evasiveness calls "the
German régime"),[20] whom Ernst Toller wanted Yeats
to recommend to the Nobel Committee for the prize for
literature. "Yeats", Hone writes, "was adamant in his
refusal to do anything of the sort. He damned Toller."
Still more crotchety, though not worse morally, was the
occasion when Professor Bose asked Yeats for a message
for India: " 'Let 100,000 men of one side meet the
other,' " Yeats answered. "He strode swiftly across the
room, took up Sato's sword, and unsheathed it dramatically
and shouted, 'Conflict, more conflict!' "[21] This was in
1937: the Spanish Civil War was in progress, China was
being invaded by Japan, Hitler was in power in Germany,
and Ireland was still, inwardly, recovering from the
Troubles. With all allowances made for age, can one expect
real poetry from a man capable of such ridiculous blood-
thirstiness? What has happened to the man who wrote
"Nineteen Hundred and Nineteen" and "A Prayer for my
Daughter"?

Yeats had always been evasive about his relations with
England. This evasiveness itself masks a deep ambivalence
and was itself an important element in his greatest poetry:
it is the function of the poet, we might say, to nurse such
ambivalences within himself: they afford him that bifocal
vision necessary to the creation of great poetry. Yet after
the death of Augusta Gregory, this ambivalence seems to
turn into sheer double-think. He can exult, cockahoop,
because the English police find a letter from Maud Gonne
on an Irish Republican Army suspect ("What a woman!
What energy!"); yet on being reprimanded by Lady
Dorothy Wellesley for encouraging "hate between nations"
in his poem "The Ghost of Roger Casement", he is capable
of replying, "How could I hate England, owing what I do
to Shakespeare, Blake and Morris? England is the only

country I cannot hate."²² Does the left hand not know
what the right hand is doing? Or has Yeats simply become
a more unscrupulous liar than ever?

The answer is really suggested in the poetry, I think. I
believe that Yeats was sincere in both of these reactions,
both in his passionate anger at English tyranny, and in his
profound attachment to English culture and to the
country itself. This is what gave body and life to some of
his greatest poetry. But it requires strength and imaginative
power to hold these poles together: that strange moving
rhythm of Yeats's, at once sturdy and subtle, rocking and
still, surely testifies to the cross-currents tamed and unified
by the poet. The separation in the later poetry shows that
Yeats simply no longer commanded the power to hold
everything in "one clear view". The politics becomes more
political, the passion simply bawdy: so we have angry vitu-
peration instead of political mediation, and, as we shall
see, Crazy Jane instead of Helen of Troy.

We do not need the evidence of Yeats's flirtation with
the Irish blue-shirts, his blindness even in the late thirties
to the horror of Nazi Germany, or even the sheer badness
— the squalid partiality — of his dreadful *Oxford Book of
Modern Verse,* to tell us that Yeats in his seventies no
longer commanded the poetic overview he had
commanded in his sixties. With the passing of Coole and
the death of Augusta Gregory, Yeats seems to have been
released from the crisis of the Anglo-Irish class. She had
always served to remind him of his obligations to England
and English culture. Lady Dorothy Wellesley to some
extent played this role later, but her influence was less
strong. Significantly, Yeats now produced the only truly
"Republican" poetry he ever thought worth publishing.
One must admire the testy honesty of the old man — the
refusal to sink into blandness. One must nevertheless also
admit that most of the poetry included in *A Full Moon in
March* and *Last Poems* is simply bad. The "vigour" often
claimed for these sins of old age is of an impish or irritable
variety. Poems like "The Curse of Cromwell", "Roger
Casement", "Colonel Martin", "Come Gather Round Me,

Parnellites", "The O'Rahilly", "Three Songs to the Same Tune", "Two Songs Rewritten for the Tune's Sake" are, at best, lively polemic. At their worst they are irascible doggerel:

> Justify all those renowned generations,
> Justify all that have sunk in their blood,
> Justify all that have died on the scaffold,
> Justify all that have fled, that have stood,
> Stood or have marched the night long
> Singing, singing a song.
>   "Three Songs to the Same Tune"

Few of the old Republican agit-prop poets wrote as badly as this, and there is a good deal of the same quality in all three of Yeats's last books. It seems that, having brought himself to some kind of identity-crisis at the time of the Free State, Yeats finally found himself – or lost himself, according to one's point of view – in a mad-dog kind of republicanism.

(vii) The synthesis of love: sex

Love, too, enters its final – synthetic – phase. In Yeats's first poetry there was the full Romantic commitment, a commitment which kept the poet from the thought of sexual consummation, so absolute was the ideal. Love in this form functioned as a drive, its physical effect experienced in poems such as "Friends" and "A Woman Homer Sung", precisely because it was unrelated to a physical fulfilment. This was the Love of Yeats's thesis – Romance, fantasy, faeryland – and it bred its own antithesis as the sought-after bondage of love became synonymous with the tyranny of hatred. Passion and politics were still fused, as with the Homeric similes of the first phase, but turned inside out. That "far-off, inviolate, and most secret Rose" of Ireland turned into the fixed stone of fanaticism. Now, finally, the remote untouchably Absolute Passion of the Romantic love re-emerges, transformed into its opposite – sex, impure and simple, ending and forestalling action rather than inspiring it. The Crazy Jane poems form a logical synthetic equivalent to the dramatic love poems of *The Wind among the Reeds*. In "Broken Dreams" in *The Wild Swans at Coole*, Yeats had had described himself rambling agedly over "Memories, nothing but memories". This drift towards a senile fondness, redeemed only by a somewhat improbable conjecture of immortality, is abruptly reversed in the Crazy Jane cycle. "A Dialogue of Self and Soul" had referred to love in terms of a foul ditch: the disgust with sexual processes in that poem belongs to the earlier Yeats. Now, we find a reversal of a kind entirely orthodox in twentieth century development: this was the era of D. H. Lawrence, we remember. (Yeats read *Women in Love* in 1932, with excitement.)[23] Possibly, too, we might predict an acceptance of the body as an element in any third-period poetry of synthesis. *Antony and Cleopatra*, which really inaugurates a new post-tragic phase in Shakespeare's drama, uses the form of the tragedy of love in order to reverse its meanings: it is not a tragedy, because it breathes a fulfilment which cancels the essential emotion of tragedy.

On the face of it, this is what we get in the Crazy Jane poems and in other late poems such as "News from the Delphic Oracle". These poems have indeed been welcomed by some critics as a new "realism" in the poet. The truth is, I think, that they mark a new cynicism in Yeats and constitute a proof, if one were thought needed, that the kind of dialectic of age I have been trying to describe, is not to be equated with a formula for wisdom or enlightenment. Wisdom — if that is what it is — does not automatically bring with it beauty and tranquillity. On the contrary, the poems which Yeats wrote after undergoing the Steinach operation, strike me as almost uniformly ugly, ugly in their very cleverness, and limited in and to their sexuality. One should, indeed, have been able to predict such a decline in poetic achievement from the fact of the operation itself. The whole essence of Yeats's poetic *oeuvre* was his constant effort to hold everything in one

clear view. Now he suddenly turns round, and interferes
with nature and time by introducing into himself the gland
of a monkey! He seems to have derived precious little joy
from the experience, even if a certain welcome randi-
ness.[24] The effect of the Steinach operation on Yeats's
attitude to love and sex was comparable to the effect
which over-use of benzedrine and other stimulants had on
the recollective faculty of writers like Jack Kerouac. If
the writer does not trust to time and memory to sort out
and articulate his memories and order them into significance, he is likely to find himself glutted with memories he
cannot use. This is exactly what we find in books like
Visions of Cody, where Proust's lesson of the wisdom of
the *mémoire involontaire* has been not so much forgotten
as turned upside down. If the mind with its schemes and
intentions fraudulates our memories, by repressing what it
does not wish to remember, benzedrine swamps it by
making all our past involuntary, and therefore without
significance.

In Yeats, the poetic crop of the Steinach operation was
a cycle of nutty, occasionally gay, usually self-consciously
bawdy lyrics which in another age would have been more
explicit, and consigned to oblivion with the *conneries*
of Rimbaud and Pushkin. There is a kind of desperate
attempt at abandon in these poems; they are obscene
gestures to an establishment that was by now far less
shockable than Yeats imagined. There is something faintly
repellent about the studied sexiness of this later love
poetry; worse, it is embarrassing, like a respectable uncle's
belated discovery that he has missed out. Is the last stanza
of "News for the Delphic Oracle", for instance,
"outrageously funny", as a fairly representative commen-
tator has put it?[25] Or is there not something rather ugly
about the insistence on foulness in the poem, the brutality,
the foulness, even the use of the word "bum":

Down the mountain walls
From where Pan's cavern is
Intolerable music falls.
Foul goat-head, brutal arm appear,

> Belly, shoulder, bum,
> Flash fishlike; nymph and satyrs
> Copulate in the foam.

"Let copulation thrive!" Lear shouted in his madness; T. S. Eliot spoke with fastidious distaste of "Birth, and copulation, and death". I see no exception in the last line of Yeats's poem to the general rule that great writers tend to use the word *copulate* and its derivatives in moods of disguist. It is nothing to do with the shifting frontiers of literary decorum: we have become accustomed to much more explicitness in good poetry than there is in Yeats's poem, yet it still strikes us — it strikes me at least — as faintly disgusting. The reason is, of course, that Yeats transmits his own inward resistance and distaste — that distaste which his renewed sexuality had opposed. "News for the Delphic Oracle" is a Tennysonian scenario directed by Luis Buñuel, and it urinates upon the Poussin picture it was "inspired by". It is a saddening spectacle. Yeats was acute enough to anticipate the accusation himself:

> You think it horrible that lust and rage
> Should dance attendance upon my old age;
> They were not such a plague when I was young;
> What else have I to spur me into song?
>   "The Spur"

The Crazy Jane poems, to be sure, are fine pieces, deftly wrought with a lifetime's knowledge behind them. Yet they, too, at centre express revulsion through their release:

> "A woman can be proud and stiff
> When on love intent;
> But Love has pitched his mansion in
> The place of excrement;
> For nothing can be sole or whole
> That has not been rent."
>   "Crazy Jane talks with the Bishop"

The plethora of puns in the last two lines (*sole/soul, whole/hole, rent/torn, hired-out*) was guaranteed to warm the cockles of the old New Critical heart: that was what poetry was supposed to be. But Yeats was not Swift; his vision was not naturally excremental. The poem tells us little about the nature of love we were not aware of: it proclaims a sexual revolution against "Romantic" love a decade too late. The cycle as a whole, witty though it is, is largely uninformative and does little to extend the range of Yeats's poetry.

Such separations may simply be characteristic of a writer's old age. We think of Shakespeare, and the almost clinical division of *A Winter's Tale* into two: an intense, mordant tragedy of Love, telling of Leontes's jealousy, and a radiant, warm Comedy of Love, eventually culminating in the healing of the breach between Leontes and his wife (and also between Leontes and himself). The older writer, perhaps, knows what he can get away with. Yet Shakespeare does get away with it, and the success of the play in dramatizing reconciliation and resurrection tells us that the wily dramatist's unscrupulousness is simply the greater scrupulousness of wisdom. We are not so confident in reading these poems of Yeats's. Those self-consciously bawdy lyrics of "love" and the querulous rabble-rousing political poems bespeak disintegration rather than resolution. The voice is shrill, the wit often spiteful.

Yet Yeats also produced in these last years a handful of poems which go a long way towards completing a repetitious yet oddly coherent *oeuvre*. He never ceased to attempt the labour of holding his life in view, though he frequently lacked the grip to do it. The old Apollonian had lost much of his force — through sickness and overwork, one must add — but his conception of his function as dream-interpreter did not waver. He had more to say — about Ireland's future, about his own last years, and about that concept of joy or gaiety, which remained with him through all his vicissitudes and vituperations.

(viii) "The Statues", "Parnell's Funeral"

The tone of Yeats's prose writings about Ireland and Irish culture over the later thirties is on the whole morbid and pessimistic. He tends to write more and more insistently yet despairingly of the role of "the Ascendancy": if Ireland is to gain or regain some of its cultural unity and with it its self-respect, it must digest and absorb the old Anglo-Irish culture in a semi-mystical act. Writing of the difficulties experienced by the Abbey Theatre, Yeats spoke of the reign of "the mob" in Ireland:[26] he meant the zealous, narrow bigotry of the new Ireland and its governors. That reign, he says, "will be broken when some government seeks unity of culture not less than economic unity, welding to the purpose museum, school, university, learned institution."

The young James Joyce had made a devastating critique of the cultural myopia of Irish nationalism half a century earlier, with Stephen Dedalus noting the peculiar narrowness of the young Fenian: "Whatsoever of thought or feeling came to him from England or by way of English culture his mind stood armed against in obedience to a password."[27] Whether modern Ireland has heeded either writer is a matter of dispute.

It is for this reason that Yeats returned once more to the theme of Parnell in what is perhaps the only other poem written after Lady Gregory's death which seriously extends the range of Yeats's political poetry. This is "Parnell's Funeral", from *A Full Moon in March*. What is first of all remarkable about this poem is the "fact" upon which Yeats bases the first stanza. Where else but in Ireland would a star oblige by falling in full view during the funeral of the country's greatest political hero? Politics in Ireland is mythology, and the Almighty has always seen to it that the myths lack neither imagery nor event to sustain themselves. "A brighter star shoots down," Yeats observes, but "What is this sacrifice?". Parnell is a sacrificial victim, but in what ceremony? Ireland is a country awaiting a destiny: hitherto its destiny has been in freeing itself from England. Is this to remain its destiny?

Commenting later in the poem upon the part played by his own caste in the downfall of the hero, Yeats remarks:

An age is the reversal of an age:
When strangers murdered Emmet, Fitzgerald, Tone,
We lived like men that watch a painted stage.
What matter for the scene, the scene once gone:
It had not touched our lives.

I take it that the verb "had" here is subjunctive: no matter what happened on the stage of politics, we (the Anglo-Irish intelligentsia) would have refused to take it seriously. It was not permitted to remain mere theatre "popular rage ... dragged this quarry down". It was the intelligentsia that was really responsible, however: "None shared our guilt". Yeats ends the stanza with a significant image:

> ...   nor did we play a part
> Upon a painted stage when we devoured his heart.

This seems a profound and profoundly metaphysical metaphor: the intellectuals ate Parnell's heart in helping to destroy him, but also in the mystical way in which the sacrificed king's body is dismembered and eaten by the priesthood in order that his power shall be inherited. The first part of the poem ends with "a thirst for accusation":

> ...   All that was sung,
> All that was said in Ireland is a lie
> Bred out of the contagion of the throng,
> Saving the rhyme rats hear before they die.

With this stripping-away of lies and factions, Yeats offers Ireland its wholeness:

> Leave nothing but the nothings that belong
> To this bare soul, let all men judge that can
> Whether it be an animal or a man.

By confessing on behalf of his own class, and by holding up the mirror to the Catholic bigots who ran down the Anglo-Irish hero who gave himself for the country, Yeats proposes a whole Ireland, one that must confess fully and wholly before it is able to take up the real burden of its own future.

The second section of the poem takes up the profound image of human sacrifice which had dominated the first:

> Had de Valéra eaten Parnell's heart
> No loose-lipped demagogue had won the day,
> No civil rancour torn the land apart.
> Had Cosgrave eaten Parnell's heart, the land's
> Imagination had been satisfied,

Clearly, de Valéra, Cosgrave and the rest of them — "even" O'Duffy, the Irish blue-shirt — did not eat Parnell's heart; did not, that is to say, complete the sacrifice of Parnell with the ritual of consuming the flesh of the dead king. While Ireland pursues the phantom of revenge upon England, it will remain incomplete, unfinished. It too must, like Parnell, pass through "Jonathan Swift's dark grove" and there pluck "bitter wisdom that enriched his blood".

With this profound and mystical image of reconciliation and transcendance, Yeats's long meditation upon Ireland and its politics approaches its conclusion. There remained but an attempt finally to unravel the mysteries of the mirror of civilization. Politics, love and the theory of culture are all bound up together in Yeats, and the image of the mirror is central to each. "The Statues" owes its origination perhaps to a passage in *The Birth of Tragedy*, where Nietzsche refers to the fact that Phidias beheld in a dream the entrancing bodies of more-than-human-beings.[28] Yeats's poem turns upon a consistent relation of deprival and thinness, of hunger and lack, to fulfilment in creation:

> But boys and girls, pale from the imagined love
> Of solitary beds, knew what they were,

Hamlet once more becomes the type of western man, wasted thin from eating flies, and is opposed to a "fat dreamer of the Middle Ages" (Aquinas, obviously). Pythagoras's bodiless numbers lacked character but they laid bare the inward proportions of absolute beauty, thus generating the art of Phidias. Passion is what generates character, and passion proceeds from "the imagined love/ Of solitary beds". Yeats now qualifies himself. "No! greater than Pythagoras" — some Asiatic inheritance went into the richness of Greek art, not the mathematical candour that produced also the warships successful at Salamis against the Persians. Europe "put off that foam" (the foam created by the beating of the warships' oars), when Phidias, the paradigmatic Greek artist, who dreamed of beautiful bodies in his sleep, according to Nietzsche, in his turn

> Gave women dreams and dreams their looking-glass.

The idea is complex: within the sculpture of Phidias there are "All Asiatic vague immensities", not mere mathematical relations. The poem hints at some Asiatic content in Greek sculpture. Culture therefore creates dreams for people, and supplies these dreams with mirror-images. Moreover, "Empty eyeballs knew/That knowledge increases unreality". The empty eyeballs are those of the statues, of course. Knowledge is what Western man characteristically appropriates, increasing his own unreality, presumably by creating only mirror-images of his own dreams, so that

> Mirror on mirror mirrored is all the show.

"Grimalkin" in the next lines presumably stands for the occult part of Western man that, dissatisfied with mere knowledge, cat-like, "crawls to Buddha's emptiness". The emptiness of the Buddha stands as a kind of polar opposite to the wasting dreaming of Western man.

What makes this arcane and hardly comprehensible poem interesting is its abrupt yet natural transition to contemporary politics in the following stanza. It is characteristic of Yeats's last poems to combine fluently and easily a wide range of disparate cultural references. The effect is the opposite of T. S. Eliot's, which is one of juxtaposition by contrast. Yeats succeeds in creating a kind of transcultural realm in which actual human issues traffic naturally with the archetypes and myths that have helped to shape them. In the present instance, the Greeks rub shoulders with Hamlet, and Hamlet with Aquinas, both with the Buddha. In the same way, Plotinus had consorted with Plato and Minos in the sacred grove of "The Delphic Oracle upon Plotinus".

Now Yeats brings all these diverse cultural allusions and sources to bear naturally upon modern Ireland:

> When Pearse summoned Cuchulain to his side,
> What stalked through the Post Office?
>
>   "The Statues"

The homely reference to the scene of the Easter Rising seems perfectly in place and not in the least bathetic. Yeats's conclusion is profoundly interesting. Pearse summoned Cuchulain because the Easter Rising was myth rather than politics, or rather it shared to a remarkably high degree the mythicality of all politics. Yeats's question is eerie:

> "What stalked through the Post Office?" What intellect,
> What calculation, number, measurement replied?

It is not rhetorical, but wittingly unanswerable. Yeats suggests that the Irish were deeper in than they knew in 1916, and he concludes by recommending that

> We Irish, born into that ancient sect
> But thrown upon this filthy modern tide
> And by its formless spawning fury wrecked,
> Climb to our proper dark, that we may trace
> The lineaments of a plummet-measured face.

The Irish, therefore, repeat the motions of the phantom children of the first stanza, those born of "the imagined love/Of solitary beds": the Irish of the Rising were born of despair; they were "wrecked" (a word frequently met with in Yeats's later poetry) by being born on the "filthy modern tide". Precisely what Yeats means by asserting that the Irish were born into "that ancient sect" (the Pythagorean) is not clear. Pythagoras based his world-view on numerology — the power of the number four, the tetrad, and included among the principal tenets of the sect the immortality of the soul, the myth of eternal recurrence, and metempsychosis. But its principal attraction for Yeats may well have been its insistence on a

strictly hierarchical social structure: Pythagoras distinguished three strata in society — lowest, tradesman; next,
entrepreneurs or merchants (our capitalists, simply, or
those with initiative enough to rise above the herd); at the
top, those mandarins capable of detached contemplation.
Such a view would strongly recommend itself to Yeats.

The implication of the poem is that Ireland properly
belongs to the dark (the dark of mysteries and mysticism),
and it should have no traffic with the "light", because in
the light Ireland is "blind and bitter". Politically, these
attitudes are about as fashionable today as the "sexist"
attitudes of "Michael Robartes and the Dancer". Yet the
visitor to Ireland today cannot help being struck by a
violent contrast between the daylight Ireland — the bright
new society which seems to out-bourgeois any other
bourgeois society in its concern for materiality — and the
old Ireland of Cashel and Glendalough, the dark mysterious
country of unconsumed dream. This is not merely a
question of the usual disparity between the "soul" of any
country, as expressed in its romantic or mythological past,
and the inevitably materialistic present. The present is
always materialistic, because man — feudal, bourgeois or
socialist — is himself materialistic. But there is a particular
instability in the Irish equation. If "September 1913" had
been Yeats's attempt to ward off the violence that was to
surprise him in "Easter 1916", these late poems may be
regarded as his attempt to guide his countrymen into a
path that would enable them to sublimate that blind
bitterness avowed so courageously in "Remorse for Intemperate Speech", and convert it into some truth great
enough to absorb the unslaked hatreds and bitternesses
of the past. Art, we remember, was for Yeats not a mirror
of what is, but a force that creates dreams and mirrors for
these dreams for the deepest part of man. Unless this
deeper part of man is satisfied, he will be unstable and
violent. So we find Yeats as an old man, as fervently as
when he was young, summoning Ireland to the old wisdom
of the dark.

(ix) The grounding of the dialectic

He had now to make his own peace. He did so in the confessional poems, "The Circus Animals' Desertion", "The
Man and the Echo" and "Under Ben Bulben". Ours is a
confessional age, and these poems have acquired a considerable reputation at least in part because of their "auto-
biographical" content. To some extent this is fair: the
poems do have a courage of "self-imposed ordeal", in
Leavis's phrase, which demands our respect. Yet there are
dangers for the critic here. In the first place, an excessive
emphasis on the confessional element of these poems may
lead us to underestimate the confessional element in
Yeats's earlier poetry. Secondly, such an emphasis may
distort our conception of the total *oeuvre* by regarding the
last poems as constituting a kind of rebuttal of the earlier.
If we see these confessions as being not the continuation
of a life-long habit of self-conception through reflection,
but rather the sudden realization that a life-time has been
wasted in delusions of grandeur, then we misread not only
the rest of Yeats's work, but the confessions themselves.

The poem which most tempts such a reductivist
approach to Yeats is undoubtedly "The Circus Animals'
Desertion". Here, it might be argued,[29] Yeats owns up to
the fact that a great deal of his poetry has been blarney —
concerned with the "painted shows" of an outworn
Romanticism rather than with those realities which
cultural empiricism has always claimed as the true terrain
of poetry. In fact, only a superficial reading of the poem
can rest content with its apparent avowals of failure. The
great significance of "The Circus Animals' Desertion" is
surely that it brings Yeats's lifelong dialectic to its final
resting-place: it is the final reversal that brooks no
opposition. If the first stanza of the poem is taken as a
mere disavowal of the poet's earlier practice (a waking-up
to the ineffable wisdom of Dr Leavis and others), it
cancels the dialectic process of Yeats's poetry as a whole;
it cancels also itself. The poem beings with a continuation:

Maybe at last, being but a broken man,
I must be satisfied with my heart, . . .

Does this betoken the final victory of *Heart* or *Self*? Surely
not: though he speaks of "being but a broken man", he
was not always broken. The poem does not suggest that
the poet should in general "be satisfied with (the) heart".
There is no suggestion here that a level of "truth" has been
reached such as reduces the poet's earlier work (with all its
circus animals) to mere myopic self-deception. On the contrary, the new "wisdom" is at best a *pis aller*.

The three inner stanzas of the poem (Part II) survey the
stages of Yeats's earlier work in an admittedly caustic
spirit. The first stanza expertly analyzes "The Wanderings
of Oisin", defining its three sections as "allegorical
dreams" motivated by "the embittered heart". Consistent
with his own theory, he suggests that he wrote the poem
out of his own need, "starved for the bosom of his faery
bride". In true dialectical spirit, Yeats then places *The
Countess Cathleen* as a "counter-truth", generated by the
otherworldliness of "Oisin". There is certainly a bitter
"confession" here: his "dear" (Maud Gonne) seemed to
destroy her own soul, "so did fanaticism and hate enslave
it". Yeats's acumen is extraordinary: he is more fully
aware of the motivations of his own work than we had the
right to expect. For he now says that this perception into
Maud-Helen's fanaticism itself

. . . brought forth a dream and soon enough
This dream itself had all my thought and love.

Finally, Yeats turns to the "heart-mysteries" allegorized in
the Cuchulain stories. Why did Cuchulain fight the sea,
Yeats now asks? It was not Cuchulain's "psychology"
that interested the poet, but the fact that he was driven by
a dream:

It was the dream itself enchanted me:
Character isolated by a deed
To engross the present and dominate memory.

Here, surely, is the quintessence of the Yeatsian theory of

man. A single action — whether it is picking an apple from a forbidden tree, cutting at an adder with a sword, or seducing another man's wife — can have the effect of "isolating" character. That is to say, it can cut a man's character off from whole series, whole life-times, of other acts: it commits, and freezes, and therefore expresses the character more truly than hundreds of thousands of trivial acts performed daily for fifty years. And this is what serves to "engross" the present, and "dominate" memory. The sequence of verbs here is arresting, and deeply characteristic: like the verb *enchant, engross* and *dominate* reveal much about Yeats and his conception of man. They direct us to remember that our actions are not uniform or equivalent to one another, nor are they to be evaluated quantitatively. One act may indeed last a lifetime. We allow ourselves to be engrossed, dominated, enchanted, driven. Our characters are "isolated" by what we do. We live in a world engrossed, dominated, enchanted.

Following this marvellously succinct and lucid *précis* of the Yeatsian world-view, the poet again attests that it was the emblems and symbols of dream that "took all my love", not "those things that they were emblems of". By now, it should not need stressing that this does not amount to a confession of failure. The last section of the poem is to bring the dialectic finally to rest in "the foul rag-and-bone shop of the heart". But this is no rueful admission that all those earlier dream-fantasies were blarney and hogwash:

> . . .   Now that my ladder's gone,
> I must lie down where all the ladders start,
> In the foul rag-and-bone shop of the heart.

The ladder has gone with age and debility, not through the accession of a new clear-sightedness. The ladders of spiritual aspiration may start in the mess of the heart, in the grounding of man in his body and his private emotional chaos. They have their origination in the fury and the mire of human blood. But this does not deny the validity of what the ladders enable man to reach while he has the strength to erect and climb them. Although the images and shows of his earlier poetry were "Players and painted stage", they still remain "those masterful images": they are "complete" — unlike the messy heart and body — because they "Grew in pure mind". The poem clearly marks out the poet's province: his traffic is with these "masterful images", not with the rag-and-bone shop of the heart. Finally acknowledged as the *Grundwerk* of the human enterprise, this original starting-point and final returning-point should not be mistaken for the scene of ·the poet's activities.

To take "The Circus Animals' Desertion" as a poem of awakening from delusion therefore — as a final belated awareness that pre-Raphaelite illusions have dominated his entire life to date — is to presuppose a theory of the creative process that Yeats never accepted — that of cultural empiricism. This is the theory that art is concerned — or ought to be — with the transmission or reflection of emotional truth, that it is reflective and realistic, that it is concerned with subjective truth; and that a fidelity to emotional experience is the criterion by which it is to be judged. As we have seen, Yeats never acknowledged that this could provide a proper basis for art. And the reason that it could not is that it is based upon a fraudulent theory of subjectivity and consciousness. We cannot know our subjectivity: what we introspect is the past, or, worse, has been doctored by the mind that introspects. We see what we want to see. Art is concerned with the dreams by which man in fact lives: it is concerned not with the mess of the subjective emotions, but with those superstructures it erects in order to live. We cannot even say that these superstructures "express" man. On the contrary, we have had to point out again and again that Yeats regarded man's artefacts as bearing an inverted (or antithetical) relationship to the "reality" that imagined them. We could even say that for Yeats man comes into existence through his artefacts. That is why his "masterful images" are "complete". It is also why most modern art, in Yeats's view, is incomplete — at best well-intentioned, at worst infantile in its megalomania. The proper business of culture is not with the transmission of "immediate" perceptions or sensations (whatever psychology might decide these were in the end), but with the ideology of dream. And if it is with man's dreams that the poet must be concerned, that is only because man's behaviour itself is dream-like. Contrary to behaviourist psychology, human action does not conform to elaborate stimulus-response patterns. We do not merely eat when we need to, as we blink. Our larger actions, and even most of our smaller ones (the gestures that rehearse our class-status for instance — the little finger raised to drink tea, the slouch of the punk, the erect carriage of the Army officer) enact some dream of a future state, a vision of an ideal being.

What we have in "The Circus Animals' Desertion", then, is the programme of a proud Apollonian, who, withered in age and willing to accept his own mortality, still remains unrepentant and undefeated. The dialectic knows no resolution except one, death: "But when I think of that, my tongue's a stone", he had said years before. It is as preparation for this death that the confessional poems play their part. Here perhaps it is as well to point out the broad difference between Yeats and existentialism in this respect. The spirit of Yeats's poetry as a whole, and of these last death-orientated poems in particular, is opposed to that of Kierkegaardian existentialism, with its emphasis upon a death-founded dread which will release man into a new freedom. The existentialist view is that by confessing our mortality — at a profound level not with that glib publicity Heidegger castigates in *Sein und Zeit* — we are freed from the lie of projects and the illusion of immortality. There is profound truth in Kierkegaard, and in such writers as Gerard Manley Hopkins and Dostoievsky. Yet there is a world of difference between the Yeatsian pride, and that snivelling-dog "awareness" that has been fostered by the existentialist cult of death — particularly in the French novelists of this century, such as Barbusse, Sartre, Camus and Gide. Kierkegaard was well aware of the dangers of reducing these matters to a new scholasticism:

it is no less easy to parrot the new existential "wisdom" than the old stale rationalism.

In the same way, certainly, Yeatsian pride easily degenerates into strutting arrogance. Bewilderingly, it does so often enough in Yeats himself: "Under Ben Bulben" oscillates between a blind bigotry and a profound courage. The courage is that of a man who was prepared to articulate what he thought valuable and to stand by it in cold print. At this late stage, the poet can do little more than offer a *rechauffée* of earlier poems. Poetically, nothing in "Under Ben Bulben" reaches the level of "The Tower", upon which it is based. At its worst, too, it degenerates into nationalistic rant, unforgivable in a man who had seen what Yeats had seen and written what he had written:

> You that Mitchel's prayer have heard,
> 'Send war in our time, O Lord!'
> Know that when all words are said
> And a man is fighting mad,
> Something drops from eyes long blind,
> He completes his partial mind,
> For an instant stands at ease,
> Laughs aloud, his heart at peace.

The degeneration of the verse into jerky near-doggerel aptly reflects the poverty of the philosophy behind these lines. Yeats, who had written so profoundly and with such courageous perceptiveness about the bigotry into which political passion led his fellow-Irishmen, himself falls foul of that blindness he had unmasked so efficiently. He fails to distinguish between that "passion" that releases man – and so completes his "partial mind" – and the foul anger of hatred that merely "bewilders" the mind. The cliché "fighting mad" sufficiently indicates the vulgarity of the thinking in these lines.

Equally vulgar is the jaunty snobbishness of section V of the poem – "Irish poets, learn your trade". Certainly the verse offers poor example for any young poet wishing to sing "whatever is well made". Still worse is it for the Irishman who wants to come to terms with his peculiarly difficult historical situation. Yeats merely illustrates the

temptations of the Irishman, oscillating between self-pity
— the Irish have been "beaten into the clay/Through seven
heroic centuries" — and arrogance — they are "still the
indomitable Irishry". If they were indomitable, Yeats leads
one to wonder, how was it they were beaten into the clay
for so long? Yeats himself had done so much to lay bare
the Irish situation that no admirer of his poetry can but
be ashamed on his behalf to read this self-contradictory
rant.

This is particularly true if we turn from this verse back
to Yeats's real "true confession", "The Man and the
Echo". Here the septosyllabics (the short lines spread
periodically to the Swiftian octosyllabic, more rarely to
pentameters) create an effect of strict self-examination,
the cruelly incisive questions ricochetting off the rock to
yield the Echo's sombre insinuations. The poem opens
with the rehearsal of a familiar theme in the poet's work —
his sense of responsibility for other men's lives and deaths.
He wonders whether his patriotic play (*The Countess
Cathleen* again is intended) sent men out to be shot; or
whether his own conversation inflamed "that woman's
reeling brain"; "All seems evil". When the Echo perverts
his words, however ("Lie down and die", it says back to
him) the poet is quick to retaliate:

> That were to shirk
> The spiritual intellect's great work,
> And shirk it in vain.

Although the poet appears here as a shrivelled little self-
questioner, like Rembrandt's late self-portrait as Saint
Paul, he does not give in to a passive resignation. On the
contrary, he insists on rigour and self-criticism:

> Nor can there be work so great
> As that which cleans man's dirty slate.

The slate is always more or less dirty; a man is responsible
for himself and others. The only escape from the self-
recrimination of the old man's sleeplessness is no escape at
all, but persistence in self-examination, until

> . . .   his intellect grows sure
> That all's arranged in one clear view,
> Pursues the thoughts that I pursue,
> Then stands in judgement on his soul,
> And, all work done, dismisses all
> Out of intellect and sight
> And sinks at last into the night.

Here is a proud *resumée* of a lifetime's practice: to arrange
everything in one clear view, to take total responsibility
for oneself — that is Yeats's answer to the human state.
The poem ends with the poet's own personality effectively
forgotten. Constant to his belief in the mind's essential
weightlessness, he shows the speaker distracted by an
irrelevancy:

> But hush, for I have lost the theme,
> Its joy or night seem but a dream;
> Up there some hawk or owl has struck,
> Dropping out of sky or rock,
> A stricken rabbit is crying out,
> And its cry distracts my thought.

Eminently distractable, the human mind pursues its
"themes" in a somnambulistic reverie, until some external
sound or sight fills it with itself. Does the human mind
really exist, outside its themes and distractions? What is
the "inner" creature that dreams the dreams of man which
are the real subject of poetry? What is the reality of which
the poet, who has awakened from these dreams, has his
visions? The poet is, according to Yeats's strict Apollonianism, concerned with the interpretation of man's dreams,
not to create new dreams, to transmit cosmic rhythms or
to release man from the bonds of time or place, as Orphic
or Dionysiac theories advocate. The poet is, Keats said,
"the most unpoetical of creatures", a mere distractable
waker, a location for infinite capacities. Paradoxically,
Yeats, the arrogant upholder of the Kantian mind against
Lockean *tabula rasa,* conforms strictly to Keatsian negative
capability; for him, too, consciousness is a vacancy.
Vacancy is the hidden theme of the one poem in *Last
Poems* which in form, structure and meaning takes its

place with the greatest of Yeats's work, "Long-legged
Fly". This lyric is tightly structured: its three stanzas are
symmetrically equivalent to one another in syntax; each
begins with the conjunction "That" (meaning, in order
that) introducing a subordinate clause of two lines, and a
main clause with an imperative main verb; the last four
lines of each stanza depict a scene, and a figure in a scene;
each stanza is rounded with the refrain,

> Like a long-legged fly upon the stream
> His mind moves upon silence.

The figure in the first stanza is the representative of War,
or human action — Caesar; in the second, of Love — Helen
of Troy; in the third, of Art — Michelangelo cradled under
the ceiling of the Sistine Chapel. In each case the figure is
caught in abstraction. Caesar's eyes are "fixed upon
nothing"; Helen's feet "practise a tinker shuffle/Picked up
on a street"; Michelangelo's hand moves to and fro "With
no more sound than the mice make".

Nowhere else does Yeats capture so beautifully the
quality of human consciousness, and the true character of
our projects and schemes. Resting on a stream of silence
and time, human consciousness pursues its dreams
knowing no more of their real nature than the fly on the
water of the stream that sustains its nimble dance. It is
appropriate that this great master of the rhythms of
English should come to rest on this imponderably subtle
dance. The attitude embodied in the poem can hardly be
called detachment, certainly not as that term suggests a
turning-aside, a disengagement of the most vital part of the
mind. The famous dictum of the Great Lord of Chou —
"Let all things pass away" — is detached in a spurious sort
of way, and Yeats's fondness for this Stoic attitudinizing
finds late expression in that famous epitaph, which,
impressive as it appears to tourists, smacks of the theatre,
as W. H. Auden pointed out.[30]

The detachment of "Long-legged Fly" is of an altogether more significant order, a product of having felt and
thought things through rather than despaired of them. The

same goes for the last great expression of that joy which we have seen to be so important in Years's last phases, "Lapis Luzuli". In the earlier poems, joy leaps up like a hidden jet, unpredictably. Therein lies its beauty and its authenticity. Inevitably, however, Yeats's long meditation on the matter produced a more philosophically grounded concept of joy: the emotion becomes a concept. Nietzsche provides support here: *La Gaya Scienza* stands in relation to the later Yeats as *Birth of Tragedy* does to the early.

"Lapis Lazuli", more than any other poem, gives articulate expression to this Nietzschean aspect of Yeats's joy, or, as he calls it in the poem, gaiety. Here is something different from the authentically personal fountain of joy that sprang up so surprisingly in the earlier poems. Rather is it a philosophically reasoned theory of experience, drawing upon much of the material of *A Vision* without using its structure. Life here is a "tragic play" (Yeats surely acknowledges now the emptiness of the Plotinian influence). No matter what roles the players perform – sad or happy, ranting or musing – ultimately they are "gay". Moreover, no matter what the actors actually say, no matter if everything comes to an end "And all the drop-scenes drop at once", still nothing can really be effected: "It cannot grow by an inch or an ounce":

> All things fall and are built again,
> And those that build them again are gay.

This is the general theory of private and public life offered in the line, "Gaiety transfiguring all that dread". The poem is written under the threat of large-scale international conflict, with every likelihood of oblivion to follow.

To give illustration to his Nietzscheam stoicism in the face of this menace, Yeats turns to the art of China. A kind of detachment, alien to the essentially tragic philosophies of the West, and attractive because of its wise elegance, seems to be an ineradicable part of China, or at least of the European's conception of China. There are many sad Chinese poems, and a profound pathos attends the greatest Chinese landscape painting. Yet it seems on the whole true to say that Chinese culture does not seem tragic to Westerners, as they understand the word. Yeats's poem is quite explicit in its relations to this implicit philosophy: it is about the poet's own imaginary China, not about Chinese thought and art itself. He describes the lapis lazuli paper-weight in fond detail, and then drifts into fantasy:

> Though doubtless plum or cherry-branch
> Sweetens the little half-way house
> Those Chinamen climb towards, and I
> Delight to imagine them seated there;

It is therefore an explicitly Western poem, with no pretence to have founded a wisdom upon actual Chinese thought or art. The spirit of China assumes a kind of mythic presence, but its relationship to a particular Western predicament is quite clear. This is not false Chinoiserie; the content of actual Chinese philosophy is irrelevant to the unforgettably tender picture conjured up in the poem's closing lines:

> There, on the mountain and the sky,
> On all the tragic scene they stare.
> One asks for mournful melodies;
> Accomplished fingers begin to play.
> Their eyes mid many wrinkles, their eyes,
> Their ancient, glittering eyes, are gay.

Thus, although the philosophical meaning we are invited to draw from the poem enjoins a gaiety that may seem fictitious in abstraction, within the poem itself this gaiety is inseparable from the sadness of the melodies the "accomplished fingers" begin to play. "Our sweetest songs are those that tell of saddest thought", said Shelley. Yeats's poem is an attempt to make us understand why.

Notes

Part One

1. References to Yeats's poems are to the *Collected Poems* (London: Macmillan, 1949), abbreviated in the notes to *CP*.
2. *CP*, p. 523 n.
3. Ibid., p. 524 n.
4. The last line originally read:
   Are shaken with earth's old and weary cry.
   See *The Variorum Edition of the poems of W.B. Yeats,* ed. P. Allt and R.K. Alspach (New York: Macmillan, 1957), p. 120.
5. H. Bloom, *Yeats* (New York: Oxford University Press, 1974), p. 40.
6. J. Hone, *W.B. Yeats 1865-1939* (London: Macmillan, 1962), pp. 145-46.
7. *CP*, pp. 526-57 n.
8. Ibid., p. 527 n.
9. D.H. Lawrence, "Edgar Allan Poe", *Studies in Classic American Literature* (New York: Doubleday, 1961): 68.
10. F.W. Nietzsche, *The Birth of Tragedy*, tr. F. Golffing (New York: Doubleday, 1956), p. 20. Nietzsche's German for "true dream" is "Wahrtraum".
11. S. Freud, *The Interpretation of Dreams*, tr. J. Strachey (London: Allen and Unwin, 1953), vol. I, gives a short account of the history of dream-interpretation.
12. See, for instance, Freud's paper, "Creative writers and day-dreaming", *Complete Psychological Works*, tr. J. Strachey (London: Hogarth Press, 1953), vol. 4.
13. In my book *The Dickens Myth* (St Lucia: University of Queensland Press, 1975), I use the modern man's dream of ultimate affluence and economic salvation as the basis for the interpretation not only of Dickens himself but of the novel as a genre.

Part Two

1. See R. Ellman, *The Identity of Yeats* (London: Faber & Faber, 1954), p. 142.
2. Hone, *Yeats*, pp. 183-85.
3. G. Moore, *Hail and Farewell: Vale* (London: Heinemann, 1947), p. 113.
4. Maude Gonne's own view of herself is amply illustrated in her book, *A Servant of the Queen* (London: Gollancz, 1938).
5. Jesse Chambers ("E.T."), *D.H. Lawrence: A Personal Record* (London: Cape, 1935), p. 98.
6. Letter to John Quinn, 15 May 1903, *Letters of W.B. Yeats,* ed. A. Wade (London: Hart-Davis, 1954), p. 403.
7. Ibid.
8. Ibid.

9. Nietzsche, *Birth of Tragedy*, p. 65.
10. See, for instance, Vyacheslav Ivanov, "Religia Dionisii", *Voprosy Zhyznyi* (St Petersburg), 1905, nos. 6–7.
11. T. Mann, *Doctor Faustus*, tr. H.T. Lowe-Porter (London: Secker and Warburg, 1949), chapter 34.
12. Hone, *Yeats*, pp. 336–37.
13. Ibid., p. 73.
14. T.S. Eliot, *The Use of Poetry and the Use of Criticism* (London: Faber, 1933), p. 148.
15. "Chard Witlow" by Henry Reed, from *A Map of Verona* (London: Faber, 1946), is only the most celebrated example of Eliot-parody.
16. W. Blake, "Auguries of innocence", *Poetry and Prose*, ed. G. Keynes (London: Nonesuch Press, 1948), p. 119.
17. Bloom, *Yeats*, p. 172.
18. See Hone, *Yeats*, p. 249.
19. Nietzsche, *Birth of Tragedy*, p. 56.
20. See Hone, *Yeats*, p. 299. Also *Letters*, pp. 612–13, to Lady Gregory.
21. A. Blok, "The Decline of Humanism", *The Spirit of Music*, tr. I. Freiman (London: Westhouse, 1946), p. 66.
22. Ibid., p. 49.
23. Quoted in Hone, *Yeats*, p. 365.
24. Ibid., p. 72.
25. Ibid., p. 327.
26. T. Roethke, "Four for Sir John Davies – The Dance", *Selected Poems* (London: Faber, 1969), p. 26.
27. G.M. Hopkins, "Author's Preface", *Poems and Prose*, ed. W.H. Gardner (Harmondsworth: Penguin, 1953), pp. 7–11.
28. Nietzsche, *Thus spake Zarathustra*, part 4, 11, "The Drunken Song" n.p. 284.
29. *Letters*, p. 742 (dated 25 April 1928).
30. Hone, *Yeats*, p. 330.
31. Ibid., p. 270.
32. Ibid., p. 253. See also *Letters*, p. 255 and p. 256: "Every influence had a shadow . . . an unbalanced – the unbalanced is the kabalistic definition of evil-duplicate of itself."
33. Hone, *Yeats*, pp. 2–3.
34. Ibid., pp. 407–408 (quoted).
35. *CP*, p. 534.
36. See *Letters*, p. 590 (dated 18 January 1915). Yeats is scathing about Wordsworth, but he laboured enough to derive substantial and important help from *The Prelude*.
37. *Autobiographies* (London: Macmillan, 1956), pp. 130–36.
38. F.R. Leavis, "Yeats: The Problem and the Challenge", in F.R. and Q.D. Leavis, *Lectures in America* (London: Chatto & Windus, 1969), p. 75.
39. J. Keats, Letter to R. Woodhouse, 27 October 1818, *Selected Poems and Letters*, ed. R. Gittings (London: Heinemann, 1966), p. 87.
40. *Autobiographies*, p. 171.
41. Ibid., p. 132.
42. Ibid., p. 135.
43. E. Goffmann, *The Presentation of Self in Everyday Life* (New York: Doubleday, 1959), p. 97.
44. Keats, *Poems and Letters*, p. 113, letter to George and Georgiana Keats, 19 March 1819.

45. Plotinus, *The Enneads*, III, 2.17, tr. S. McKenna (London: Faber, 1956).
46. P. Calderon de la Barca, "El Gran Teatro del Mundo", *Obras Completas*, 3.199 (Madrid: Aguilar, 1967).
47. T. Sturge Moore, *W.B. Yeats and T. Sturge Moore: Their Correspondence 1901-1937*, ed. V. Bridge (London: Routledge, 1953).
48. Ibid., p. 64, letter to Sturge Moore, January 1926.

Part Three

1. F.R. Leavis, *Lectures in America*, p. 75.
2. "Friends", *CP*, p. 139.
3. Ibid.
4. W.H. Auden, "D.H. Lawrence", *Selected Essays* (London: Faber, 1962), p. 128.
5. F.R. Leavis, "The Great Yeats: and the Latest", *Scrutiny*, 8 no. 4 (March 1940) 437-40. Also, "The Latest Yeats", *Scrutiny*, 2 no. 3 (December 1933), pp. 293-95.
6. Leavis, "Lectures in America", pp. 66 and 69.
7. Ibid., p. 66.
8. Ibid., p. 69.
9. Ibid.
10. Ibid.
11. Auden, "Writing", *Selected Essays*, p. 28.
12. J. Lacan, " 'Le stade du miroir' comme formateur de la fonction du Je", (1936) *Ecrits* (Paris: Seiul, 1966), p. 93-100.
13. *CP*, p. 537.
14. Letter to Maurice Wollman, 23 September 1935, *Letters*, p. 840.
15. Hone, *Yeats*, p. 313 for details of Irish reaction.
16. *The Senate Speeches of W.B. Yeats*, ed. D.R. Pearce (London: Faber, 1960), p. 99.
17. Hone, *Yeats*, p. 264.
18. Hone, *Yeats*, p. 435.
19. Ibid., p. 401.
20. Ibid., p. 450. For Yeats's interest in the Nazi Regime see pp. 467-68. See also E. Cullingford, *Yeats, Ireland and Fascism* (London: Macmillan, 1981), esp. pp. 198-99.
21. Hone, *Yeats*, p. 459.
22. Ibid., p. 450.
23. Letter to Olivia Shakespeare, 1 January 1935, *Letters*, p. 803.
24. Hone, *Yeats*, pp. 436-37.
25. R. Snukal, *High Talk: The Philosophical Poetry of W.B. Yeats* (Cambridge: Cambridge University Press, 1973), p. 37.
26. Letter to Edith Shackleton Heald, 4 September 1938, *Letters*, p. 915.
27. J. Joyce, *A Portrait of the Artist as a Young Man* (London: Cape, 1944), pp. 205-206.
28. Nietzsche, *Birth of Tragedy*, pp. 19-20.
29. See, for instance, Denis Donoghue, *An Honoured Guest* (London: Edward Arnold, 1965), pp. 140-41. Harold Bloom, *Yeats*, pp. 456-59 argues along lines similar to my own, though reaching different ends.
30. Auden, *Selected Essays*, p. 163.

Index to Poems

Index